Philip Massinger

Philip Massinger

A Critical Reassessment

Edited by

DOUGLAS HOWARD

St John Fisher College, Rochester, New York

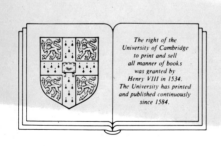

The right of the
University of Cambridge
to print and sell
all manner of books
was granted by
Henry VIII in 1534.
The University has printed
and published continuously
since 1584.

CAMBRIDGE UNIVERSITY PRESS

Cambridge
London   New York   New Rochelle
Melbourne   Sydney

Published by the Press Syndicate of the University of Cambridge
The Pitt Building, Trumpington Street, Cambridge CB2 1RP
32 East 57th Street, New York, NY 10022, USA
10 Stamford Road, Oakleigh, Melbourne 3166, Australia

© Cambridge University Press 1985

First published 1985

Printed in Great Britain by
Woolnough Bookbinding, Wellingborough

Library of Congress catalogue card number: 84–21359

British Library Cataloguing in Publication Data
Philip Massinger: a critical reassessment.
1. Massinger, Philip, 1583–1640—Criticism
and interpretation
I. Howard, Douglas
822'.3   PR2707
ISBN 0 521 25895 2

Contents

Contributors

ANNE BARTON, Professor of English Literature, University of Cambridge

MARTIN BUTLER, Lecturer in English, University of Leeds

PHILIP EDWARDS, King Alfred Professor of English Literature, University of Liverpool

COLIN GIBSON, Professor of English, University of Otago, Dunedin

DOUGLAS HOWARD, Assistant Professor of English, St John Fisher College, Rochester, New York

CYRUS HOY, Trevor Professor of English, University of Rochester, New York

NANCY S. LEONARD, Associate Professor of English, Bard College, Annandale-on-Hudson, New York

RUSS McDONALD, Assistant Professor of English, University of Rochester, New York

MICHAEL NEILL, Associate Professor of English, University of Auckland

their names being associated with plays written by Fletcher and others – Massinger chief among them – long after Beaumont's retirement from the stage in 1613. In fact, of the 35 plays in the 1647 folio of 'Beaumont and Fletcher', Massinger is, according to Cyrus Hoy's disintegrations,[3] responsible for parts of at least 14 plays. The second folio of 1679 adds 3 others in which Massinger had a hand, though he is again unmentioned on the title page. Massinger's friend, Aston Cokayne, took up the dramatist's cause and beginning in 1658 protested the injustice of such omissions,[4] but not until the twentieth century was Massinger given full credit for his extensive collaborative work.

In spite of these uncertain beginnings, Massinger emerged in the 1620s as an important playwright, and in 1625 he succeeded Fletcher as chief dramatist for Shakespeare's company, the King's Men. The bulk of his early collaborations and two early tragedies, *The Duke of Milan* (?1621–2) and *The Unnatural Combat* (?1624–5), were acted by the King's Men, but beginning with *The Maid of Honour*, Massinger wrote a series of tragicomedies and comedies for Christopher Beeston's companies at the Phoenix (or Cockpit) in Drury Lane. The other plays Massinger wrote for Beeston's companies in the early 1620s include *The Bondman* (1623), *The Renegado* and *The Parliament of Love* (1624), and *A New Way to Pay Old Debts* (1625). After 1625, however, with the single exception of *The Great Duke of Florence* (1627), another Beeston play, Massinger's name was associated exclusively with the King's company, for which he wrote nearly 20 plays before his death in 1640. The plays extant from this period are *The Roman Actor* (1626), *The Picture* (1629), *Believe As You List* (1631), *The Emperor of the East* (1631), *The City Madam* (1632), *The Guardian* (1633), *A Very Woman* (1634), and *The Bashful Lover* (1636).

Massinger's dramatic output extends beyond these extant plays. His most recent editors credit Massinger with work on 33 surviving plays, 18 of which are collaborations and 15 of which Massinger wrote on his own; including lost works attributable to Massinger, the Clarendon editors count some 55 plays in which he appears to have had a hand.[5] Extracts from the office-book of Sir Henry Herbert, Master of the Revels, record licences for 9 plays by Massinger that are no longer extant. This number is greatly increased if one includes works attributed to Massinger

Introduction

OVERSHADOWED in his own day by his flashier mentor and collaborator, John Fletcher, and suffering in more recent times, like all his contemporaries, from unfavourable comparison with Shakespeare, Massinger has never enjoyed a secure reputation as a major dramatist. Considering that he was, along with Ford and Shirley, one of the three most important dramatists of the later Stuart period, the fact of his neglect is somewhat surprising. Part of the cause is no doubt Massinger's own view of his art. The dedications prefixed to his individual plays are self-deprecating, even if we allow for the conventional humility of such documents, and they suggest that Massinger was a dramatist largely by default. As late as 1639, the year before his death, Massinger spoke of the 'necessitous fortunes' that made playwriting his profession.[1] Similarly, whether the reason was reluctance to commit himself to the humble trade of playwright or lack of confidence in his abilities, Massinger's failure to strike out on his own as a dramatist until he was nearly 40 also indicates something less than genuine enthusiasm for his craft. Born in 1583, Massinger appears to have been active as a writer for the stage by the early 1610s, but the first extant plays of his sole authorship date from the 1620s.

If we take *The Maid of Honour* (?1621–2) to be his earliest unaided work,[2] then Massinger had collaborated on no fewer than a dozen plays before venturing to write on his own. Although he may have written non-collaborative plays during these formative years, none survives, and his work with other dramatists, especially Fletcher, regularly went unacknowledged. By about 1616, when Massinger had become a frequent collaborator with Fletcher, the names Beaumont and Fletcher were already inextricably linked, and the popularity of plays like *Philaster* (1609) and *A King and No King* (1611) had resulted in

1

Acknowledgements

Our individual contributions to this volume owe a debt to earlier studies of Massinger and to generous colleagues and fellow contributors who have read and commented upon our essays, but as editor I should like to acknowledge the kind assistance of Sarah Stanton, humanities editor at Cambridge University Press, and of Professor Cyrus Hoy, who has steadily encouraged my own interest in Massinger for nearly a decade. I am grateful to the editors of *The Times Literary Supplement* for permission to reprint Anne Barton's review of the Clarendon edition of Massinger. I should also like to express my gratitude to my colleagues, Dr Kenneth Mason and Dr Charles Natoli, to my research assistant, Daniel McGurk, and to St John Fisher College for a Summer Research Grant that allowed me to complete work on this volume.

February 1984   DOUGLAS HOWARD in Humphrey Moseley's important entries in the Stationers' Register in 1653 and 1660, whereby he sought to secure copyright for as many as 13 titles neither extant nor mentioned by Herbert. Moseley's credibility is diminished by his ruse of trying to protect two plays for the price of one in his 1653 entry with double titles like 'Alexius the Chast Gallant or The Bashfull Louer.' Moseley's entries are also notorious for misattributions of authorship, among them the assigning of *The Parliament of Love* to Rowley instead of Massinger, but his two entries in the Stationers' Register, even if they contain other such errors, certainly prove that Massinger was a more prolific dramatist than his surviving plays indicate. Philip Edwards and Colin Gibson give a detailed account of the evidence for lost plays in their edition of Massinger, including the horrifying possibility that John Warburton (1682–1759) collected many of them in manuscript, only to have his cook destroy them by using the pages to line pie bottoms.[6]

Massinger was clearly a successful dramatist in the later years of his life, but his popular appeal, even during his heyday in the late 1620s, seems to have been limited, and the commendatory verses attached to editions of individual plays are sometimes less than laudatory. Thomas Jay's contribution to the 1630 edition of *The Picture*, for example, compliments Massinger for not envying the praise accorded Beaumont and Jonson, 'whose worth long since was known/And justly too preferr'd before your own'. On the whole, judging from the bulk of dedicatory poems which are more generous than this one, Massinger seems to have gained some fair popularity, and only once, in the early 1630s, is there clear evidence that he was out of favour with the public.[7] From 1625 until the end of his life, then, Massinger played a significant enough role in the theatre of his day to remain an important figure even when individual plays were not well-received. The closing of the theatres followed soon after Massinger's death, and when they reopened in 1660, he was among the old dramatists whose plays were revived. At least five Massinger plays were performed during the first years after the Restoration: *The Bondman*, by which Pepys was so impressed, *The Renegado*, *The Virgin Martyr*, *A Very Woman*, and *A New Way to Pay Old Debts*.[8]

There was even greater interest in his plays in the eighteenth century, in part because they are highly sententious and provided apt material for anthologies like Oldys's *The British Muse* (1738) and, much later, Lamb's *Specimens of the English Dramatic Poets* (1808). With Coleridge's serious, if sometimes unflattering, critical attention to Massinger, and Kean's great successes as Sir Giles Overreach in *A New Way to Pay Old Debts* (beginning in 1816), the early nineteenth century showed a general enthusiasm for the dramatist which culminated in Henry Hallam's verdict that 'Massinger, as a tragic writer, appears to me second only to Shakespeare; in the higher comedy, I can hardly think him inferior to Jonson'.[9] From this laudatory assessment of the late 1830s up to the appearance of Philip Edwards and Colin Gibson's edition, *The Plays and Poems of Philip Massinger* (5 vols., Oxford, Clarendon Press, 1976), little favourable attention was accorded this author, the nadir of whose reputation was no doubt reached when T. S. Eliot found his verse anaemic and held him personally responsible for the dissociation of sensibility that marked the end of the great (metaphysical) period of English literature and the onset of Milton and the baroque.[10]

While the editors of the Clarendon edition did not attempt a critical appraisal of Massinger's plays (their task was clearly a monumental one already), their general introduction does trace in some detail these and other, less extreme differences of opinion about Massinger. One of the virtues of Edwards and Gibson's survey is that it presents both the excessive praise and peremptory dismissal Massinger has inspired over the years with an analytical reserve and detachment on both sides. The Clarendon editors do not take Hallam's encomium as a rallying cry, nor do they feel obliged to counter the provocative, though finally insupportable, accusations of Eliot. Their tacit assumption is that Massinger's plays are artful and self-conscious constructions and as such can be judged on their own merits.

In the almost ten years since the publication of the Clarendon edition, other students of Massinger have begun to build upon Edwards and Gibson's foundation, and there are encouraging signs that Massinger is undergoing, if not an apotheosis, at least a serious critical examination of the sort to which he has never been treated, and of which he has frequently and wrongly been thought unworthy. The first critic to take the appearance of the

Introduction

Clarendon edition as an occasion for further study of the dramatist was Anne Barton in her lengthy and comprehensive *TLS* review, 'The Distinctive Voice of Massinger',[11] which, because of its seminal importance, is reprinted as an appendix to this volume. Professor Barton's review not only provided a stimulating look at the entire Massinger canon, but also predicted that the edition under consideration seemed certain 'to spark off a much-needed critical re-evaluation of Massinger's work as a whole'. Another spur to Massinger studies was the decision of Cambridge University Press to issue a one-volume, modern-spelling anthology of *Selected Plays of Philip Massinger* (1978), based on the Clarendon texts and edited by Colin Gibson. This was the first such representative collection of Massinger's works to appear in nearly seventy years, and it was no doubt issued with the expectation that Massinger was about to acquire a wider audience than he had previously known. Other signs of interest in the dramatist include Professor Gibson's work on a book-length survey of critical response to Massinger's work, and a projected Twayne series study by Professor Doris Adler of Howard University.

Although other books on Massinger by individual scholars are certain to appear in the next few years, the present volume of essays provides an occasion for a number of critics and scholars interested in the dramatist to take a collective look at his works and thereby help establish that, *pace* Eliot, Massinger's place in the history of English drama is not yet fully determined. These eight essays grew from a wish to initiate a long-overdue critical reappraisal of Massinger's plays and a desire to commemorate the quatercentenary of the dramatist's birth in 1983, but prior commitments on the part of contributors have meant that the volume itself could not appear in time to mark the anniversary.

A number of different approaches and assessments are contained in these eight essays, but they have in common the wish of their authors to provide a fresh and constructive assessment of Massinger's works. Our collective effort has been directed towards a broad range of subjects, treating major plays as well as important general aspects of Massinger's dramaturgy. We have tried to correct long-held misconceptions about Massinger, as Colin Gibson does in his essay on 'Massinger's Theatrical Language', and we have attempted to explore previously neglected areas of the canon, as Cyrus Hoy does in 'Massinger as Collaborator', a detailed study of Massinger's plays with Fletcher and other dramatists. In a third essay on a general topic, 'Massinger's Men and Women', Philip Edwards extends Colin Gibson's arguments about the theatrical effectiveness of Massinger's verbal patterning to recurring dramatic situations in the plays, and in doing so lays to rest long-standing objections that this dramatist's characters lack, in Coleridge's words, 'a guiding point', that we 'never know what they are about'.[12]

Like these essays on broader topics, those on particular plays examine works by Massinger in the light of the whole canon and with a view to their dramatic and historical context. Russ McDonald's study of *The Maid of Honour* shows Massinger's individuality as a writer of tragicomedy and examines his dual inheritance from Shakespeare and Jonson as well as his departure from the Fletcherian norm of tragicomic practice. My essay on 'Massinger's Political Tragedies' sees *The Roman Actor* and *Believe As You List* as evidence of Massinger's increased political involvement in the Caroline period and of his shift towards more appropriate subject matter for tragedy than he had hit upon in his earlier plays. Martin Butler's study, 'Romans in Britain', also focuses upon *The Roman Actor*, but it examines the play in the context of other classical plays of the 1620s and '30s, thereby establishing Massinger's role in the intellectual and political ferment that eventually led to civil war.

The volume concludes with new studies of Massinger's best-known plays, his two satiric comedies. Nancy Leonard offers a tantalizingly original perspective on *A New Way to Pay Old Debts* in her essay, 'Overreach at Bay', and Michael Neill deepens our understanding of the social implications of *The City Madam* in 'The Tongues of Angels', his study of the theme of charity in Massinger's play.

NOTES

1 Dedication to *The Unnatural Combat* (1639).
2 Philip Edwards dates the play *c.*1621–2 in *The Plays and Poems of Philip Massinger*, ed. Philip Edwards and Colin Gibson (5 vols., Oxford Clarendon Press, 1976), vol. 1, pp. 105–6. All dates for Massinger's plays given here are those established by the Clarendon editors.
3 See Hoy's series of articles, 'The Shares of Fletcher and his Collaborators

in the Beaumont and Fletcher Canon', *Studies in Bibliography*, 8 (1956), 129–46; 9 (1957), 143–62; 11 (1958), 85–106; 12 (1959), 91–116; 13 (1960), 77–108; 14 (1961), 45–67; 15 (1962), 71–90.

4 Cokayne addresses the publishers of the 1647 folio directly in '*To Mr. Humphrey Mosley, and Mr. Humphrey Robinson*', one of the verses in his book, *A Chain of Golden Poems*. See Edwards and Gibson, vol. 1, p. xix.

5 Edwards and Gibson, vol. 1, p. xxvii.

6 Edwards and Gibson, vol. 1, pp. xxvi–xxvii.

7 See the 'Prologue at the Blackfriars' written for *The Emperor of the East* (1631) and the Prologue to *The Guardian* (1633); the matter is discussed in Edwards and Gibson, vol. 1, pp. xl–xlii.

8 Edwards and Gibson, vol. 1, p. xlvii.

9 Edwards and Gibson, vol. 1, p. lxiii.

10 T. S. Eliot, 'Philip Massinger', in *Selected Essays* (New York, Harcourt, Brace and World, 1964), p. 187.

11 Anne Barton, 'The Distinctive Voice of Massinger', *TLS* (20 May 1977), pp. 623–4, reprinted as an appendix in this volume.

12 Edwards and Gibson, vol. 1, p. lx.

Massinger's Theatrical Language

COLIN GIBSON

FOR MORE THAN three hundred and fifty years the merits and demerits of the language of Massinger's plays have been debated by theatregoers, poets, professional critics and general readers. Massinger's dramatic style has never excited the praise lavished on Shakespeare's writing, against which his work is usually measured, nor has it received an equal share in the general modern admiration for the poetic language of the greatest Elizabethan and Stuart dramatists.

Edmund Gosse, one of Massinger's severest critics, wrote:

If the truth be told, Massinger is scarcely a poet, except in the sense in which that word may be used of any man who writes seriously in dramatic form. What we delight in in the earlier Elizabethans, the splendid bursts of imaginative insight, the wild freaks of diction, the sudden sheet-lightning of poetry illuminating for an instant dark places of the soul, all this is absent in Massinger. He is uniform and humdrum; he has no lyrical passages; his very versification, as various critics have observed, is scarcely to be distinguished from prose, and often would not seem metrical if it were printed along the page. Intensity is not within his reach, and even in the aims of composition we distinguish between the joyous instinctive lyricism of the Elizabethans, which attained to beauty without much design, and this deliberate and unimpassioned work, so plain and easy and workmanlike.[1]

Modern critics like T. S. Eliot and Massinger's biographer T. A. Dunn, agreeing with Gosse that the dramatist's work lacks the marks of absolute poetic genius, have specified other charges. Not only is there an absence of striking phrases; Massinger's diction suffers from a blight of abstraction, a general enervation. His style betrays a fatal separation of thought and feeling from immediate sense experience. The feebleness of his imagination is said to be evidenced by his habit of self-repetition, and by the borrowings he makes from other dramatists. Massinger's style is characteristically eloquent and long-winded; his convoluted periodic sentences make delivery difficult even for intelligent and

9

experienced actors. In short, as an earlier critic reviewing Gifford's 1805 edition of Massinger's plays wrote:

Massinger's talents appear to have been better fitted by nature for heroic than dramatic writing: he excels in dignified scenes; he describes both character and passion with skill; but is unable to give them appropriate language and expression: he is eloquent, indeed, in every species of description; but his flowing, stately periods, are perhaps too lofty for the stage, and contribute to render his plays heavy and wearisome to the reader.[2]

Of course Massinger has his supporters, numbering among them poets, critics and men of the theatre. C. H. Terrot's opinion that 'Blank verse is upon the whole much more difficult to write than any of our rhyming measures. The best example of its Tragic form is Massinger',[3] is not likely to find much sympathy today, but the dramatist's stage-poetry has been praised in less extreme terms by George Colman, Lamb, Coleridge, Thomas Campbell, Keats, Hallam, Beddoes, Elton and Swinburne. Like T. S. Eliot's more famous piece, John Middleton Murry's critique of Massinger's style in *The Problem of Style* (London, 1922) acknowledges some considerable merits — 'The odd thing is that this blank verse is really excellent prose — lucid, well shaped, and sinewy. Massinger's sentence-management (as Coleridge noted) is beautiful' — and modern critics like L. C. Knights and Anne Barton have written sympathetically of the dramatist's handling of his medium.

Still, the counterview is weightily supported, detailed and widely held. A single essay could scarcely hope to address all its aspects, let alone overthrow it. But it may be possible to turn the flank of the attack a little by insisting on something that is self-evident but frequently ignored. Massinger wrote for the theatre; his language, poetical or not, is theatrical, and by considering its working in the fuller context of the stage it may be possible to identify qualities, even virtues, easily missed if the text is read as though it were a long narrative poem.

It is a curious fact that the critical debate about Massinger's stage language has largely been conducted by readers. And since performances of the plays other than *A New Way to Pay Old Debts* have been few and isolated (in the present century only *The Duke of Milan* at Merton College, Oxford, in 1923; *The City Madam* at the Birmingham Repertory Theatre in 1964; and *The Roman Actor* at the Bouwerie Lane Theatre, New York, in 1980, and at the Glasgow Citizens Theatre in 1982), even when those readers have been habitual playgoers and in some cases practising dramatists there has been little opportunity to confirm impressions or test readings against the actualities of stage production. It is of course possible to imagine a stage production, even to visualize a performance while reading the words. But no such theatre of the mind is likely to reproduce the stream of local and particular aural, visual, emotional and mental impressions which constitute the experience of the playgoer watching a performance by live actors.

Unlike the theatre audience, a reader is in complete personal control of the scanning process. He can repeatedly scrutinize a line, a passage of dialogue or a whole scene, or skim over what fails to interest him. He can virtually reassemble the given text by reading its parts in a chronological order different from that established by the author. He is able to anticipate and digress; or suspend the reading process in order to consult other sources of information. The two or three hours' traffic of the stage becomes a time span of indeterminate length. The particular theatrical representation is replaced by a free imaginative experience, richer or poorer by the measure of what the solitary reader brings to the reading.

The playgoer cannot count images, compare at will different parts of the play, track down sources or objectify at leisure his response to the play in progress. He must attend to the words, sounds, images and experiences as they are projected by the actors in the temporal sequence determined by the playwright. And his individual reaction may be modified or even overridden by the collective response of the group of which he is a member.

Given such a major shift from a stage audience to a reading public of the kind which took place after the closing of the theatres in 1642, the little surviving evidence for contemporary response to Massinger's theatrical language assumes special interest.

Unfortunately there is no direct evidence of a theatregoer's response to a Massinger play. If a latter-day Simon Forman ever sat on a Blackfriars bench and watched a performance of *The Duke of Milan* or *The Roman Actor* his journal entry is still to be found. But there is strong circumstantial evidence of popular favour in the fact of Massinger's selection to succeed Shakespeare and Fletcher as the principal dramatist for the King's Men, the most famous professional company of its time. We know that there were occasional failures in the theatre,[4] but such information is more than balanced by the records of royal command performances, the company's protection of a number of scripts from their dissemination in print, and by the brief acknowledgements of theatrical success on the title page of play quartos. Of the plays of Massinger's single authorship all but *The Unnatural Combat* carry a reference to frequency of performance or favourable reception. Even if the phrases are conventional ones it is doubtful that a printer would apply them to a known theatrical flop, and not all playtexts carried such advertisements. The players who spoke the lines of Shakespeare, Jonson, Webster, Fletcher, Middleton and Ford performed the dramas of Massinger, and the leading actor Joseph Taylor publicly associated himself with the publication of *The Roman Actor*.

We know of some playgoers or readers who appreciatively entered passages from Massinger plays in their private journals. Thomas Frewen collected a number of extracts from *The Bondman*, and William How excerpted material from *The Great Duke of Florence* and *The Maid of Honour*. Two songs from *The Fatal Dowry*, the Citizen's Song of the Courtier and the Courtier's Song of the Citizen (IV.ii), enjoyed a wide currency in commonplace book collections and in the miscellany *The Academy of Complements* and its related publications.[5]

However, Massinger's lines did not please Abraham Wright, a fellow of St John's College, Oxford, and a student of the theatre. Wright, who was engaged in collecting striking passages and phrases from the dramatists of the period, abandoned his reading of *A New Way to Pay Old Debts* in Act III, and entered this comment: 'for yᵉ lines they are very poore, noe expressions, but onely plaine downright relating yᵉ matter; wthout any new dress either of language or fancy'.[6] Since he did note down such expressions as 'manumizd from yᵉ *porters lodge*' and 'Thou barathrum of yᵉ shambles' he may have been looking for an Alexandrian sophistication of language not to be found in the material before him.

An even more hostile reader was the author (perhaps Davenant) of a diatribe against Massinger addressed to Thomas Carew, the leading figure in a literary quarrel between the supporters of

the Blackfriars Theatre and those defending the Queen's
players at the Cockpit. Replying to an aggressive prologue to
The Maid of Honour, prepared by Massinger for a revival of
his play in 1630, the anonymous writer denounces the 'flat dull
dialogues fraught wth insipit chatt' of 'this Mechanicke playwright' (lines 6–8). 'I haue read his workes', he declares,

>   & by the bay
> That crownes Apollo, I can nothinge finde
> but a wilde desert, emptie aire & winde;
> only some shreds of Seneca.
>   . . . lines forcd, ruffe,
> Botch'd & vnshap'd in fashion, Course in stuffe.
> Yet hee this spurious issue poems calls.   (lines 12–15, 19–21)

Carew's poetry, he goes on, may claim a station in the first
rank, 'farre boue the humble forme of his [Massinger's] lame
blanks' (line 26).[7]

There is vague praise of Massinger's character as a writer in
William Hemminge's *Elegy on Randolph's Finger* (?1630–2):

>   Messenger that knowes
> the strength to wright or plott In verse or prose,
> Whose easye pegasus Can Ambell ore
> some threscore Myles of fancye In an hower.

George Wither, in his poem 'The Great Assizes Holden *in Par-
nassus by* Apollo and his Assessors' (1645) ranks Massinger
with Beaumont, Fletcher and Shakespeare as 'Poets good and
free; / Dramatick writers all', and in 1650 Richard Wash-
ington, in a copy of *The Picture* inscribed a laudatory verse
entitled 'To the Memory of that great Architect of Poetry M^r.
Phillip Massinger'.

The poems by Massinger's friends and supporters prefixed to
some of the play quartos occasionally contain specific remarks
about the language of the plays. They cannot be discounted as
conventional flattery, for several of the writers are critical
enough of the dramatist on other heads, and there seems to
have been no tradition that style should be singled out for
discussion.

In a prefatory poem (1623) W. B. (probably William
Bagnall, the minor poet) praised *The Duke of Milan* in these
terms:

13

> *Here* witt *(more fortunate) is ioyn'd with* Art,
> *And that most sacred* Frenzie *beares a part*
> *Infus'd by* Nature *in the* Poet's *heart.*
>
> *Here, may the* Puny-wits *themselues direct,*
> *Here, may the* Wisest *find what to affect;*
> *And* Kings *may learne their proper* Dialect.

In a poem (1633) prefixed to *A New Way to Pay Old Debts*
Thomas Jay takes the opposite view to Abraham Wright, paying
tribute to

> *The craftie* Mazes *of the cunning plot;*
> *The polish'd phrase; the sweet expressions; got*
> *Neither by theft, nor violence; the conceipt*
> *Fresh, and vnsullied.*

The Roman Actor appeared in print (1629) with no fewer than
six attendant poems. Like Bagnall's remarks, they anticipate the
praise of Massinger's dignity, loftiness and eloquence which was
to become a commonplace in later discussions of the dramatist's
theatrical style and something of an embarrassment to his
modern defenders. Thomas Gough addresses a Latin poem to the
poeta elegantissima. Thomas May declares that in Massinger's
tragedy

> Paris, the best of Actors in his age
>   Acts yet, and speakes vpon our Roman Stage
> Such lines by thee, as doe not derogate
>   From *Romes* proud heights, and Her then learned State.

Robert Harvey says of Domitian's words,

> Each line speakes him an Emperour, eu'ry phrase
> Crownes thy deseruing temples with the Bayes;
>   So that reciprocally both agree
>   Thou liu'st in him and Hee surviues in Thee.

John Ford, Massinger's dramatist friend, takes up the same
theme; the story of Domitian, his wife, and Paris

>   meerly were related
> Without a Soule, Vntill thy abler Pen
>   Spoke them, and made them speake, nay Act agen
> In such a height, that Heere to know their Deeds
> Hee may become an Actor that but Reades.

So does Thomas Jay:

> Such power lyes in this loftie straine as can
> Giue Swords, and legions to DOMITIAN.
> And when thy PARIS pleades in the defence
> Of Actors, every grace, and excellence
> Of Argument for that subject, are by Thee
> Contracted in a sweete Epitome.

But Jay adds the interesting remark,

> Nor doe thy Women the tyr'd Hearers vexe,
> With language no way proper to their sexe,

interesting because T. S. Eliot was later to level the accusation that 'When Massinger's ladies resist temptation they do not appear to undergo any important emotion; they merely know what is expected of them; they manifest themselves to us as lubricious prudes.'[8]

Eliot, as I have already noticed, mixes praise with his criticism of Massinger. There is striking agreement between his admiration for a passage from *The Fatal Dowry* for its 'language … pure and correct, free from muddiness or turbidity' and Sir Aston Cokayne's praise (1632) of Massinger prefixed to *The Emperor of the East*:

> *Thou more then Poet, our* Mercurie (*that art*
> Apollo's *Messenger, and do'st impart*
> *His best expressions to our eares*) *liue long*
> *To purifie the slighted English tongue,*
> *That both the* Nymphes *of* Tagus, *and of* Poe,
> *May not henceforth despise our language so.*

But a finer if less extravagant tribute than this occurs in John Ford's poem (1636) on *The Great Duke of Florence*. Ford, who as a man of the theatre himself knew the power of the actor to give dramatic life even to a lifeless script, insists that it was the quality of Massinger's writing that made a good performance possible, and not the delivery:

> Action *gives many Poems right to live,*
> This Piece *gave life to* Action; *and will give*
> *For state, and language, in each change of Age,*
> *To Time, delight; and honour to the stage.*

In what follows I am concerned to explore some of the theatrical virtues of Massinger's dramatic language, by which I mean its effective operation in the full context of stage presentation. I shall begin with some instances of poetic imagery taken from his tragedy *The Unnatural Combat*, the play which Eliot counted among Massinger's three best, and which Kean is said to have 'longed to bring upon the stage, yet dare not'.[9]

What is particularly evident is the coherence of image and action through which this dramatist expresses the powerful conception which controls all the parts of the play. Verbal images are supported by and in turn reinforce visual stage imagery at key points, and although Massinger does not attempt to create the kind of figurative density which distinguishes the poetic style of the earlier Jacobean tragedy, image iteration throughout the drama brings into being a verbal and theatrical grid of pictures strongly reinforcing the total structure of the play. That the images themselves are not strikingly original or poetically remarkable may seem less important in the theatre than that they should work so consistently towards the effect of the tragedy as a whole.

I begin by drawing attention to the working of a local image which occurs at the point where Malefort, Admiral of Marseilles, and his son, the renegade leader of pirates who have been ravaging the port, are about to fight a duel to the death, the father having agreed to accept his son's sensational challenge to single combat in order to clear himself from a charge of complicity with the pirates. Malefort rejects the offers of three of his supporters to fight alongside him, and asks the seconds on both sides:

> Now if you please
> On both parts to retire to yonder mount,
> Where you, as in a Roman Theater,
> May see the bloudy difference determin'd,
> Your favours meet my wishes.
> *Malefort junior.*   'Tis approv'd of
> By me, and I command you lead the way,
> And leave me to my fortune.
> *Beaufort junior.*   I would gladly
> Be a spectator (since I am deni'd
> To be an Actor) of each blow, and thrust,
> And punctually observe 'em.
> *Malefort junior.*   You shall have
> All you desire; for in a word or two
> I must make bold to entertaine the time,
> If he give suffrage to it.
> *Malefort senior.*   Yes, I will,
> I'll heare thee, and then kill thee: nay farewell.
> *Malefort junior.*   Embrace with love on both sides, and with us

16

> Leave deadly hate, and furie.
> *Malefort senior.*   From this place
> You nere shall see both living.
> *Belgarde.*   What's past help, is
> Beyond prevention.   (II.i.97–114)

While the others are out of sight and hearing, climbing to their places (in Massinger's theatre, ascending to the upper stage), father and son express a personal hatred and enmity whose real cause is only half-revealed to the audience when the son names his dead mother and the Admiral immediately throws himself at him, before the group of supporters can appear '*Above*' to watch the beginning of the combat.

Malefort's allusion to 'a Roman Theater' is not a casual one. The idea of a Roman theatre is carried forward in the dialogue, both in Beaufort's remarks and in repeated references to seeing and watching. It is visually reinforced by the stage circumstances, with a number of actor-spectators taking their places to observe two men engaged in gladiatorial combat. Such a conception anticipates, as does this scene as a whole, the final scene of the play, in which Malefort will stand with his daughter beneath the battlements of Montreville's fortress, while above him Montrevile appears, '*the curtaine suddenly drawn*' (a direction surely more appropriate for a theatre than for a stronghold). When Montreville is called away by news of an attack on the fort he is succeeded by the ghosts of Malefort's victims, his son and first wife, who, though the stage directions do not require it, probably walk the same battlements before the old man is struck down by a flash of lightning. At least some of the audience must have experienced the action of the play as leading from a Roman theatre, the scene of Malefort's triumph, to a theatre of divine judgement.

The theatre image has more than a structural function of this sort. It also prompts the audience to see the Admiral and his son as *actors*, performing a dreadful but mysterious show for the astonished spectators on the stage and in the auditorium, a spectacular public display of sword-fighting whose true cause lies hidden from both groups of observers.

The Admiral and young Malefort are actors in another sense: they mask the true springs of their behaviour not only from those watching them but also from each other and from themselves. Both father and son avoid direct expression of the truth; young

Malefort choosing to speak 'in a perplext forme and method' which only his father can interpret, even when there are no stage listeners. Massinger in fact here uses the actor-in-a-theatre image to hint at a profound disjunction between the deepest levels of his two characters' personalities and their public behaviour towards each other and their associates. Beneath the formal arrangements for a public duel lie the son's insensate rage against the murderer of his mother, and the father's unacknowledged blood-guiltiness (typically this dramatist exploits primitive emotional conflicts).

Such a disjunction is like that between the true personality of the actor (the real man) and the language and behaviour which manifests his assumed role. Malefort is in actuality 'a wicked man' confronting the knowledge of his own crimes, but he adopts the part of the injured commander of the naval forces of Marseilles, the outraged parent dealing with a defiant child. The insistently theatrical language of the son's cry to his father,

> not as with a father, (all respect,
> Love, feare, and reverence cast off,) but as
> A wicked man I thus expostulate with you.
> Why have you done that which I dare not speake?
> And in the action chang'd the humble shape
> Of my obedience, to rebellious rage
> And insolent pride? (II.i.128–34)

expresses the chaos in his mind in terms of a bewildering confusion of roles; an identity crisis, in which conflicting moral positions are imagined as costumes chosen by an actor.

Image counting of the kind which recognizes such a passage as this only as a statistical unit in a catalogue of Massinger's imagery drawn from the theatre does little justice to such theatre-poetry or to the cooperation of image and stage action in the representation of character and the construction of the play as a whole.

My second example of the local richness and larger ramifications of a Massingerian image comes from an earlier scene in *The Unnatural Combat*, in which the out-of-work soldier Belgarde approaches the young Beaufort, son of the Governor of Marseilles, to appeal for employment and money. But Beaufort's attention is distracted by a second suitor, a beautiful woman:

Massinger's Theatrical Language

> *Beaufort junior.*   Away, you are troublesome,
>   Designes of more weight –
> *Belgarde.*   Ha faire *Theocrine*,
>   Nay if a velvet peticote move in the front
>   Buffe jerkins must to the rere, I know my manners;
>   This is indeed great businesse, mine a gugawe,
>   I may dance attendance, this must be dispatchd,
>   And suddainly, or all will goe to wracke.
>   Charge her home in the flank my Lord, nay I am gone sir.
>   *Exit* BELGARDE.
>   (I.i.116–23)

Studies of Massinger's imagery are inclined to point out that the second and third lines of this passage supply instances of metonymy, that Massinger frequently uses this figure and that textiles often provide the subject of such figures. But such observations contribute little to any appreciation of the theatrical vitality or the literary quality, the particular aptness, of the imagery here.

First, the passage demonstrates Massinger's ability to find words appropriate to his character's experience and situation. 'Velvet peticote' conveys exactly the speaker's explosive scorn for women and for an influence stronger than his own, as well as his acute awareness of the sources of that influence in Theocrine's sexual attractiveness and her social rank, whose mark is the money he himself so desperately needs. 'Buffe jerkins' is the soldier's appeal to hearty, masculine toughness and military sentiment. (The modern term 'leather jacket' has much the same connotations.) Massinger combines these expressive textile images with military jargon appropriate to his soldier, and the verse is constructed to provide a rough and emphatic stress pattern.

There is careful provision, too, for an amusing piece of stage action in the last line when Belgarde speaks out too freely to Beaufort, rouses a strong gesture of disapproval, and has to exit apologetically: 'nay I am gone sir'.

But like the previous theatre image this image functions in ways that reach beyond the infusion of local life into a piece of dialogue. Belgarde's reference to velvet petticoats and buff jerkins forms part of a whole chain of clothing images, which in Shakespearian manner is introduced in the opening lines of the play with Montreville's remark:

Now to bee modest Madam, when you are
A suitor for your father, would appeare
Courser then bouldnesse; you a while must part with
Soft silence, and the blushings of a virgin,
Though I must grant (did not this cause command it)
They are rich jewells you have ever worne
To all mens admiration.   (I.i.1–7)

There is no space for a complete catalogue of similar instances, but a short collection of representative passages will serve to illustrate the range and extent of this vein of imagery:

> *Malefort senior.*
> though my deeds wore Hels blacke liverie,
> To thee they should appeare triumphall robes,
> Set off with glorious honour, thou being bound
> To see with my eyes, and to hold that reason,
> That takes or birth or fashion from my will.   (II.i.160–4)

> *Malefort.*   Welcome Girle:
> My joy, my comfort, my delight, my all,
> Why dost thou come to greet my victorie
> In such a sable habit? this shew'd well
> When thy father was a prisoner and suspected;
> But now his faith and loyaltie are admir'd,
> Rather than doubted, in your outward garments
> You are to expresse the joy you feele within.   (II.iii.59–66)

> *Belgarde.*   I would I were aquainted with the players,
> In charity they might furnish me, but there is
> No faith in Brokers, and for believing Taylors
> They are only to be read of, but not seene,
> And sure they are confinde to their owne hells,
> And there they live invisible; well I must not
> Be fubd off thus – pray you report my service
> To the Lord governour. I will obey him
> And though my wardrop's poore, rather then loose
> His company at this feast, I will put on
> The richest suite I have, and fill the chaire,
> That makes me worthy of.   (III.i.101–12)

> *Usher.*   Why had I beene borne a Lorde, I had beene no servant.
> 1. *Woman.*   And where as now necessity makes us wayters,
> We had been attended on.
> 2. *Woman.*   And might have slept then,
> As long as we pleas'd, and fed when we had stomackes,
> And worne new cloths, nor liv'd as now in hope
> Of a cast gowne, or petticote.

Page.   You are fooles,
   And ignorant of your happinesse; ere I was
   Sworne to the pantofle, I have heard my tutor
   Prove it by logicke, that a servants life
   Was better then his masters.
        . . .
                              And as a horse
   Is still a horse, for all his golden trappings,
   So your men of purchas'd titles, at their best are
   But serving-men in rich liveries.   (III.ii.101–10, 130–3)

Malefort senior.   O that I was ever
   Accurs'd in having issue: my sonnes bloud,
   (That like the poyson'd shirt of *Hercules*
   Growes to each part about me) which my hate
   Forc'd from him with much willingnesse, may admit
   Some weake defence; but my most impious love
   To my faire daughter *Theocrine*, none.
        . . .
   Why was I tender of her? cover'd with
   That fond disguise, this mischiefe stole upon me.   (IV.i.7–13, 20–1)

Belgarde.   What ere you thinke, I am not master at
   This instant, of a livre.
2. Wench.   What, and in
   Such a glorious suite?
Belgarde.   The liker wretched things
   To have no mony.
Bawd.   You may pawne your clothes, Sir.
1. Wench.   Will you see your issue starve?
2. Wench.   Or the mothers beg?
Belgarde.   Why, you unconscionable strumpets, would you have me
   Transforme my hat to double clouts and biggins?
   My corselet to a cradle? or my belt
   To swaddlebands? or turne my cloke to blankets?
   Or to sell my sword and spurs for sope and candles?
   Have you no mercy? what a chargeable divell
   We carry in our breeches!   (IV.ii.121–32)

Montrevile.   How her heart beats!
   Much like a Partridge in a Sparhawkes foot,
   That with a panting silence does lament
   The fate she cannot flie from! sweet, take comfort,
   You are safe, and nothing is intended to you
   But love and service.
Theocrine.   They came never cloth'd
   In force, and outrage.
                              (V.i.14–20)

This sequence of impressions, signalled through the language, is designed to catch the eye as well as the ear. Stage pictures, many of them carefully specified by the dramatist, reinforce the verbal costume images. Theocrine makes her first appearance on stage still and silent, veiled and dressed in black.[10] She last appears raped and helpless, *'her garments loose, her haire disheveld'* (v.ii). Belgarde on his first entrance is dressed in a soldier's rough uniform. Then in a fine *coup de théâtre* of the kind Massinger was specially skilled in he arrives at Beaufort's banquet in full armour, *'a case of Carbines by his side'* (III.iii). Later he comes on *'in a gallant habit'* (IV.ii), wearing ostrich feathers and perfumed gloves, and finally goes into action, still in his finery, now made ridiculous by the circumstances and the bad weather:

> *Belgarde.*   Here is a night
> To season my silkes. Buffe-jerkin, now I misse thee,
> Thou hast endur'd many foule nights, but never
> One like to this; how fine my feather looks now!
> Just like a Capons taile stolne out of the pen
> And hid in the sinke, and yet 't had beene dishonour
> To have charg'd me without it.   (v.ii.306–12)

Malefort is involved in an equally important series of episodes in which dress and appearance play a main part. They include his transformation from released prisoner to honoured guest of the Governor of Marseilles, and the younger Beaufort's report (III.ii) of his extraordinary attention to the details of Theocrine's dress, a convincing and pathetic picture of sexual frustration. The apparition of the ghost of Malefort's son, *'naked from the wast, full of wounds'*, and his dead wife, *'her face leprous'* (v.ii), is part of the dramatist's careful attention to emblematic action.

Such a strict selection of vocabulary, imagery and scenic action works powerfully to express the controlling idea of the play, one which has little to do with the trite moralizing of old Beaufort at the conclusion. The dramatist's conception is a genuinely tragic one; Massinger is interested in Malefort's human experience rather than in the power of heaven to 'punishe murther and unlaw-full love'. His imaginative energy goes into the effort to represent the effects of an overmastering passion in a divided human per-sonality; to explore stage-moment by stage-moment what it is like to be a Malefort, and to measure that tragic experience in a world at once as natural (whole) and as deviant (fragmented) as the character of the tragic protagonist himself. Buff jerkins, glorious suits, outward forms, curious dressings, veils and sable habits are part of the concrete, allusive language of the stage through which such a mastering idea is given life in the theatre.

The pattern of characters underscores the same thoughtful design of the play. Beaufort and his son, secure in the normal world (though not idealized), point up the tragic relationship of Malefort and his son. The natural affection of Theocrine for her father and stepbrother, the casual sexual looseness of Belgarde, the romantic love of young Beaufort, the knowing wit of the precocious page boy, the brazenness of the wenches and the passion-crazed hatred of Montreville place and define for us the special nature of Malefort's sexuality.

Belgarde occupies a unique position in such a pattern. In a world of extraordinary warfare (father against son) and unnatural desire (father for daughter) he is the ordinary man, *l'homme sensuel moyen*, the soldier 'in ... his naturall, and proper shape'. His capture of the fort the desperate Malefort fails to enter, and his displacement of its treacherous commander Montreville, assert the reappearance of professional competence and conventional integrity.

But simple contrast of this kind is not his only function. Throughout the play his fortunes are intertwined with Malefort's, a linkage which the dramatist stresses in several ways. He uses, for instance, parallel episodes, such as the double petition to Beaufort which opens the play, or the banquet scene in which both men appear splendidly dressed and are honoured by the Governor. Malefort and Belgarde also have in common the language of war applied in radically different contexts, as in Malefort's passionate speech to his daughter:

> Wherefort art thou
> So cruell to me? This thy outward shape
> Brought a fierce warre against me, not to be
> By flesh and blood resisted: but to leave me
> No hope of freedome, from the Magazine
> Of thy minds forces, treacherously thou drewst up
> Auxiliary helpes to strengthen that
> Which was already in it selfe too potent:
> Thy beauty gave the first charge, but thy duty
> Seconded with thy care, and watchfull studies
> To please, and serve my will in all that might

Raise up content in me, like thunder brake through
All opposition, and my rankes of reason
Disbanded, my victorious passions fell
To bloody execution, and compeld me
With willing hands to tie on my owne chaines,
And with a kinde of flattering joy to glory
In my captivity.   (IV.i.107–24)

Another instance is Malefort's weak explanation to Beaufort of
his request to observe his son's courtship of Theocrine:

But now pray you pardon me, and if you please
Ere she deliver up her virgin fort,
I would observe what is the art he uses
In planting his artillery against it;
She is my only care, nor must she yield
But upon noble termes.   (III.iii.151–6)

But such language is habitual with him.

Massinger uses the close counterpointing of Belgarde with
Malefort to direct attention to the profounder disjunctions
which distinguish Malefort's tragic experience from Belgarde's
misfortunes. The old Admiral's criminal self is masked, desperately concealed beneath his public selves as natural parent and
famous commander. But that darker self gradually forces itself to
the surface, disrupting and finally destroying Malefort's life and
the lives of those closest to him. Belgarde, on the other hand,
suffers no such deep psychological disruption; his change in
fortunes is on the surface, his discomfiture social. New clothes
bring him swarms of hangers-on and prove ridiculously unsuit-
able for the practice of his profession. But the process is
reversible:

Beaufort senior. Why in this heat, *Belgarde*?
Belgarde.   You are the cause of't.
Beaufort senior. Who, I?
Belgarde.   Yes, your pied liverie, and your gold
     Draw these vexations on mee, pray you strip me
     And let me be as I was: I will not lose
     The pleasures and the fredome which I had
     In my certaine povertie; for all the wealth
     Faire France is proud of!   (IV.ii.139–45)

For Malefort, no such reversal is possible. Locked in unnatural
combat with himself, he destroys the one person in the play who
possesses a simple innocence, his own daughter Theocrine. And

her doomed perfection, like Malefort's deformed and divided nature, is articulated in part by means of the principal verbal and visual images of the play. When Theocrine is brought to Beaufort, wearing the 'rich and curious dressings' which her father has lavished on her, Malefort remarks:

> View her well brave *Beaufort*,
> But yet at distance; you hereafter may
> Make your approaches neerer, when the priest
> Hath made it lawfull, and were not shee mine,
> I durst alowd proclaime it, *Hymen* never
> Put on his saffron coloured robe to change
> A barren virgin name with more good omens,
> Then at her nuptialls. Looke on her againe,
> Then tell me if she now appeare the same
> That she was yesterday.   (III.ii.55–64)

To which the lover replies, unconscious of the ironic application to her presenter:

> Being her self
> She cannot but be excellent, these rich
> And curious dressings, which in others might
> Cover deformities, from her take lustre
> Nor can adde to her.   (III.ii.64–8)

The Unnatural Combat is no special case. Massinger writes poetry-for-the-theatre, and Massingerian drama as a whole evinces a similar concern for the coordination of theatrical and verbal imagery, and its coherence with the central conception of each play.

The nexus of imagery and action in Massinger's own preferred drama, *The Roman Actor*, 'the most perfit birth of my Minerua', as he called it, has been the subject of a number of critical studies. It is a kind of theatrical *tour de force*, in which no fewer than four inset plays generate poetic and dramatic images for the larger skein of actions which enfolds them. A virtuoso piece, with a histrionic hero, written for the actors of his company by a professional playwright. *The City Madam*, with its tissue of images drawn from animal life (more than fifty of them), evoking the life of the city in terms of its opposite, the countryside, has still to attract a careful analysis of the interconnection of local theatrical effect, structural design and intellectual theme. So too does the interweaving of the language of war and sex in *The Picture*. And there are others like them.

The City Madam is also a play which demonstrates another important and neglected quality of Massinger's theatrical language: the change of registers and tones within a single drama which is so gratifying to any acting company and its audiences.

It must be admitted that it is possible to gather from the chorus of Massinger's admirers the impression that this dramatist was perpetually standing on his dignity; to use Gosse's sour phrase, that Massinger is 'uniform and humdrum'. Eighteenth- and nineteenth-century critics, concerned to express their admiration for Massinger in terms of the values of classicism, become almost obsessive about 'the harmony and dignity of his dramatic eloquence' (Thomas Campbell).[11] John Hamilton Reynolds found an appropriate metaphor for Massinger's usual language in 'the calm and majestic gliding of a river'.[12] W. J. Courthope, making the common reservation about Shakespeare's agreed superiority, wrote: 'The nobility of style is one of Massinger's characteristics ... Without ever rivalling the sublime flights of Shakespeare's figurative eloquence he avoids the roughness and obscurity of his late manner. Compared with Fletcher he is less exuberant and flowing but more lofty and poetical. His verse moves with an even and majestic march.'[13] Even Elizabeth Barrett Browning, who thought that Massinger lacked passion – 'he writes all like a giant – a dry-eyed giant', she said – was otherwise content to repeat in her essay *The Book of the Poets* the received character of his writing: 'His gesture and enunciation are slow and majestic ... From Massinger's more resonant majesty we turn back to [Shakespeare's] artlessness of art.'

To all of which it might be replied that no theatre audience would tolerate such a monotonous diet within a single play or the products of a working lifetime, as any professional dramatist would know.

Harmony, dignity and eloquence are key elements in Massinger's linguistic strategy, but they are not the only timbres available to him. Not infrequently in his plays eloquence and dignity are taken for a ride, subverted by their dramatic context or subtly reharmonized by the addition of another 'voice', as in *A New Way to Pay Old Debts*, III.i, where the page Alworth hesitantly expresses his fear that his master Lord Lovell will compete for the affections of Overreach's daughter, Margaret:

Alworth.   Were you to encounter with a single foe,
   The victorie were certaine: but to stand
   The charge of two such potent enemies,
   At once assaulting you, as Wealth and Beauty,
   And those too seconded with Power, is oddes
   Too great for *Hercules.*
Louell.   Speake your doubts, and feares,
   Since you will nourish 'em, in plainer language,
   That I may vnderstand 'em.   (III.i.50–7)

Lovell's request releases a 23-line speech from the boy in Massinger's most extravagant and orotund manner; a high-flown description of Margaret's beauty which only provokes a one-sentence reply from Lovell, 'Loue hath made you/Poeticall, *Alworth.*' To treat such a speech simply as an example of lofty Massingerian rhetoric, and to criticize its artificiality, its derivative imagery or its long-winded syntax is to miss the point. The comic contrast of the voluble, enthusiastic boy with his plain-speaking master, and the ludicrous nature of such a reply to a request for 'plainer language,/That I may vnderstand' is what Massinger is after. The dramatist is deliberately manipulating language to give his audience a direct impression of both the force and the adolescent quality of Alworth's love for Margaret. He is the conscious controller, not the victim, of his own eloquence.

But to return to *The City Madam.* Certainly there is dignity and eloquence to be found in the play, expressed in the convoluted syntactical structures that Dunn found to be a vice of Massinger's style:

Luke.   Your affability, and mildnesse cloath'd
   In the garments of your debtors breath
   Shall every where, though you strive to conceal it
   Be seen, and wondred at, and in the act
   With a prodigall hand rewarded. Whereas such
   As are born only for themselvs, and live so,
   Though prosperous in worldly understandings,
   Are but like beasts of rapine, that by odds
   Of strength, usurp, and tyrannize o're others
   Brought under their subjection.   (I.iii.64–73)

But Luke is here speaking the language of reformation and hypocrisy. He offers an almost perfectly convincing imitation of a good man's exhortation. His persuasion to licentious living

addressed to his brother's apprentices is couched in very different terms:

> Did'st thou know
> What ravishing lechery it is to enter
> An Ordinarie, *cap a pe*, trim'd like a Gallant,
> (For which in truncks conceal'd be ever furnish'd)
> The reverence, respect, the crouches, cringes,
> The musical chime of Gold in your cram'd pockets,
> Commands from the attendants, and poor Porters?
> *Tradewell.*   Oh rare!   (II.i.79–86)

The concrete vocabulary, the strong rhythmic patterns and the incremental sentence structure perfectly express the deliberately infectious excitement of the speech and at the same time subtly convey the speaker's own emotional commitment to the delights he is describing in order to deceive others. '*Cap a pe*' and 'Gold' are skilfully placed for maximum effect on the hearers, and the parenthesis has just the right touch of a piece of professional advice to junior partners in crime. But Luke is also savouring his past delights. We know him from within.

Further down the social scale there is even less of dignity, harmony or eloquence, for this is a comedy about social class and Massinger carefully adjusts the language to distinguish each social stratum. The following episode, in which two city toughs break into a brothel, is at once an exceptionally lively piece of theatre and a thematic illustration of pride followed by humiliation. It also demonstrates the variety of style within a single play which refutes Gosse's charge that Massinger is 'uniform and humdrum'. Here the language is predominantly monosyllabic, concrete and vulgar. There are frequent colloquialisms and slang terms. And in such a passage, the verse achieves that remarkable fluidity which is the despair of textual editors, but which Coleridge so admired as 'the nearest approach to the language of real life at all compatible with a fixed metre'. It is not a flexibility allowed everywhere in this play:

> *Enter* RAMBLE *and* SCUFFLE.
> *Scuffle.*   Are you grown proud?
> *Ramble.*   I knew you a wastcotier in the garden allies,
>   And would come to a saylors whistle.
> *Secret.*   Good Sir *Ramble*,
>   Use her not roughly. Shee is very tender.

Ramble. Rank and rotten, is she not?
                    She draws her knife. RAMBLE *his sword.*
Shavem.   Your spittle rogueships
  Shall not make me so.
Secret.   As you are a man, Squire *Scuffle*,
  Step in between em. A weapon of that length
  Was ne're drawn in my house.
Shavem.   Let him come on,
  I'le scoure it in your guts, you dog.
Ramble.   You brach,
  Are you turn'd mankind? You forgot I gave you,
  When wee last join'd issue, twenty pound.
Shavem.   O're night,
  And kickt it out of me in the morning. I was then
  A novice, but I know to make my game now.
  Fetch the Constable.
          Enter GOLDWIRE *like a Justice of Peace,* DINGEM *like a
              Constable, the Musicians like watch men.*
Secret.   Ah me. Here's one unsent for,
  And a Justice of Peace too.
Shavem.   I'l hang you both you rascalls,
  I can but ride. You for the purse you cut
  In Powl's at a sermon. I have smoak'd you. And you for the bacon
  You took on the high way from the poor market woman
  As she road from Rumford.
Ramble.   Mistris *Shavem.*
Scuffle.   Mistris *Secret*,
  On our knees we beg your pardon.
Ramble.   Set a ransom on us.

                                        (III.i.42–61)

In *The City Madam* Massinger not only discriminates verti-
cally, as it were, between stylistic levels which correspond to
differences in social rank. He differentiates between modes of
language appropriate to different modes of feeling and intellectual activity.

Beside the eloquence and passion of his brother, Sir John shows
a refreshing bluntness and plainness of speech. Luke has the
chameleon-like variety appropriate to his nature. As we have
seen, he can imitate the accents of pleading or high moral indignation. To the Frugal women he speaks a Marlovian language of
enticement, bitterly remembered when he imposes his puritanical
regime:

      Ladie.   O good brother!
        Do you thus preserve your protestation to me?

> Can Queens envy this habit? or did *Juno*
> E're feast in such a shape?
> *Anne.* You talk'd of *Hebe*,
> Of *Iris*, and I know not what; but were they
> Dres'd as we are, they were sure some Chandlers daughters
> Bleaching linnen in Moor-fields.
> *Mary.* Or Exchange-wenches,
> Comming from eating pudding-pies on a Sunday
> At *Pemlico*, or *Islington*. (IV.iv.31–9)

He can talk to the apprentices Goldwire and Tradewell with the heartiness of a good fellow or with an obdurate coldness. Stumbling out of Sir John's strongroom he speaks the language of emotion carried to the point of trance:

> 'Twas no phantastick object, but a truth,
> A reall truth. Nor dream; I did not slumber,
> And could wake ever with a brooding eye
> To gaze upon't! It did indure the touch,
> I saw, and felt it. Yet what I beheld
> And handl'd oft, did so transcend beleefe
> (My wonder, and astonishment pass'd ore)
> I faintly could give credit to my senses.
> Thou dumb magician that without a charm
> Did'st make my entrance easie, to possesse
> What wise men wish, and toyl for. *Hermes* Moly;
> *Sybilla's* golden bough; the great Elixar,
> Imagin'd onely by the Alchymist
> Compar'd with thee are shadows, thou the substance
> And guardian of felicity. (III.iii.1–15)

This is a brilliant piece of dramatic writing; a musical score for the actor, through which we are admitted to the process of Luke's mind as he recovers from his amazement to grasp what he takes for reality, the key stuck fast in his hand, 'the substance / And guardian of felicity'. (Massinger, the man of the theatre, is at work again, supplying his actor with clues for physical behaviour as well as creating in Luke's new assurance a delectable irony.) Luke's rapt conversation with himself, then with the key, the verbal reiterations as he compels his own belief ('no phantastick object ... truth ... reall truth ... Nor dream ... not slumber'), and the rapid change of mood from incredulity to rapture convincingly represent a mental experience never repeated in the play, and provide the actor with a great theatrical occasion.

A comparable passage, though one expressing a very different set of emotions, occurs in v.ii, when Luke turns on Lord Lacy:

Lord.   Such a cut-throat. I have heard of
   The usage of your brothers wife, and daughters.
   You shall find you are not lawlesse, and that your moneys
   Cannot justifie your villanies.
Luke.   I indure this.
   And good my Lord, now you talk in time of moneys,
   Pay in what you owe me. And give me leav to wonder
   Your wisedome should have leisure to consider
   The businesse of these gentlemen, or my carriage
   To my Sister, or my Neeces, being your self
   So much in my danger.
Lord.   In thy danger?
Luke.   Mine.
   I find in my counting house a Mannor pawn'd,
   Pawn'd, my good Lord, Lacie-Mannour, and that Mannour
   From which you have the title of a Lord,
   And it please your good Lordship. You are a noble man
   Pray you pay in my moneys. The interest
   Will eat faster in't, then *Aqua fortis* in iron.
   Now though you bear me hard, I love your Lordship.
   I grant your person to be priviledg'd
   From all arrests. Yet there lives a foolish creature
   Call'd an Under-sheriffe, who being well paid, will serve
   An extent on Lords, or Lowns land. Pay it in,
   I would be loth your name should sink. Or that
   Your hopefull son, when he returns from travel,
   Should find you my lord without land. You are angry
   For my good counsell. Look you to your Bonds: had I known
   Of your comming, believe it I would have had Serjeants ready:
   Lord how you fret! but that a Tavern's near
   You should taste a cup of Muscadine in my house,
   To wash down sorrow, but there it will do better,
   I know you'l drink a health to me.   *Exit* LUKE.
                                         (v.ii.54–83)

    The style here is at the utmost remove from the dignified rheto-
ric of morality, with its short sentences, enjambements and
syllabic licence. Luke's sentence beginning 'I find in my counting
house a Mannor pawn'd' offers a superb example of colloquial
speech (and syntax). Expressive words are set in fluid line structures with an instinctive understanding of the right place for
them. There is no mistaking the nastiness of 'self' or 'son'. But
there is an emotional coherence established in part by the repetitions which seam the speech. Massinger insistently plays off the
command 'Pay' against the sneering honorific 'your Lordship' to
convey more than the words themselves can tell us about Luke's

feelings and attitude. And the speech moves through a concaten-
ation of moods and tones that would delight any actor: 'And give
me leav to wonder / Your wisedome should have leisure ... You
are angry / For my good counsell. Look you to your Bonds ...'
This is theatrical language of a high order. Through it we know
Luke as he cannot know himself.

There are many other kinds of language in *The City Madam*. The
language of the 'Indians', Holdfast's culinary catalogue, Luke's
list of damnable fashions; and the language of astrological quack-
ery, played off in detail against Plenty's honest indignation ('our
own language' ... 'our vulgar tongue') and Lady Frugal's affected
enthusiasm:

> *Ladie.*   Be silent,
>   And ere we do articulate, much more
>   Grow to a full conclusion, instruct us
>   Whether this day and hour, by the planets, promise
>   Happie success in marriage.
> *Stargaze.*   *In omni*
>   *Parte, et toto.*
> *Plenty.*   Good learn'd Sir, in English.
>   And since it is resolved we must be Coxcombs,
>   Make us so in our own language.
> *Stargaze.*   You are pleasant:
>   Thus in our vulgar tongue then.
> *Ladie.*   Pray you observe him.
> *Stargaze. Venus* in the West-angle, the house of marriage the
>   seventh house, in Trine of *Mars*, in Conjunction of *Luna*, and *Mars*
>   Almuthen, or Lord of the Horoscope.
> *Plenty.* Hoy day!
> *Ladie.* The Angels language, I am ravish'd! forward.   (II.ii.50–63)

Variety of language in this richly varied play serves many purposes, then, and not the least of them discriminations in character.
When Lacy and Plenty attempt to negotiate marriage terms with
Sir John's daughters, Mary Frugal shows the tougher temper of her
mind through her greater command of the resources of language. It
is instructive to set side by side her sister Anne's childlike chatter
about city pleasures and her own expression of downright scorn
for country life:

> *Lacie.*   Is there ought else
>   To be demanded?
> *Anne.*   Yes Sir, mine own Doctor;
>   French, and Italian Cooks; Musicians, Songsters,
>   And a Chaplain that must preach to please my fancie;

A friend at Court to place me at a Mask;
The private Box took up at a new Play
For me, and my retinue; a fresh habit,
(Of a fashion never seen before) to draw
The Gallants eies that sit on the Stage upon me;
Some decay'd Ladie for my Parasite,
To flatter me, and rail at other Madams;
And there ends my ambition.
. . .

Mary.   And can you in your wisedom,
Or rusticall simplicity imagine,
You have met some innocent Country girle, that never
Look'd further then her fathers farm, nor knew more
Then the price of corn in the Market; or at what rate
Beefe went a stone? that would surveigh your dayrie,
And bring in mutton out of Cheese, and butter?
That could give directions at what time of the Moon
To cut her Cocks, for Capons against Christmas,
Or when to raise up Goslings?
Plenty.   These are arts
Would not mis-become you, though you should put in
Obedience and duty.
Mary.   Yes, and patience,
To sit like a fool at home, and eye your thrashers;
Then make provision for your slavering Hounds,
When you come drunk from an Ale-house after hunting,
With your Clowns and Comrades as if all were yours,
You the Lord Paramount, and I the drudge;
The case Sir, must be otherwise.   (II.ii. 113–24, 143–60)

It must be admitted that when he is working in modes other than comedy Massinger offers a more restricted stylistic range, but only in *The Roman Actor*, in which on his own admission his object is 'grauity and height of subject', does he confine himself to a single, narrowly austere style, fit only for noble Romans.

A tragicomedy like *The Picture* is more typical of his linguistic strategy, and it is a strategy which aims at maximum theatrical contrast from language variation.

Although the staple of the play is blank verse, there is one major comic variation and two minor variations, lyric and moralizing. When Hilario, in a disastrous attempt to cheer up his mistress Sophia, dresses himself as an ancient warrior bearing a fake message about her husband Mathias, he speaks in rhymed couplets whose content is a clever parody of military jargon and the phrases of the old heroic romances:

> The Reere march'd first, which follow'd by the Van,
> And wing'd with the Battalia, no man
> Durst stay to shift a shirt or louze himselfe;
> Yet ere the armies ioyn'd, that hopefull elfe,
> Thy deere, my dainty duckling, bold *Mathias*
> Aduanc'd, and star'd like *Hercules* or *Golias*.
> A hundred thousand *Turkes*, it is no vaunt,
> Assail'd him, euery one a Termagaunt,
> But what did he then? with his keene edgde speare
> He cut, and carbonadode 'em, heere, and there,
> Lay leggs and armes, and as 'tis sayd truely
> Of *Beuis*, some he quarter'd all in three.　　(II.i.111–22)

Hilario's excitement and self-assurance here, well caught in the swing of the verse, make an amusing contrast with his next appearance, banished from the house and cold and hungry. The echo of military language, as well as the heavy verse rhythms, underlines the change:

> Thinne, thinne prouision, I am dieted
> Like one set to watch hawkes, and to keepe me waking
> My croaking guts make a perpetuall larum.
> Heere I stand centinell, and though I fright
> Beggers from my ladies gate, in hope to haue
> A greater share, I find my commons mend not.　　(III.i.1–6)

There are three songs in the play, one of which gained inclusion in a long-lived anthology of contemporary lyrical and amatory poetry. The close of Eubulus's speech in honour of soldiers and the final 'moral' of the play are both delivered in traditional rhymed couplets.

Throughout *The Picture* the usual decorum is observed, providing further stylistic variation. Servants speak in a lower register, as when Sophia's noble farewell to her husband is followed by her woman's leavetaking:

> *Corisca.*　　　　　　　Though you are my Lord,
> 　Yet being her gentlewoman, by my place
> 　I may take my leaue; your hand or if you please
> 　To haue me fight so high, ile not be coy
> 　But stande a tiptoe for't.
> *Mathias.*　　　　　　O farewell gyrle.
> *Hilario.*　A kisse well begg'd *Corisca*.
> *Corisca.*　　　　　　　Twas my fee,
> 　Loue how he melts! I cannot blame my ladies
> 　Vnwillingnesse to part with such marmulade lips.
> 　There will be scrambling for 'em in the campe,

34

And were it not for my honesty I could wish now
I were his leager landresse. I would finde
Sope of mine owne, enough to wash his linnen
Or I would straine hard for't.
Hilario.   How the mammet twitters!
Come, come my ladie staies for vs.
Corisca.   Would I had beene
Her ladiship the last night.
Hilario.   Noe more of that, wench.

                                 (1.i.94–108)

The broken rhythms and short sentences, the vocabulary of domestic activity, colloquial terms like 'mammet' and 'wench' and the generally bawdy tone make for a simple, heightening contrast with the previous episode.

Soldiers, by convention, are blunt speakers, and Massinger constructs an amusing scene (II.ii) out of 'a fight at complement' between the foppish courtiers, Ricardo and Ubaldo, and General Ferdinand. However, there are degrees of bluntness, and the dramatist introduces four soldiers, the knight Mathias, his commander Ferdinand, the old fighter Eubulus and the pretended warrior Hilario, each with his distinctive range and speaking voice.

The two central and complementary actions of the play, the temptation of Mathias by Queen Honoria and that of his wife Sophia by the two courtiers, are given distinguishing modes of language. Abstract moral rhetoric for the first, and physical, witty sex-talk for the second.

Contrasts and parallels in content, action and style are at the heart of Massinger's method here. Both Mathias and Sophia are given passionate speeches of anger at apparent betrayal by their partner (III.vi.126–61 and 1.i.41–53). Stylistically they are much alike, but the man repeatedly accuses all womankind, 'these Aspicks,/These weeping Crocadiles'; the woman refers only to herself and her husband, hers is a personal rather than a generalizing response. When Queen Honoria gives Mathias diamonds, as Ubaldo offers Sophia gems, the language of temptation, like the character of the tempters, is different in each case:

Honoria.   You are rude,
And by your narrow thoughts proportion mine.
What I will doe now, shall be worth the enuie
Of *Cleopatra*. Open it; see heere   HONORIA *descends.*

The Lapidaries Idol, gold is trash
And a poore salarie fit for groomes, weare these
As studded stars in your armour, and make the Sun
Looke dimme with iealousie of a greater light
Then his beames guild the day with: when it is
Expos'd to view, call it Honorias guift,
The Queene *Honorias* guift that loues a souldier,
And to giue ornament, and lustre to him
Parts freely with her owne.   (II.ii.245–57)

Vbaldo.   This chaine
   Of pearle was a great widdowes, that inuited
   Your Lord to the masque, and the wether prouing foule
   He lodg'd in her house all night, and merry they were,
   But how he came by it I know not.
Sophia.   Periurd man!
Vbaldo.   This ring was *Iuliettas*, a fine peece
   But very good at the sport; this diamond
   Was Madam *Acanthes* giuen him for a song
   Prick'd in a priuate arbor, as she sayd
   When the Queene askd for it, and she hard him sing to,
   And danc'd to his hornepipe or there are lyers abroad.
                                        (III.vi.102–12)

Such thematic variety is common in this play which displays
the remarkable adaptability of Massinger's poetic idiom. In
representing a violent action or fluent conversation, such as that
between Sophia and Ricardo in IV.ii.80 ff., it can relax to become
virtually indistinguishable from prose. It will acommodate
parody, sober moral instruction, satire or high passion.

But Massinger's most considerable triumph in *The Picture* is
the creation of the voice of Sophia. Angry at the test her husband
has put her to and apparently failed himself, she can respond to
his fury with exactly the accents of controlled but passionate
indignation:

Mathias.   Forbeare.
   Or you will rayse my anger to a height,
   That will descend in fury.
Sophia.   Whie? you know
   How to resolue your selfe what my intents are,
   By the helpe of *Mephostophiles*, and your picture,
   Pray you looke vpon't again. I humbly thanke
   The Queenes great care of me, while you were absent.
   She knew how tedious 'twas for a young wife,
   And being for that time a kind of widdow,
   To passe away her melancholly howers

36

Without good company, and in charity therefore
Prouided for me: out of her owne store
She culd the Lords *Ubaldo*, and *Ricardo*,
Two principall courtiers for Ladies seruice,
To do me all good offices, and as such
Imployd by her. I hope I haue receaud,
And entertaind 'em, nor shall they depart
Without the effect arising from the cause
That brought 'em hither.   (v.iii.74–92)

But she has other tones. In this play, she is the guarantee of Mathias's faith, and her integrity is unquestionable after we have heard her speaking her farewell to her husband. It is a speech which shows more than Massinger's skill in modulating his theatrical language and his keen sense of the unity of speech and action on stage.[14] On occasion this craftsman-poet of the theatre could command that eloquent simplicity of language which is the mark of some of the very greatest dramatists:

Sophia.   My soule
Shall goe along with you, and when you are
Circl'd with death and horrour seeke and finde you:
And then I will not leaue a Saint vnsu'd to
For your protection. To tell you what
I will doe in your absence, would shew poorely,
My actions shall speake me; 'twere to doubt you
To begge I may heere from you, where you are,
You cannot liue obscure nor shall one post
By night, or day passe vnexamined by me.
If I dwell long vpon your lips, consider
After this feast the griping fast that followes
And it will be excusable. Pray turne from mee.
All that I can is spoken.   (i.i.77–90)

NOTES

1   Gosse, *The Jacobean Poets* (London, 1899), pp. 206–7.
2   *The Edinburgh Review*, 12 (April 1808), 114.
3   Quoted in *The Collected Letters of Thomas and Jane Carlyle*, ed. Charles R. Sanders and Kenneth J. Fielding (9 vols., Durham, NC, Duke University Press, 1970–81), vol. 2, p. 291, from a letter written in 1814.
4   See, for instance, the discussion of the Prologue to *The Guardian* in *The Plays and Poems of Philip Massinger*, ed. Philip Edwards and Colin Gibson (5 vols., Oxford, Clarendon Press, 1976), vol. 1, pp. xl–xlii. All quotations from Massinger's plays and their accompanying poems are taken from this edition.

5   The manuscript evidence is conveniently documented in Peter Beal's *Index of English Literary Manuscripts, Vol. 1, 1450–1625* (London, Mansell; New York, Bowker, 1980), pt 2, pp. 335–40, 631. Massinger's presence in printed and manuscript verse anthologies of the seventeenth century is the subject of a forthcoming study.

6   Printed in Edwards and Gibson, vol. 2, pp. 378–9.

7   Quotations are from the transcript printed in Peter Beal's 'Massinger at Bay: Unpublished Verses in a War of the Theatres', *The Yearbook of English Studies*, 10 (1980), 190–203. See pp. 193–5.

8   I quote Eliot's essay from his *Selected Essays* (London, Faber and Faber, 1932), p. 213.

9   Quoted in an unsigned review of the 11 May (1834) performance at the Royal Victoria Theatre of Elton's adaptation of *The Unnatural Combat*; *British Museum Theatrical Cuttings*, vol. 3 (1832–4).

10 The effect strongly resembles that of the silent presence of the black-clad Charalois at the beginning of *The Fatal Dowry*. Some verbal resemblances suggest that Massinger was consciously reworking a scene he had previously found successful in the theatre. Compare, for instance, *The Unnatural Combat*, 1.i.67–73, with *The Fatal Dowry*, 1.i.54–60.

11 Campbell, *Specimens of the British Poets; with Biographical and Critical Notices, and an Essay on English Poetry* (7 vols., London, John Murray, 1819), vol. 1, p. 201.

12 Reynolds, *On the Early Dramatic Poets*, an essay printed in *The Champion* on January 7, 1816, reprinted in *Selected Prose of John Hamilton Reynolds*, ed. Leonidas M. Jones, (Cambridge, Mass., Harvard University Press, 1966), p. 36.

13 W. J. Courthope, *A History of English Poetry* (6 vols., London, Macmillan, 1895–1910), vol. 4, pp. 367–8.

14 The kiss which Sophia gives her husband at the close of the speech, the natural action confirming the sincerity of her words, is not forgotten by Massinger. In the final scene of the play, Sophia wantonly kisses the returned Mathias's companions, showing him the woman he suspected her of having become.

Massinger's Men and Women

PHILIP EDWARDS

An extended session with Massinger's plays is likely to give a reader a frequent sense of *déjà vu* as similar images, protestations, situations and even characters come round again and again. But repetitiousness is not necessarily a sign of a lack of inventiveness, and Massinger's pronounced tendency to do things more than once often shows him absorbed in the ramifications of some particular issue or problem. His two satirical comedies, *A New Way to Pay Old Debts* and *The City Madam*, show general similarity in treating the war between the nobility and the city, but the scrupulous attention to social detail in these two plays reveals Massinger extending, not repeating, his views of the problem. I shall try to show that in dealing with the relations between the sexes Massinger's tendency to repeat patterns of conflict shows him exploring perennial problems about domination and submission with subtlety and shrewdness.

A king or duke who is a besotted and infatuated husband embarrassing his court by his public declaration of the pleasure he gets from his wife's embraces is a piece of theatre which Massinger gives us twice, in *The Duke of Milan* and *The Picture*. Here is Sforza in the former play:

> Such as are cloyd with those they haue embrac'd,
> May thinke their wooing done: No night to mee,
> But is a brydall one, where *Himen* lights
> His torches fresh, and new: And those delights,
> Which are not to be cloth'd in ayrie sounds,
> Inioyd, beget desires, as full of heat,
> And Iouiall feruor, as when first I tasted
> Her virgin fruit.   (I.iii.41–8)

We might feel that we need not be detained by the psychology of this, but we are on the threshold of what goes beyond mere theatre. The devotion of Ladislaus, the comic king in *The Picture*, 'drownd in dotage', takes the form of a fervent masochism. 'He forbeares / The duety of a husband, but when she calles for't' (I.ii.70–1). He publicly kisses the hem of her robe 'in signe of my subiection, as your vassall' (I.ii.161). This submissiveness with all its grovelling delights – 'hugging his fetters' as Eubulus calls it – belongs to an intense possessiveness: 'But then adde this, she's mine, mine *Eubulus*' (I.ii.109). The necessary relationship between doting servility and a possessiveness that verges on the insane becomes a main issue in *The Duke of Milan* and *The Bondman*.

The Duke of Milan is a sensational play and all emotions tend to be at an extreme. Sforza has made his own way to the dukedom (III.i.156–7; hence the 'supposed' Duke of Milan, that is, supposititious or not genuine, in the list of characters). Massinger shows us the fearless soldier-statesman in the excellent scene (III.i) in which, having backed the wrong side, Sforza makes a spirited defence of his conduct to the victorious Emperor – and so retains his title and averts the sack of his city. But the rest of the play is his private life, the private life of an autocrat. We do not know until towards the end of the play what instigates and explains the whole of the action. Three years before, Sforza seduced Eugenia on a promise of marriage, then threw her off. He then advanced her brother Francisco in order to buy his silence. It is to this apparently trustworthy aide that he imparts the dreadful secret instruction as he leaves Milan in order to meet the Emperor; namely, to kill his wife if he doesn't return. Francisco has been waiting for an opportunity to avenge his sister's disgrace; in the possession of this secret he now has all he needs, and proceeds to the mischief which culminates in Sforza stabbing his own wife in jealous fury.

What makes Sforza issue this secret instruction that his wife is not to outlive him if he fails in his desperate mission to placate the Emperor? He has publicly honoured and expressed in the extreme terms I have quoted his adoration for this woman whose life he now proposes to snuff out if it continues beyond his own. It is but justice, he says, that she should not outlive him, because *he* would refuse to outlive *her*! So his immoderate affection is not freely bestowed but stipulates an equivalent return. He basks in the thought of receiving the adoration he bestows, and indeed it is the *honour* to him of a voluntarily offered death that he is crazily exacting from her:

> The slauish Indian Princes when they dye
> Are cheerefully attended to the fire,
> By the wife, and slaue, that liuing they lou'd best,
> To doe them seruice in another world:
> Nor will I be lesse honor'd, that loue more.   (I.iii.361–5)

Within this vanity is also the strange idea that heaven may permit sexual intercourse. 'There is no heauen without her' (356). It is the ultimate reduction of the worshipped person into an eternal sex-object that chiefly inspires Marcelia's indignation when Francisco betrays Sforza's secret to her:

> But that my Lord, my *Sforza* should esteeme
> My life fit only as a page, to waite on
> The various course of his vncertaine fortunes,
> Or cherish in himselfe that sensuall hope
> In death to know me as a wife, afflicts me.   (III.iii.58–62)

That his wife should (compulsorily) offer him the adoration of not surviving him, and that they should together experience what heaven may perhaps allow them is still not the whole story. It may seem an indifference to Marcelia as a person that her life is valued only in its continuance with him, but indifference is hardly the word for his nauseated contemplation of her sexual life if she continues to live. The need to placate the Emperor and stop him sacking Milan is the more urgent because he cannot bear the thought of her becoming one of the spoils of war. It is curious, however, that he should picture this ravishment with himself as observer – when he presumably would have been the first victim:

> But should that will
> To be so be forc'd *Marcelia*! and I liue
> To see those Eyes I prize aboue mine owne,
> Dart fauours (though compel'd) vpon another!
> Or those sweet Lips (yeelding Immortall Nectar)
> Be gently touch'd by any but my selfe!
> Thinke, thinke *Marcelia*, what a cursed thing
> I were, beyond expression.   (I.iii.201–8)

This is the jealousy which sums up and explains Sforza and is finally exhibited in the play's climax, when, goaded by suspicions which Francisco has carefully fomented, he stabs his wife and kills her. It is a jealousy which takes a secret pleasure in imagining the loved one being defiled in compelled sexual encounters with rough captors. The passage I have quoted takes extra force when put alongside passages from the companion study of possessive jealousy in Leosthenes' part in *The Bondman*. Such insistent fantasies of capture and rape seem a very poor basis for the ethic of masculine supremacy which society in these plays takes for granted. And there is no doubt that Massinger is taking trouble to expose these shadowy foundations.

The difficulty, for us, about the Leosthenes–Cleora relationship in *The Bondman* is that Cleora is such a prig. She is certainly not meant to be; it is she, a mere woman, who shames the decadent aristocracy of Syracuse into an awareness of their duty to fight for their country. It is one thing for a young woman to congratulate herself that she has not let herself go with her young man, but quite another to express to the young man the hope that the love between them may

> burne heere,
> And as a Sea-marke, serue to guide true Louers,
> (Toss'd on the Ocean of luxurious wishes)
> Safe from the rockes of Lust into the harbour
> Of pure affection. (II.i.73–7)

But since her chastity – the firmness of her will to say no – is of great importance in the play, we shall have to put up with the way Massinger makes her talk about it. Leosthenes is an immensely distrustful man, distrustful of his power to engage or keep Cleora's affection. It is 'excesse of loue', he says, that convinces him that in his absence at the wars Cleora's attractiveness will make some rival replace him. 'Can you thinke,' she asks, 'I may be tempted?' 'You were neuer prou'd', he replies brutally, explaining that he never attempted to get past her guard.

> When you are courted
> By such as keepe a Catalogue of their Conquests,
> Wonne vpon credulous Virgins; when nor Father
> Is here to awe you; Brother to aduise you;
> Nor your poore seruant by, to keepe such off,
> By lust instructed how to vndermine,
> And blow your chastity vp; when your weake senses
> At once assaulted, shall conspire against you;
> And play the traytors to your soule, your vertue;
> How can you stand? (II.i.150–9)

To counter a jealousy born of such an undervaluing of her intelligence and self-control, Cleora swears to stay blindfold until Leosthenes returns from the wars. Being blindfold makes rather more plausible than usual the non-recognition of a disguised character. Her former admirer Pisander, returned in the guise of a slave, engineers a slaves' revolt and rather unfairly wins her esteem by acting as her protector instead of ravishing her, which is what a slave-leader in rebellion is supposed to do. On his return Leosthenes of course expects that Cleora's virginity has not survived the revolt. 'Come', he says to her maid, 'discouer/What kinde of looke he had, that forc'd thy Lady' (IV.iii.53–4). Cleora finds it as hard to accept his domineering possessiveness (IV.iii.177–9) as his continuous suspicion that she has in fact yielded (188–200). Leosthenes accepts her word that she is still chaste, and acknowledges to himself an abnormality in his suspiciousness (209–11), which, however, breaks out again immediately he hears that Pisander has been found in her rooms. 'This confirmes/All she deliuer'd, false' (IV.iv.56–7). In a further moment of remorse he explains that

> Distrust of other springs, *Timagoras*,
> From diffidence in our selues.   (v.i.68–9)

But is this really true? Timid adoration, and fearfulness that he may lose or have lost Cleora, seem paradoxically rooted in approval of himself and a contempt for Cleora. Feeling that he is losing ground to this astonishing slave Pisander, he sinks to an odious protestation of his own niceness:

>   If my pride,
> Or any bold assurance of my worth,
> Has pluck'd this mountaine of disgrace vpon me,
> I am iustly punish'd, and submit; but if
> I haue beene modest, and esteem'd my selfe
> More iniur'd in the tribute of the praise,
> Which no desert of mine priz'd by selfe-loue
> Euer exacted; may this cause, and minute
> For euer be forgotten.   (v.iii.59–67)

It is he who loses control, and his bitter taunt to Cleora surely reveals his basic fear of her as the insatiable female. Perhaps, he says,

>   you haue seene
> This gallant, pitch the barre, or beare a burthen
> Would cracke the shoulders of a weaker bond-man;
> Or any other boistrous exercise,
> Assuring a strong backe to satisfie
> Your loose desires, insatiate as the graue.   (v.iii.89–94)

A notable concluding image! Of course, he loses her, and it is bad luck on Timandra that the plot requires her to take for a husband such a bundle of arrogance and fear as Leosthenes.

Leosthenes is Massinger's closest study of the psychology of jealousy. There is an extended study of the masculine complacency and self-approval which Leosthenes exhibits in Mathias in *The Picture*. Here, the partner (Sophia) is much more interestingly and extensively written up. The dialogue of the opening scene is outstanding. The patronizing self-assurance of Mathias is beautifully struck. He is parting from her to go to the wars and there try to make his fortune. There is more than a little of the seven-year itch about him. He is obviously exhilarated at the prospect of war and a holiday from his wife, but he puts on a puritan censoriousness:

> We haue long inioyd the sweets of loue, and though
> Not to Satietie, or lothing, yet
> We must not liue such dotardes on our pleasures
> As still to hugge them to the certaine losse
> Of profit, and preferment.   (I.i.30–4)

His values are very superficial. He needs the fortune which is the goal of his expedition to enable him to keep state and show off Sophia (it is notable that he admits he is of lower social rank than she (I.i.14)). It embarrasses him (46) that she should 'passe vnregarded' because their poverty will not allow jewellery or an extensive wardrobe. He knows women, of course, and knows that 'want breeds dissention/Euen in good women' (35–6).

To all this bland chatter, Sophia's replies are brief and simple. Has he seen any sign of discontent in her with this standard of living? She doesn't want the ostentation of superfluities. But Mathias better understands the duties of a husband:

> I should be censur'd
> Of ignorance, possessing such a Iewell
> Aboue all price, if I forbeare to giue it
> The best of ornaments. Therefore *Sophia*
> In few words know my pleasure and obey me,
> As you haue euer done.   (I.i.55–60)

But, as we shall now expect, this masterful man, so condescending to his wife's inferior understanding and so confident of her obedience, is plagued by the possibility that in the absence of his control this dear creature will suddenly become a beast with a ravenous sexual appetite – 'those wanton heates in women/Not to be quench'd by lawfull meanes' (144–5). So he procures a magic picture which will perfectly reflect his wife's constancy in his absence.

Of course, it is he who falls, a victim of the wiles of the vain queen whose besotted husband Ladislaus I have already talked about. Or nearly falls: 'Is it in man/To resist such strong temptations?' (III.v.168–9). It would be too much to describe in detail the amusing stop-go of his relations with the queen. He preserves his loyalty to Sophia and even manages to give a sanctimonious lecture on virtue to the queen who tempted him. He has been very successful in his main venture, achieving glory and prosperity, and the king and queen accompany him back to his modest home.

The final act of *The Picture* is one of Massinger's very best. When Sophia learns from an informant of her husband's adventure with the queen, and of his secret method for keeping a record of her own constancy, it is the latter that fires her extreme indignation. 'Was I growne so cheape in his opinion of me?' (v.ii.7). She refuses the consolation that as everything has turned out so well Mathias's conduct could be excused. To justify people's actions by the way things turn out is preposterous, she says. Such a defence is

> The sanctuary fooles and madmen flie to,
> When their rash and desperat vndertakings thriue well.
>
> (V.ii.10–11)

And she hits Mathias where he is most vulnerable, namely in his anxiety to make a good show, by providing absolutely no reception for the royal train and not even being on hand herself to welcome them. 'How shall I begge/Your maiesties patience?', asks Mathias, beside himself with vexation. When he finds his wife, he quite fails to impress her with the greatness of the occasion and the 'wrong' she is doing both of them by her crazy indifference to royal guests (v.iii.37–44). She publicly challenges him with his affair with the queen, torments him by pretending that she too has been unchaste, and finally sues for a divorce. (The 'inchanter' in her speech is the man who fashioned the magic picture.)

> When you went to the warrs
> I set no spie vpon you to obserue
> Which way you wandred: though our sex by nature
> Is subject to suspitions and feares,
> My confidence in your loyalty freed me from 'em.
> But to deale as you did gainst your religion
> With this inchanter to suruey my actions
> Was more then womans weaknes, therefore know
> And tis my boone vnto the King, I doe
> Desire a seperation from your bed,
> For I will spend the remnant of my life
> In prayer, and meditation.   (V.iii.171–82)

But she relents when they all, king and queen included, beseech her to change her mind. Sophia's challenging assertion of herself makes an excellent ending, morally and theatrically, and shows very well how Massinger does not accommodate his morality to theatrical requirements but exploits and utilizes those requirements for moral ends.

All these male self-approvers we have been looking at, Sforza, Leosthenes, Mathias, overestimate themselves and undervalue their partners. Their sense of superiority accompanies a deep insecurity; they assume a position of control over women because, they argue, the inferior sex needs guidance; but in fact they fear that without strict guard the rapacity of women's sexual appetite will take over and they will lose their monopoly. Yet nothing in the women's actual behaviour can justify these fears. No one could call Massinger's drama male-oriented, and it would not be improper to call it feminist. The insufficiency of men is more often shown than the insufficiency of women; the weak structure on which an ethos of male dominance is founded seems all the weaker for the constant demonstration of great fortitude and moral tenacity in women, and their self-knowledge.

The ending of *The Picture*, with Sophia's determination to seek a religious celibacy, has obvious affinities with *The Maid of Honour*. There is also, as I have pointed out, a severe comment by Sophia on the philosophy that all's well that ends well. Now the parallels between *The Maid of Honour* and Shakespeare's *All's Well That Ends Well* are striking enough to suggest that Massinger intended to invite a direct comparison, challenging with his ending the moral and theatrical soppiness of the ending provided by his great predecessor. Both plays have the feature of a war which is fought by volunteers only after a king has refused official assistance. In both plays the strong-minded heroine, rather surprisingly in love with a man of patently weaker character, forces a marriage on to him as the payment of a debt. In *The Maid of Honour*, the obligation is a kind of jest. Camiola ransoms Bertoldo from captivity and as payment demands only the marriage that he himself has sought. But the bond and obligation are still there. Bertoldo falls like Bertram to the attractions of another woman. From these Camiola proposes to rescue him by direct confrontation, and she utters the following perplexing words:

> You perhaps
> Expect I now should seeke recovery
> Of what I have lost by teares, and with bent knees
> Beg his compassion. No; my towring vertue
> From the assurance of my merit scornes
> To stoope so low. I'll take a nobler course,
> And confident in the justice of my cause,
> The king his brother, and new mistrisse, judges,
> Ravish him from her armes.
> . . .
> He shal be then against his wil my husband
> And when I have him, I'll so use him —   (V.i.102–13)

This speech, so strangely out of character, is mere play-acting, to deceive both the person she is speaking to and the audience, and so lead to the grand surprise of the final set-piece which is of course not marriage and reconciliation but a repudiation of Bertoldo and the world for the life of the convent. This is a drastic response to the fickleness and instability of men, but there is a particular fitness here in that Bertoldo was a Knight of Malta who had broken his vow of celibacy in even seeking Camiola's hand in the first place. In later offering him marriage, Camiola connived at his sin. Her final action redeems them both and drives him back to his order. The idea of marriage becomes only a brief interlude and weak indulgence. So far as the parallel with *All's Well* goes, Camiola's final choice of a religious life makes a pointed comment. Shakespeare's Helena gave up her pilgrimage in order to regain her erring husband and to become fully his wife. The ending of *The Maid of Honour* at one blow rejects such trifling with religion and such disconcerting moral choices as Helena's final union with Bertram.

The Maid of Honour is strict and grim, and its ending is in strong contrast to that of *The Great Duke of Florence* where the patience of Fiorinda for the erring Sanazarro is without limit; she persuades a perplexed Duke to let the happy ending arrive by a forgiveness beyond reason. Endings may differ, but the constant material is the greater strength of women.

But what about the erring women? Given such sexually excitable females as Beaumelle in *The Fatal Dowry*, Domitia in *The Roman Actor*, Donusa in *The Renegado*, might Massinger's possessive males not have some reason for wishing to keep the closest eye on their women? No one can say that Massinger ignored the libido of women. The sexy maid-in-waiting is just a cliché, of course, and perhaps the aristocratic nymphomaniacs of *The Bondman*, Corisca and Olimpia, amusing though they are, seem too exaggerated to form part of any writer's view of the world. But these errant people, however stereotyped or caricatured, belong in the Massingerian mimesis. It is not that they are the only women with sexual desires; they are those who do not succeed in controlling and channelling them. The offence that the jealous possessive males are guilty of is a total inability to observe and recognize the women they claim to love. They simply do not discriminate. They see Woman not individual women. This impercipience, parading as knowingness, is a real crime against the person.

Massinger tried to make a whole play out of the mistakes of men whose philosophy is *così fan tutte*. This was *The Parliament of Love*, but it is a failure. What *are* we to think of a Leonora who is so outraged at the 'brutality' of Cleremond in trying to get her to sleep with him just before their marriage that she pursues a limitless vendetta? The rest of the action is more comprehensible, being a series of outwittings of philanderers and adulterers who believe that women can very easily be persuaded to give themselves to them. But the play never comes alive. I think the failure of *A Very Woman*, a rewriting of an earlier collaboration with Fletcher, is a very different kind of failure. Here the leading woman, Almira, is incorrigibly light and inconstant. She falls in love with Don John, whom she has rejected in his own person, when he is disguised as a slave. (*The Bondman*, with its somewhat similar plot, explores a quite different moral issue, and well illustrates Massinger's tendency to look for new aspects of familiar material.) Almira is quite unable to perceive and judge the person, in the way Massinger more often makes the man misjudge the woman. The final union of Almira and Don John is a patched-up thing that offends against the standards of *The Maid of Honour* and *The Great Duke of Florence*. By writing his share of the original of *A Very Woman* and liking the play well enough to revise it, Massinger shows himself ready to accept the dramatic rendering of an irresponsibility in women equal to the male irresponsibility he so often anatomized. (It is interesting, though, that the two plays built on female inconstancy and infidelity are collaborative plays: *The Fatal Dowry* with Field and *A Very Woman* with Fletcher.) Yet because of the unfamiliarity of the theme, or because it was not really his kind of play, the ending, unusually for him, betrayed what had gone before.

Massinger's satirical comedies are intensely observant of the social scene and (for their time) rather high-minded and old-fashioned about social change. His tragedies and tragicomedies are, I think, for all the operatic manoeuvrings of the plots, similarly observant and sensitive about the male–female relationship, and his views on sexual restraint and indulgence are similarly high-minded and (in a rather general and perennial way) 'old-fashioned'. But his extensive criticism of the exponents of male dominance and his recognition of the rights of women as people strike a much more modern note than can be found in many of his contemporaries.

Massinger as Collaborator:
The Plays with Fletcher and Others

CYRUS HOY

THE first reference that we have to Massinger as a dramatist finds him writing in collaboration with others: in the famous 'tripartite' letter (written sometime around 1613) wherein he, Nathan Field and Robert Daborne – all in prison for debt – appealed to Philip Henslowe to come to their aid with a loan which they planned to repay from the sum that would be due them when they completed a play on which they were collaborating for him.[1] Although by the end of the decade that followed, Massinger had begun to write plays on his own (e.g. *The Maid of Honour, c.* 1621–22; *The Duke of Milan, c.* 1622; *The Bondman,* 1623), his work for the stage during these years chiefly consisted in writing plays in association with one or more other dramatists. He wrote *The Fatal Dowry* with Field (*c.* 1616–19) and *The Virgin Martyr* with Thomas Dekker (*c.* 1620), but the dramatist with whom he most regularly worked was John Fletcher; their partnership continued until Fletcher's death in 1625. Most of the Fletcher–Massinger collaborations were printed for the first time in the Beaumont and Fletcher Folio collection of 1647, where Massinger's share went unacknowledged, to the indignation of his friend, Sir Aston Cokayne.[2] They continue to lead their textual and editorial lives as part of the Beaumont and Fletcher corpus to the present day.

There are, it seems, 19 plays that contain the work of Fletcher and Massinger, or of Fletcher and Massinger and one or more other playwrights. It will be well to list them here, together with their approximate dates (unless otherwise indicated, the play was first published in the 1647 Beaumont and Fletcher Folio).

Fletcher and Massinger (11 plays)
   The Custom of the Country, c. 1619–20
   The Tragedy of Sir John van Olden Barnavelt, 1619

(preserved in manuscript; unpublished until 1883)
The False One, c. 1620
The Little French Lawyer, 1619–23
The Double Marriage, c. 1621
The Spanish Curate, 1622
The Prophetess, 1622
The Sea Voyage, 1622
The Elder Brother, ?1625 (first printed in quarto in 1637
    with a title-page attribution to Fletcher)
The Lovers' Progress, 1634 (Massinger's revision of a
    Fletcherian original of 1623)
A Very Woman, 1634 (Massinger's revision of a Fletcher–
    Massinger collaboration of indeterminate date; first
    printed in Massinger's *Three New Plays,* 1655)
Fletcher, Massinger, Field (3 plays)[3]
The Honest Man's Fortune, 1613
The Queen of Corinth, 1616–17
The Knight of Malta, 1616–18
Fletcher, Massinger and others (5 plays)
Thierry and Theodoret, c. 1613–16 (first printed in quarto
    in 1621 without attribution of authorship)
Beggars' Bush, 1615–22
Rollo, Duke of Normandy, 1616–24 (first printed in
    quarto in 1639 under the title *The Bloody Brother,* and
    attributed to 'B.J.F.')
Love's Cure, ?1625 (Massinger's revision of a Beaumont
    and Fletcher original of indeterminate date)
The Fair Maid of the Inn, 1625–6

The purpose of this essay is to describe the kinds of play to which Massinger contributed: to give some general sense of the sort of plot materials with which the dramatists concerned are dealing, and of the particular elements of plot which Massinger contributed to the various plays on which he worked.[4]

The most immediately striking fact about Massinger's work as a collaborator is the frequency with which he writes both the opening and closing scenes of a play.[5] He does so in *The Fatal Dowry* and *The Virgin Martyr,* and in his collaborations with Fletcher he opens and closes *The Double Marriage, The Little French Lawyer, The Spanish Curate,* and *A Very Woman.* In all of these plays, Massinger contributes as well to the scenes that intervene between the opening and the close, but sometimes he seems to have been employed for the express purpose of setting a play in motion, and providing it with a finale. He sometimes seems to have been called on, in effect, to put a frame around a play's various actions. This is the case in his share of *The False One*, *The Elder Brother*, *The Queen of Corinth*, *The Fair Maid of the Inn*, *Rollo Duke of Normandy*, and *Beggars' Bush*.[6]

There is nothing particularly striking about Massinger's opening scenes in these plays, but they accomplish with clarity and economy the work of dramatic exposition that it is the business of opening scenes to provide. The best of them move with a professional efficiency and assurance, for Massinger knew how, even as he went about the business of dramatic exposition, to lay the groundwork for the complications of plot that the play as a whole would explore and eventually resolve. The opening scene of *The Spanish Curate* is a good example of how he goes about his work. Milanes and Arsenio, two lords of Cordova, discuss: (1) Leandro, whose rich father has recently died, leaving him a considerable fortune; (2) Leandro's friendship with Don Jamie, the badly treated younger brother of the rich Don Henrique; (3) 'the young lad' (1.i.46) Ascanio, who is generally admired and who is said to be 'the son/Of a poor cast captain, one Octavio;/And she that once was call'd the fair Jacintha' (1.i.52–4).[7] Don Jamie and Leandro enter with Ascanio; they would like to set him up in a career, but Ascanio declines their offer because he cannot leave his adoring parents, to whom he is everything. Don Henrique enters and quarrels with Don Jamie, who taunts him with the fact that he will be Don Henrique's heir since the brother, after 16 years of marriage, has not managed to beget a child. When Don Henrique has left, Don Jamie mentions the beautiful wife of the jealous lawyer, Bartolus, and sets Leandro's imagination aflame. Leandro determines to win her despite her watchful husband.

In the course of the 305 lines of this scene Massinger introduces all of the play's principal plot materials, but his share of the play thereafter is confined to the story of Don Henrique and his relations with Violante, the haughty heiress whom he has married, and with Jacintha, his first wife whom he divorced in order to marry Violante, and with Ascanio, who is in fact his son by Jacintha. The remainder of Massinger's first act immediately sets about dramatizing the story of these characters. In i.ii, Jacintha has written to Don Henrique for aid but he has scorned her letter. Ascanio enters with money from his friends which he gives to his mother and his supposed father. In i.iii, Don Henrique and Violante bitterly lament their lack of an heir, and the fact that the despised Don Jamie will inherit their estate. Don Henrique says that he can frustrate Don Jamie's expectations if Violante will bear with patience his 'dishonour' (i.iii.39), and she agrees.

Massinger's next scene (iii.iii) shows Don Henrique carrying through with his promise. The scene is a court of justice, and Don Henrique (through his lawyer, Bartolus) confesses that Ascanio is his legitimate son by Jacintha. She acknowledges this, but protests against his exposure of the truth at this late date. Don Jamie is indignant at his own consequent disinheritance. After an intervening Fletcherian scene, Massinger's next (iv.i) shows the effects of Don Henrique's disclosure on his home life. Violante is not enduring his dishonour with patience, as she had promised, but is furious to learn that another woman has borne what she is pleased to term her husband's bastard (iv.i.19). To placate her, Ascanio offers to leave the home of his father, and Don Henrique permits this, but Violante is not pacified. She vows revenge.

Two brief scenes by Fletcher follow, and then in Massinger's iv.iv we have the effects of Don Henrique's disclosure on the household of Jacintha and Octavio, where both grieve the loss of the beloved Ascanio. Jacintha fears for his treatment at the hands of a stepmother. Ascanio enters with Don Jamie, announcing his banishment from his father's house. Then a servant from Violante enters and privately summons Don Jamie to her: if he dare make himself a fortune, she will propose the means, Don Henrique being now from home (iv.iv.43–5). Though this be an ambush laid for his life, Don Jamie is determined to sound the secret (iv.iv.47–8). When Massinger resumes his share in the play four scenes later (v.i), Don Jamie is being ushered into the presence of Violante. He denounces her for her pride and her arrogance, but she says his rude speech wins her favour, and invites him to join with her in revenging themselves on Don Henrique and Ascanio by killing both. Don Jamie seems to consent. Violante will reward him with her person and her fortune when both murders have been committed.

The play's final scene (v.iii), which is the work of Massinger, is a stagey exposure of Violante's perfidy. Don Jamie causes Don Henrique, Ascanio, Jacintha and Octavio to be seized and bound, and when Violante enters to 'triumph in their misery' (v.iii.72), he lures her on to pronounce sentence of death on them all, and to make avowal of the favours she has in store for him by way of reward. But then the officers of the law who have witnessed the scene seize her. Don Jamie expresses his satisfaction at having been able to show Don Henrique how much his 'love was cozen'd' (v.iii.113). He feels no envy that Ascanio will now replace him as his brother's heir, and is promised a 'moiety' of his brother's estate (v.iii.134). Don Henrique is repentant. He will marry Jacintha (where this will leave the faithful Octavio, who stood by her and her son during the years of her abandonment, the play neglects to mention). Violante's dowry will be used to build a nunnery where she will spend the rest of her life.

The story of Don Henrique, his brother, his son, and his wives, provides only one strand in the double plot of *The Spanish Curate*: the strand that poses, however superficially, problems of moral or ethical behaviour. Interwoven with it is Fletcher's brisk account of how Leandro manages the seduction of Amaranta, Bartolus's beauteous wife (he disguises himself as a naive but rich student who obtains a room in Bartolus's house for the ostensible purpose of studying the law under his direction, aided and abetted in his schemes by Lopez, the roguish curate of the play's title, and Diego, his sexton, who are gleeful at the prospect of Bartolus's cuckoldry). Though Massinger's share in the play is by no means negligible, *The Spanish Curate* is essentially Fletcherian in spirit, and Massinger's sententious and somewhat sentimental plot serves as but a pale foil for setting off the witty ironies of Fletcher's mischievously amoral comedy of romantic and legal and commercial intrigue.

For a collaborative play, *The Spanish Curate* is remarkably well unified, and this is because Massinger's share is confined to the beginning, the end, and one plot strand in between. When the two dramatists both contribute to the same plot, the play is in for trouble, as *The Little French Lawyer* proves. The first act of this play finds Massinger going about the work of dramatic exposition with his usual efficiency and dispatch. Dinant, frustrated in his love for Lamira who has married the elderly but rich Champernel, enlists the services of his friend Cleremont in insulting the wedding party. Angry words fly back and forth, and the bride's brother, Beaupré, with the groom's nephew, Verdone, challenge Dinant and Cleremont to a duel. But Lamira, concerned for her brother's safety, demands of Dinant that, if he still loves her, he will not take part in the duel, but will go instead to an opposite side of the city from that where it is scheduled to take place, and there defend her honour against an unidentified person who has insulted her. Fletcher's Act II gives us the plight of Cleremont when Dinant fails to appear at the appointed hour, and he is confronted with both opponents. He appeals to various passers-by to aid him against Beaupré and Verdone, but to no avail until he manages to persuade a choleric little lawyer who bustles onto the scene to assist him. The lawyer (La Writ by name) has never been a fighting man, but takes to the sword with such alacrity that he drives both Beaupré and Verdone from the field.

The dramatic situation that has emerged by the end of Massinger's Act I – wherein a vengeful woman causes her despised suitor to imperil the life of his friend on the duelling ground – is of the problematic sort that could produce a rich yield of the moral and emotional imbroglios characteristic of Jacobean drama. Versions of it figure prominently in the design of two other contemporary plays (Marston's *Dutch Courtesan* and Webster and Rowley's *A Cure for a Cuckold*), and Massinger would employ it again – to distinctly greater problematic effect – in *The Parliament of Love*.[8] But a character like La Writ has a doubtful place in such a design. He is entirely Fletcher's creation, and he brings into the play an air of humorous whimsy that affects the shares of both dramatists. In Massinger's III.i, Lamira declares Dinant to be 'a lustful villain' who is seeking to solicit her to her dishonour. This is her quarrel with him, which she 'will so revenge/As it shall fright such as dare only think/To be adulterers' (III.i.123–8).[9] As Fletcher presents it (in III.iv–v), her revenge takes the form of summoning Dinant to a midnight assig-nation (accompanied by Cleremont, who is needed to take Lamira's place in her husband's bed), plying him with wine, setting his nerves on edge with the noise of loud laughter and music which he fears will awaken the household, and finally, after tantalizing him to near distraction, denouncing him for his lascivious designs and dismissing him. The entire household is summoned to witness Dinant's shame, as well as the humiliation of Cleremont when he awakens to find that he has been sleeping, not with Lamira's elderly husband but with her husband's lovely niece, Annabell.

If *The Little French Lawyer* ended here, it would be an unusual play (in that it allowed the woman to frustrate her rejected lover's attempts on her honour, and to expose him to public ridicule), but a more effective one than the play as it is, which goes on for two more acts. There is no mystery, however, as to why the dramatists considered this to be necessary. Fletcher's Act IV is almost entirely given over to putting La Writ out of his humour; he has taken so avidly to issuing challenges, picking quarrels and fighting duels, that the legal affairs of his clients have suffered. The last two scenes of Act IV and the whole of Act V, which contain the work of both dramatists, comprise a cumbersome piece of dramatic carpentry designed to give the gentlemen their revenge, and the last word. Lamira and her household, en route to their summer house in the country, are set upon by 'ruffians' (actually friends of Dinant) and made captive. Dinant and Cleremont come on the scene in their own persons and attempt a rescue but they too are seized (this in the first 96 lines of Massinger's IV.vi). When their story is resumed in Massinger's IV.vii, the gentlemen-ruffians have Lamira and Annabell imprisoned in a cave and are about to ravish them. The ladies call for Dinant and Cleremont, who are brought on, bound, to 'see,/And suffer in the object' (IV.vii.29–30). They take the occasion to remind the women how the honour that each might sweetly have surrendered to one of them is now going to be forced from them by licentious villains. The women are properly abashed at this prospect, and Act V continues the process of bringing them to their knees. In Fletcher's share of V.i, Cleremont tells Annabell he can rescue her if she will marry him, and she readily consents. In the second half of the scene (which is Massinger's), Dinant, alone with Lamira, reveals that he has masterminded the plot that now has her in his power, and gloats at the prospect of defiling her much-vaunted honour. This reduces her to an abject confession of guilt. Lamira has been a scornful lady. The conversation between Dinant and Cleremont in Act I has been explicit about the rude reception she accorded Dinant's long and devoted suit to her before her marriage (I.i.99–112). And the play has shown her tendency after her marriage to go on exploiting the hold she knows she has on his affections. Her confession of guilt produces one of those surprising turns for which Jacobean drama is notorious: Dinant announces that he will not touch or hurt her, 'nor had ever/Such a lewd purpose' (v.i.271–2). She vexed him in fooling him so often, but he has repaid her on that score, and now renounces all unchaste love. The play ends in a general reconciliation.

A decade or so before *The Little French Lawyer*, Beaumont and Fletcher had written a comedy entitled *The Scornful Lady*, and it is one of their airiest, most buoyantly witty productions. The obligatory transformation of the lady from scornful to yielding is amusingly but gracefully managed. When eventually she is caught by one of the tricks to which her long-suffering lover has at last resorted, she can surrender without humiliation and he can rejoice in his triumph without appearing a brute. When the subject came to be treated again in *The Little French Lawyer*, it apparently was deemed advisable to give it a new twist, whereby the lady (Lamira) has been so very scornful of the ardent suit of her young lover that, as the play begins, she has given herself in marriage to a wealthy old man. This was bound to make for an unconventional comedy, one in which, at the end, Jack would not have Jill, and it puts quite a strain on the character of Lamira, who must be by turns the respectable young wife of an old man, resolutely defending her honour against the lustful attacks of a rejected young suitor; a witty strategist who is determined to outmanoeuvre her adversary, and is not above resorting to the devices of a sexual tease in order to do so (a sort of merry wife of Windsor); finally, a penitent who pleads guilty to all the charges of vanity and arrogance her rejected lover brings against her. But if inconsistencies are to be noted in the character of Lamira, there is nothing inconsistent in the character of Dinant. He cheerfully admits that his love for Lamira is scarcely distinguishable from lust, that his designs on her are ill ones; he assumes that, under cover of her marriage, she will be willing to have an affair with him (i.ii.35–9). In his breezy immorality, he is a typically Fletcherian comic figure, even though Massinger wrote most of the scenes in which he appears. In the end, he has outplayed her in their running contest of insult and reprisal; she acknowledges him the victor as well as the injured party in their quarrel, and begs his pardon. It is as if the merry wives of Windsor were caught in a trap set by Falstaff, and when he releases them from it, apologize to him for having spurned his suit and tried to trick him.

I have discussed *The Little French Lawyer* in this detail because it seems to me one of the clearest examples among all the Fletcher–Massinger collaborations where the dramatists are of two mind about the nature of the play they are writing. The comic design of the play seems essentially Fletcherian, with the humorous figure of La Writ darting in and out between the mazes of intrigue and counter-intrigue presided over by Dinant and Lamira. La Writ, the little French lawyer, is to this play what Bartolus, the Spanish curate, was to that one: a centre of humorous comic interest amid the romantic complications of a plot that turns on the efforts of a young man to seduce a married woman. One wonders, indeed, if *The Little French Lawyer* is not the later play, written to the formula that had proved successful in *The Spanish Curate*, the formula varied just enough to offer a few new twists for the appreciation of knowing audiences. Thus, for a Spanish curate we are given a French lawyer, and for a seduction scheme that succeeds we are presented with one that fails, or at least is given over when the young man has had his revenge on his scornful lady. *The Little French Lawyer* has the marks of a play written to repeat a recent success but which is in fact rather less successful than its model. La Writ is not nearly so well integrated into the total design of his play as Bartolus, his opposite number, is into his. The role of La Writ is very much a star turn. After he comes to Cleremont's aid in Act II, nothing he does furthers any of the play's various actions; his subsequent appearances are all aimed at exploiting the comic incongruity of his transformation from dapper bureaucrat to swaggering duellist, and while audiences probably enjoyed the antics of this character more than anything else in the play, his prominence throws the rest of the play off balance. There is not enough in the surrounding action for his particular humour to relate to. The two romantic principals are sometimes put to disconcertingly different uses by the two dramatists. Lamira, stage-managing the discomfiture of Dinant at their midnight rendezvous (III.iv–v), is a typically Fletcherian comic heroine, very unlike Massinger's Lamira, with her earnest decorum and moral intensity. As for the announcement of Massinger's Dinant, to the effect that he never intended any such lewd purpose as the violation of Lamira's honour: this is the sort of thing characters say in plays by way of providing an edifying end to a comic action that could go on indefinitely.

Things are better managed in *The Custom of the Country*. Fletcher, exceptionally, begins this play, and lays out the dramatic situation: the newly married Arnoldo and Zenocia, to prevent their ruler from exacting his *droit de seigneur* on their wedding night, flee their Italian city along with Arnoldo's brother, Rutilio. In Massinger's Act II, the scene has shifted to Lisbon, and a new group of characters enters: the governor Manuel, his sister Guiomar, and her son, Duarte, whose violent pride and reckless behaviour are cause of great concern to mother and uncle. Then the characters from Act I begin to arrive. The ship carrying Zenocia, Arnoldo and Rutilio has been captured and the brothers have managed to escape, leaving Zenocia in the hands of the captain, Leopold, who is favourably disposed towards her, and promises to introduce her into the service of his beloved, Hippolyta. The brothers arrive, looking for Zenocia, in II.iii, and they are immediately beset with adventures. Arnoldo, without knowing it, has caught the eye of Hippolyta, who is both rich and wanton; he is approached by her servant, Zabulon, who gives him money, and tells him that there is more where that came from if he will follow. Arnoldo, feeling he has nothing to lose, does so. Rutilio, left alone, witnesses a quarrel between Duarte and one Alonzo, intervenes, and wounds Duarte, who falls, apparently dead. Advised that he has killed the governor's nephew, Rutilio takes refuge in what turns out to be the house of Guiomar. He begs for sanctuary and she promises to conceal him; but when the officers in search of the fugitive enter, they bring with them Duarte's body and Guiomar realizes she has protected her son's murderer. She remains true to her promise to him, but alone with him again, she orders him to leave his hiding place and to cover his face so that she will never be able to recognize him, gives him money and sends him on his way.

The block of action that follows is Fletcher's: Zenocia is received into the service of Hippolyta (III.i); Zabulon brings the bewildered Arnoldo to Hippolyta's house, where she welcomes him with a rich banquet. He is much struck by her beauty but displeased by her immodest wooing of him. She gives him jewels. At last her importunities become so insistent that he says he abhors her and leaves. Furious, she sends Zabulon after him to charge him with the theft of the jewels (III.ii). Rutilio's misadventures continue. He has stumbled by accident into a cellar containing the city's munitions (a punishable offence), and since he cannot pay the stipulated fine, he is about to be assigned to the galleys for six years when Sulpitia, on the look-out for lusty men to stock her male brothel, discovers him. She pays his fine, tells him what she expects of him, and he happily enters her service.

Massinger resumes the story. In III.iv, Hippolyta, musing sourly on her rejection by Arnoldo, recognizes the limitations of the power of her beauty. 'They flatter'd me / That said my looks were charms', she says (III.iv.23–4) in a King Lear-like moment of truth.[10] But when Zabulon enters to announce that at her suit Arnoldo has been arrested and sentenced to death for the theft of her jewels, she now realizes that if he is killed she can never satisfy her passion for him. She rushes off to save him, followed by the faithful Leopold and by Zenocia. III.v contains only 126 lines in the Variorum edition, but it is full of announcements of what has been happening to characters off-stage, and brings all the principals together in what could have been, and to an extent is, a recognition scene but in which the fruits of recognition are not yet to be enjoyed. Clodio, the governor of the country with the accursed custom that has driven Arnoldo and Zenocia into exile, arrives in Lisbon in the company of Zenocia's father, Charino, both disguised. Clodio has had a change of heart and will no longer plague the lovers. Manuel, the governor, enters in conversation with the Doctor who attended on his wounded nephew, and we learn that Duarte has not died of the effects of his fight with Rutilio. Manuel asks the Doctor to conceal this news, for the time being, from Duarte's mother. Manuel, as governor, has Arnoldo under guard. Hippolyta rushes in, followed by Zenocia, Leopold and Zabulon. She dismisses them impatiently, but not before Arnoldo, to his surprise, has recognized Zenocia as a servant in Hippolyta's house. Hippolyta confesses her guilt in accusing Arnoldo, and bears witness to his virtue that has stood out against her immodesty. Manuel sets him free. Arnoldo realizes he can gain access to Zenocia only through Hippolyta, so he offers to escort her to her house. Clodio and Charino have recognized both Zenocia and Arnoldo, and Clodio reveals himself to the governor, Manuel, as the act ends.

Massinger's share of the play continues through the first two scenes of Act IV. In IV.i, Duarte acknowledges his gratitude to the Doctor for having given him a second life. He sees the error of his previous proud ways. He will go in disguise for a time (which, for purposes of the plot, nicely accords with his uncle the governor's proposal in III.v that his recovery be for the present concealed), and test his mother's grief; also he will seek to find and to help the man who was charged with killing him, for it was the wound he received from him that, in Duarte's opinion, set him on the way to true health.[11] In Massinger's IV.ii, the sea captain, Leopold, distraught to find that his years of dedicated but unrequited devotion to Hippolyta count for nothing before the fury of her passion for Arnoldo, discusses with a bravo the price for disfiguring Arnoldo, but changes his mind. Since both Zenocia and Arnoldo were previously his prisoners, he knows of their love, and suspects this to be the reason why Arnoldo scorns Hippolyta. He arranges with Zabulon to allow Zenocia and Arnoldo to meet in Hippolyta's house, and to see to it that Hippolyta witnesses their meeting. He hopes that, when she sees herself scorned for her servant, she will cease doting on Arnoldo.

Fletcher dramatizes the meeting (IV.iii) which is interrupted by the arrival of the governor, Manuel, come to restore Zenocia to her father. Hippolyta's plans to avenge herself on her rival are thus temporarily thwarted, but Zabulon holds out to her the prospect of other ways in which her lust for vengeance can be satisfied. Fletcher's IV.iv presents the plight of Rutilio, nearly worn out by the crowds of women who flock to Sulpitia's brothel for his services. Duarte has managed to track him down there, and presents himself, disguised, as an enemy of Duarte; he gives Rutilio 1,000 ducats for having killed him. Rutilio is thus able to buy his freedom from Sulpitia, and he promptly launches a plan with the request that the disguised Duarte carry a letter to a lady. Meanwhile, Zabulon has come to Sulpitia for a powerful spell to be used against Zenocia.

Almost all of Act v is Massinger's. It begins with the disclosure of Rutilio's plan. He has managed to convince himself that Guiomar is in love with him, and that he can best repay her for having saved his life by offering to marry her. The letter in which he sets forth his proposal is to be delivered to her by the disguised Duarte. Alone, Duarte is dashed to learn that his mother saved the man whom she believed had killed her son. In v.ii, Zenocia has been suddenly and mysteriously stricken with a deathly illness (the result of Sulpitia's spell). Hippolyta glories in the anticipated demise of her rival. In v.iii, Duarte, disguised, gains entry into his mother's chamber and finds her grieving over his picture. He delivers Rutilio's letter. She is secretly furious at its contents, but also triumphant now that she has the means to revenge herself on her son's murderer. Outwardly, she appears to welcome Rutilio's proposal, and Duarte is more outraged than ever. At the outset of v.iv, Zenocia is dying, and Arnoldo will die with her. All present are much affected: Charino, her father; Manuel, the governor of Lisbon; Clodio, who regrets his role in separating the lovers and renounces henceforth his *droit de seigneur*. Even Hippolyta, when she appears, is moved with sympathy for the unfortunate lovers, and regrets her action; she orders Sulpitia to undo the spell, and announces to the company that Zenocia will recover. A servant enters and whispers news of a marriage to Manuel. He leaves and asks the others to accompany him.

Fletcher's single contribution to this final act consists of the first 198 lines of v.v. Here we find Guiomar, alone, wondering why her kindness to Rutilio should make him so bold as to propose marriage to her. Rutilio and Duarte (the latter in disguise) arrive. Rutilio is sure she lusts after him, but she summons her servants and they bind him. She denounces him, to Duarte's private satisfaction (v.v.124). Manuel, Clodio, and Charino arrive, and she asks Manuel, her brother, for justice against Rutilio. He, now chastened, is ashamed and makes his own self-accusation. Guiomar is so moved by his manner that she begins to waver in pressing for justice against him. Duarte settles the matter by discovering himself, and declaring that while the physician healed his body, the lesson Rutilio's sword read to him saved his soul (v.v.185–8). He urges his mother to love this man, and she announces that she will take him for her husband. Massinger provides a 37-line close: Hippolyta enters with Zenocia, now cured, and Arnoldo, plus Leopold, Zabulon and Sulpitia. She vows to lead a better life, and to reward Leopold who has sought her for so long (v.v.220). She assures all that her behaviour was worse in appearance than in reality:

> though my violent dotage did transport me
> Beyond those bounds my modesty should have kept in,
> Though my desires were loose, from unchaste act
> Heaven knows, I am free. (V.v.223–6)

Arnoldo, united with Zenocia at last, points the moral: their example shows that while good purposes are long withstood, 'The hand of Heaven still guides such as are good' (v.v.236).

The Custom of the Country is the most dramatically satisfying play that Massinger and Fletcher ever wrote together. The story of Arnoldo and Zenocia and Arnoldo's brother, Rutilio, unfolds with irresistible ease, gathering more and more materials to itself; and the dramatists pass it back and forth, each contributing his characteristic flourishes to the *dramatis personae*, with surprisingly rich and harmonious results. No character in the play is the exclusive property of either dramatist. The Guiomar who protects Rutilio is Massinger's creation, but the Guiomar who accepts him as a husband is Fletcher's, even as the Rutilio who accepts employment in Sulpitia's male stews is Fletcher's as well. Episodes from different regions of plot and from different authorial shares are nicely balanced. Hippolyta, having spied Arnoldo, dispatches her servant to bring him to her in Massinger's II.iii; Sulpitia sees Rutilio and promptly employs him in Fletcher's III.iii. Hippolyta accuses Arnoldo in Fletcher's III.ii, but relents in Massinger's III.iv. Guiomar accuses Rutilio but subsequently relents in Fletcher's v.v.

At the centre of *The Custom of the Country* is a triangular romantic plot that occurs repeatedly in Massinger and Fletcher's collaborations of the early 1620s. It features a pair of lovers whose devotion to each other is severely strained when circumstances separate them and the man finds himself obligated against his will to a woman of a far more passionate nature who lusts after him with unabashed abandon. The trio composed of Zenocia, Arnoldo and Hippolyta in *The Custom of the Country* is a paradigmatic one for a number of plays in which Massinger is concerned. In *The Sea Voyage*, for example, Albert and his beloved Aminta are shipwrecked. When, in Massinger's II.ii, he goes in search of help, he comes upon an island governed by women where Clarinda, daughter of the Amazonian governess, falls fiercely in love with him, the first man she has ever seen. To ensure her continued aid to him and his beloved in their shipwrecked need, Albert tells

and the whole of Act I and a portion of v.ii of *Beggars' Bush* (inner scenes by Beaumont and Fletcher).

All this is journeyman work: professionally competent but hardly distinguished. The two scenes that comprise Massinger's first act of *The False One* are good examples of his professional expertise. Scene i quickly establishes the atmosphere of moral expediency that reigns in the court of Ptolemy, where a corrupt counsellor, Photinus, persuades the King to abandon his loyalty to Pompey whose defeat at the battle of Pharsalia is reported in the course of the scene, and to seek to make his peace with Caesar. Scene ii brings us into the presence of the King's sister, Cleopatra, whose rival claim to the Egyptian throne has caused him to place her under guard. She learns of Caesar's victory, and as Act I ends, has managed to persuade her admiring guardian, Apollodorus, to take her to Caesar, on whom she is confident her royalty and her beauty will have a happy effect. With this introduction, the main action of the play can begin with Fletcher's Act II and the dramatic entrance of Septimius (the false one of the title), who has been employed by Photinus to murder Pompey and who now enters with Pompey's head, intended as a gift for Caesar. By Act V, when Massinger sets about concluding the play, Caesar has had occasion to taste the full measure of Photinus's and Septimius's treachery. A palace revolt has broken out under their direction, and Caesar is hard pressed to avoid falling victim to their plotting. But while there is much talk of the urgency of the situation, Caesar's speeches exude an imperturbable assurance; and Cleopatra, who is threatened with capture by the rebellious forces, faces her situation with the 'masculine constancy' (v.iv.18)[14] which is Massinger's highest tribute to the kind of fortitude great ladies are capable of displaying in adversity (cf. *The Custom of the Country*, II.i.51; *The Queen of Corinth*, v.iv(p.483)).[15] The gravity of the situation is belied by the unruffled grandeur with which both principal characters speak.

The Act I–Act V frame which Massinger provides for Fletcher's charming comedy, *The Elder Brother*, seems intended to strike a somewhat lower – and therefore more appropriately comedic – stylistic key than that which had seemed to be required for *The False One*, with its subject drawn from ancient history, but the characters whose humours and follies, quirks and affectations are so sharply defined by Fletcher's dialogue in the play's inner acts tend to speak with one voice in Massinger's outer ones. There is indeed very little of dramatic interest in these. The comedy's principal business (the transformation of the titular character from unworldly bookworm to responsible man of affairs and gallant lover when he realizes that his coxcomb of a younger brother is about to win both his inheritance and the hand of a lovely woman) is completed by the end of Act IV. There is an air of desperation about much of the fifth act, as new plot developments are introduced in an effort to keep things going. The principal business Massinger was able to devise here shows us the reformation of the younger brother, who finally comes to realize the error of his dandified ways and the worthlessness of his elegant but craven companions. The effect is dully didactic.

More lively are the opening and closing acts which Massinger provided for *The Queen of Corinth*. The first of these, like Massinger's Act I of *The Spanish Curate*, sets all the play's principal plots in motion: (1) the plan to seal a peace between Corinth and Argos by marrying Merione, sister to the Corinthian general Leonidas, to Agenor, prince of Argos; (2) the fury of the Queen's son, Theanor, who has 'made love' (1.i.(p.398)) to Merione formerly with his mother's approval but has now been commanded by her to give over his suit for the sake of peace with Agenor, and who – urged on by his villainous companion Crates – is bent on revenge; (3) the love of the noble lady Beliza for Euphanes, younger brother of Crates, who is as virtuous as Crates is treacherous; (4) a comic sub-plot involving the foolish middle-aged gallant Onus, his guardian Uncle, and his Tutor. The first act ends on a sensational note when, on the eve of her wedding to Agenor, Merione, praying in the temple of Venus, is seized and ravished by Theanor, aided by Crates and a trio of courtiers, all disguised. When Massinger resumes his share of the play with Act V, the insatiable Theanor is plotting to ravish Beliza on the eve of her wedding to Euphanes, but Crates, now reconciled with Euphanes, exposes the danger to his brother and they meet it by presenting Theanor with Merione, disguised as Beliza, thus causing him to rape that lady a second time. He is caught and brought before the Queen, his mother, who condemns him to death. This leads to the rhetorical bravura of the final scene (based, as Eugene Waith has shown, on one of the *Controversiae* of Seneca),[16] where at Theanor's trial Beliza (who has lent herself to the trick) accuses him of rape and demands his death, while Merione accuses him of rape and demands that he marry her, the law of the land permitting either penalty. He acknowledges his guiltiness, and asks to be allowed to restore Merione's honour by marrying her before he is executed. The Queen agrees and, the executioner standing by, wishes 'that now the gods would shew some miracle,/That this might not divorce it' (v.iv.(p. 484)), whereupon Crates tells all. Matters by the end of the play have turned to 'unexpected comedy' (v.iv.(p. 486)). Theanor will wed Merione, Euphanes will have Beliza, and the Queen offers herself to Agenor, who receives her 'with all joy' (v.iv.(p. 486)).

Massinger's first acts of *The Fair Maid of the Inn* and *Rollo, Duke of Normandy* are among the best examples of his command of the architectural principles on which first acts of Jacobean plays are built if they are to accomplish their purpose: provide the necessary dramatic exposition concerning events and relationships prior to the beginning of the play, introduce the various lines of dramatic business that will be complicated and eventually resolved in the play's subsequent action, and end this first movement of the dramatic action on a strong note. The first scene of *The Fair Maid of the Inn* tells us of the friendship between two Florentine naval commanders, Alberto and Baptista, and their respective sons, Cesario and Mentivole, and of the budding love affair between Mentivole and Alberto's daughter, Clarissa. We are told how Baptista's life has been saddened by the loss of his wife, Juliana, whose family objected to his marriage to her and brought about their separation. In a pleasant dialogue that opens the play, Cesario (à la Laertes to Ophelia) counsels his sister against being too free with her favours to the young gentlemen who make suit to her, and she responds by informing him of the public notice that is being taken of his visits to Bianca, daughter of a local inn-keeper. But by the time Act I ends, the concord that has bound the two families is seriously threatened. Cesario and Mentivole quarrel over whose horse is the finer bred; the quarrel leads to a duel, and Cesario is wounded by Mentivole. Baptista high-mindedly orders his son to gain Cesario's pardon or he will disown him.

Jacobean tragicomedy is famous for the surprising turns its various actions can take, but few plays of the period can outdo *The Fair Maid of the Inn* where surprising twists of plot and startling disclosures are concerned. In Act II, Mentivole dutifully presents himself at the home of the wounded Cesario, but not only is his effort to make peace rebuffed, he is physically threatened by Cesario's enraged father. When he reports his reception to his own father, Baptista is outraged in his turn, and vows revenge against the whole family of the Alberti. Meanwhile Alberto, who in Massinger's I.ii had been ordered to active duty against the Turks, is now reported lost at sea, and his terrified wife, Mariana, fearful for the fate of her son at the hands of the vengeful Baptista, makes declaration in open court that Cesario is not in fact of the house of the Alberti. He is, according to her story, the son of her faulkner's wife whom she passed off for her own when her husband repined at her failure to present him with an heir; in the manner of such deceits, she shortly thereafter found herself pregnant with her husband's child, their daughter Clarissa, and she tells the court that, now that her husband is dead, she cannot endure that his true child should share her inheritance with the base-born Cesario.[17]

This announcement leads to a number of complications: the Duke who hears it takes pity on Cesario for the sudden collapse of his fortunes, and decrees that, since Mariana is now a widow, she should mend his state by taking him for her husband. She is horrified at such a proposal, tells Cesario that if she is forced to marry him he will never be her bedfellow, whereupon he suggests that he marry Clarissa instead. The mother finds this equally revolting; in any case, Clarissa loves Mentivole, whose father, now that Alberto is reportedly dead and the hated Cesario disinherited, is reconciled to his son's marriage to the daughter of the enemy house. When, at the beginning of Act V, Alberto reappears, not having been lost at sea after all, he is understandably shocked to hear of his wife's disclosure concerning Cesario, whom he continues to regard as his son, and outraged to learn of her consent to the marriage of their daughter to the son of his enemy.

It is Massinger's unenviable task in the play's final scene to resolve all this, together with the story of Cesario's relationship with Bianca, of which I have made no mention but which threads its way in scenes that alternate with the action just described through the play's inner acts. The finale (v.iii) is not one of Massinger's more successful undertakings. The scene opens with a monologue by Mariana, in which we have the first indication the play has given that her declaration concerning the parentage of Cesario was not true. The wedding of Clarissa and Mentivole is about to take place when Alberto and Cesario burst in. Alberto is furious with wife and daughter, and denounces the Duke for countenancing the marriage of his daughter to the son of his enemy. Fathers and sons of the opposing houses square off. At the height of the turmoil, Mariana asks for a private word with the Duke, and according to the stage direction, he takes her aside (v.iii.132). We do not hear what they say; Clarissa is appealing to the others to cease their quarrelling. When Mariana has finished talking apart with the Duke, the following exchange occurs:

> Duke.   Was it to that end then
>   On your religion?
> Mar.   And my hope in heaven Sir.
>   (v.iii.167–8)

We must surmise from this that she has confessed the truth about her son's parentage (namely, that he is her and Alberto's child), but nobody on stage hears her except the Duke, and nothing more is said in the play on the score of Cesario's paternity. The rest of Massinger's share of the scene is given over to what amounts to narration: Juliana, Baptista's long-lost wife, has appeared and she is restored to her husband, and we now learn that Bianca is their daughter. How all this can be, Massinger explains in the last hundred lines of his share of the scene (v.iii.184–297), in the course of which the reconciliation of Alberto and Baptista is confirmed by the marriage of their children. No attention is given to the reconciliation – if there is to be one – of Alberto and his wife. The last thirty-odd lines of the scene – from the entrance of the Host who has passed for Bianca's father, and of the comic figures who have been prominent in the scenes set in his inn – are by another hand than Massinger's.

Massinger may not be altogether responsible for this botched final scene. Though the play's first act seems to be entirely his, he may be present in v.iii as a reviser, though of what it is difficult to say: perhaps of an old play, perhaps of a new one left incomplete by Fletcher on his death in August 1625 (*The Fair Maid of the Inn* was licensed for performance on 22 January 1625/6).[18] The possibility of revision hovers around Massinger's contribution not only to this play but to his share in *Rollo, Duke of Normandy* as well.[19] Whether as reviser or original collaborator, Massinger unquestionably wrote the first act of *Rollo*, and in itself it is one of his most effective introductory pieces, with its quarrelling ducal brothers and their factions, and the efforts of their mother to bring about an accord between them: efforts that issue in plans for celebrating the uneasy peace that has been patched together by the end of the scene. But the relation of this first act to what follows is in some ways curious, and opens the question of whether Massinger is present in the play as collaborator or reviser. The factions of the quarrelling brothers (Grandpree and Verdon, servants to Rollo; Trevile and Du Prete, servants to Otto), so prominent in Act I, never appear again in the play. On the other hand, Act I gives no hint of the threat that Latorch will pose throughout the rest of the play, though he does appear in Act I along with the rest of the factious followers (I.i.147 SD) and speaks one line (at I.i.172).[20] But it seems unlikely that, if Massinger is present in the play simply as a reviser and not one of the original authors, he would have introduced the factious servants (including Grandpree, an important role in Act I) in the first act only. As for the almost total silence of Latorch during the first act, it may be intentional. Since his treachery becomes immediately apparent with the beginning of Fletcher's Act II, the dramatists may have waited until this point to reveal him for what he is, and he has been kept by design to a virtually silent presence throughout his previous stage appearance, like Ortrud in the first act of *Lohengrin*.

Massinger certainly had a principal hand in devising the fifth-act catastrophe for the tragedy of *Rollo*. He wrote all of v.i. with the possible exception of Aubrey's soliloquy after the exit of Hamond (v.i.90–116), though there are touches of Massinger here, as there are throughout the first 135 lines of v.ii, a scene that is often attributed entirely to Fletcher and was probably originally his, but which Massinger seems to have revised.[21] Here Edith, getting ready to murder Rollo, sounds like Juliana in *The Double Marriage* getting ready to kill the man she thinks is Ronvere. Each lady will sink the soul of her enemy. Here is Edith (*Rollo*, v.ii.11–13):

> Stormelike may my destruction fall upon him,
> My rage like roving Billowes as they rise,
> Pour'd on his soule to sinke it.

This seems in fact to echo two passages from Massinger's share of *The Double Marriage*. Juliana, watching her intended victim as he stands musing, declares how

> In the full meditation of his wickedness,
> I'll sink his cursed soul. (v.ii.(p. 403))

And the unrepentant Martia, confronted at the end by her furious father, thus defies him:

> let your rage run higher
> Than billows rais'd up by a violent tempest. (v.iv.(p. 413))

Edith's soliloquy in *Rollo* is followed by the song 'Take ô take those lipps away' which somebody (Fletcher? Massinger? an unknown hand?) has transported into the play (in a somewhat variant version) from Shakespeare's *Measure for Measure*.

The text of *Beggars' Bush* resembles that of *Rollo*, with a first act and part of the fifth (v.ii) by Massinger. It is not altogether clear whether Massinger is present in the play as collaborator or reviser. If as collaborator, his share must represent some of his earliest work, for since the play also contains the work of Beaumont and Fletcher, it must date in its original form from sometime prior to Beaumont's death in March 1616. The play was acted at court on 27 December 1622,[22] and it is possible that it was revised for this occasion by Fletcher or by Massinger or by both. Be that as it may, I tend to the view that Massinger had had a share in it from the beginning. The plot of *Beggars' Bush* is extraordinarily complicated, and Massinger was assigned his inevitable task of setting forth its antecedent actions in the opening scene. He sets about his formidable job gamely, if routinely. At I.i.7–10, one of the two characters who has entered at the beginning says to the other:

> My ten yeares absence, hath kept me a stranger
> So much to all the occurrents of my Country,
> As you shall bind me for some short relation
> To make me understand the present times.[23]

There follows an efficient if not exactly graceful account of wars between Flanders and Brabant, of a royal guardian who has become a usurping tyrant, of missing royal children, and members of the nobility who have vanished into exile. Where would Massinger's expository style be without his English equivalent to the ablative absolute?

> This war upon't proclaim'd,
> Our Earle, being then a Child, although his Father
> Good *Gerrard* liv'd, yet in respect he was
> Chosen by the Countesse favour for her Husband
> And but a Gentleman, and *Floriz* holding
> His right unto this Country from his Mother,
> The State thought fit in this defensive war,
> *Woolfort* being then the only man of marke,
> To make him Generall. (I.i.23–31)

The two remaining scenes of Massinger's first act are more dramatic than this. Scene ii contains quite an effective confrontation between the tyrant Wolfort and Hubert, one of the most honourable of the Flemish noblemen who has tried to flee the court and has been brought back forcibly to it. Scene iii shows us what has happened to the exiled Flemish heir; he has become a flourishing merchant of Bruges, and at the end of the scene he is approached by a friendly beggar whom he has aided over the past three years, and who requests his support on the morrow when the fraternity of vagabonds elects its king. *Beggars' Bush* is very much a comedy of disguises. Most of the principal characters have assumed identities other than their real ones, and when Massinger returns to the play at the beginning of v.ii, it is time to launch the dénouement, which largely consists in revealing who a sizeable number of characters in fact are (beginning with the disclosure that the seeming beggar of I.iii is father of the seeming merchant). Massinger does not handle the play's finale, with its sentences of punishment and provisions for marriage; this seems to be the work of Beaumont.

Massinger contributed to another Beaumont and Fletcher collaboration, *Thierry and Theodoret*, and there is little doubt that he was one of the play's original authors. It is one of the more lurid of Jacobean tragedies, with its lascivious queen, Brunhalt, and the ruin she brings down on her princely sons when they seek to restrain her lustful ways. Fletcher opens the play with a noisy confrontation between her and her son Theodoret, in which he orders her to a monastery (I.i.79).[24] Alone, she defies his orders, and accompanied by her male entourage, departs for the court of her other son, Thierry. Massinger takes up the story here and dramatizes it over the next two scenes (I.ii–II.i). I.ii finds Theodoret, in the aftermath of his scene with his mother, questioning the wisdom of the course he has taken with her. If he were to have acted at all, it were better to have rendered her powerless than simply to use words which are bound to make her furious and dangerous. Yet, after all she is his mother, and he cannot bring himself to take such courses with her as discretion suggests ought to be taken. During the scene, word comes of Brunhalt's departure for the court of Thierry, and Theodoret promptly sets out to try and prevent the discord that he knows his mother will seek to bring about between him and his brother.

In II.i, Brunhalt is received with great favour by Thierry, who is indignant at her account of the wrongs she says Theodoret has done her. But when Theodoret arrives and recounts his version of his dealings with his mother, Thierry begins to wonder about the truth of what Brunhalt has told him. He effects a reconciliation between her and his brother, and sets off to meet Ordella, his contracted wife, who is arriving at his court. The prospect of being displaced as Queen adds new fires to Brunhalt's rage. Among her entourage of panders is a physician, Lecure, who suggests that on his bridal night, Thierry be given a drink that will render him impotent for five days. This, it is assumed, will bring about a breach between the new husband and wife. Brunhalt approves the plan. Two brief Fletcherian scenes follow, concerned with a plot for the exposure of Brunhalt's cowardly lover, Protaldye, whom Thierry has unwisely made general of his army. Massinger returns with II.iv, the wedding feast. Ordella, all mildness, offers to make room in the place of honour for Brunhalt, but Thierry will not allow this. Brunhalt proposes a toast, and Thierry drinks from the drugged cup, and then retires with his bride. Brunhalt retires to bed with Protaldye, but is beginning to make plans for the murder of Theodoret.

Much of the dramatic design of *Thierry and Theodoret* seems like some monstrous inversion of Shakespeare's *King Lear*: the passionate parent at the centre of the play is a mother, not a father; the passion that works chaos in the play is lust, not anger (the concupiscent, not the irascible passion); the children to whom the parent resorts by turn are sons, not daughters, and Thierry and Theodoret, unlike Goneril and Regan, would like to respect their parent if they could. Beaumont is responsible for

Act III, which contains a number of surprising turns. In III.i, Thierry in his impotence finds Ordella undemanding and a model of virtuous restraint (and thus we are given another of those scenes of enforced continence on the wedding night which Beaumont and Fletcher had depicted in *The Maid's Tragedy*, and which Fletcher had dramatized in *A Wife for a Month*). In III.ii, Protaldye stabs and kills Theodoret under cover of a scene of courtly revels. When Thierry threatens to burn the palace to discover the murderer, Brunhalt, to protect her lover, takes Thierry aside and tells him that she killed Theodoret because he was not in truth her son. According to her story (III.ii.154–73), she was pregnant but lost her unborn child, and to keep her husband's affections, replaced the dead infant with a gardener's child; within the next year, Thierry was born. The story is similar to the one concocted by Mariana when she would disown Cesario in *The Fair Maid of the Inn*; behind both, so far as the Beaumont and Fletcher canon is concerned, is the account (presented as truth) of Arane's dealings in the births of her presumptive son and real daughter in *A King and No King* (v.iv.202–50).[25] Thierry accepts this tale. Seeking a cure for his impotence, he goes (in III.iii) to a local magician-astrologer (actually, Brunhalt's physician in disguise) and is told that he will be capable of begetting a child if before sunrise he will kill the first female he sees coming out of the temple of Diana. He is waiting to do so at the beginning of Fletcher's IV.i, but the first female who presents herself is (by Brunhalt's design) Ordella, and Thierry cannot go through with the deed, though she would gladly die for his sake.

The following scene (IV.ii) is Massinger's final contribution to this elaborately contrived plot. Brunhalt and Protaldye await news from the temple. The physician, Lecure, arrives with a new device in case the other fails: a poisoned handkerchief that will cause the eyelids that it touches never to close. Thierry arrives and gives an hysterical account of what has happened at the temple. Word comes that Ordella has killed herself (this is not, in fact, true), her dying request being that Thierry should marry again. Though distraught, he is inclined to do so. The daughter of the dead Theodoret is present at court, and Thierry will marry her and thereby make amends for the murder of her father. Brunhalt tries to discourage this, and is finally brought (shades of Mariana in *The Fair Maid of the Inn*) to deny her previous declaration that

Theodoret was not her son. Marriage to his daughter, she now tells Thierry, will be incestuous, but Thierry declines to believe her. Whereupon she hands him the fatal handkerchief to wipe away a tear shed in memory of Ordella. It is left to Beaumont and Fletcher in, respectively, the two scenes that comprise Act v, to handle the play's catastrophe, which includes the deaths of Thierry and Ordella, and the suicide of Brunhalt.

For all its garish convolutions, the plot of *Thierry and Theodoret* is an effectively unified one, and Massinger's scenes are far more integral than they often are in his subsequent collaborations with Fletcher. His share of *Thierry and Theodoret* is not confined to opening and closing acts or scenes, or to a single strand of a multifarious plot, and his contribution is dramatically impressive. In the years after *Thierry and Theodoret*, however, something happened to Massinger's role as a collaborator, at least with Fletcher. Though in the period *c.* 1616–18 he contributed significantly (along with Fletcher) to the inner acts of *The Knight of Malta* (a play for which Field provides the Act i–Act v frame), and although through some busy weeks in the summer of 1619 the pen must have passed rapidly back and forth between him and Fletcher as they worked together creating a play out of a recent news sensation (the downfall and execution of the Dutch patriot Sir John van Olden Barnavelt),[26] Massinger's share in the Fletcherian plays of the early 1620s takes on a more and more routine quality. He had evidently become typed as a dramatist whose talents were better suited for handling certain assignments than for others. Only in *The Custom of the Country*, *The Double Marriage* and *The Little French Lawyer* (the latter with not altogether happy results) does his share in the central movements of a play equal Fletcher's. For the rest, he is consigned to doing openings and closings, to explaining the motivating factors that set a play in motion and to accounting for (but not designing) the factors of circumstance and choice that bring it to an end.

The timbre of his own dramatic language may have had something to do with this. Massinger's verbal style, with its limited repertoire of image and analogy and its oft-repeated phrases,[27] is unmistakable, and it does not change; that is one reason why it is so relatively easy to differentiate his work from Fletcher's in a collaborative play. There is a gravity, a studied seriousness, a reserved dignity about the style that very considerably limits the sort of dramatic story material to which it can be effectively applied. It is best suited to tragedy, or to the more serious, less hare-brained kind of tragicomedy; it is very ill-suited to all but the most morally earnest variety of comedy. Occasionally, in Massinger's career as an independent dramatist, he found a subject that fitted his style very well indeed: *The Roman Actor* and *Believe as You List* in tragedy, *The Maid of Honour* and *The Bondman* in tragicomedy, *A New Way to Pay Old Debts* and *The City Madam* in comedy. But these occasions were rare in his own career – where his own choice of dramatic subject may be presumed to have prevailed – and they were even rarer among the assignments that came his way in the Fletcherian *atelier* where he was so largely employed during the early 1620s. The competence of his style – its clarity and coherence, its Latinate syntactic constructions and its capacity for sustaining a certain weight of rhetorical ornamentation – could always be counted on to carry him through the composition of scenes that probably held no great interest for him, and that were not really appropriate to his peculiar stylistic timbre. His general competence as poet and dramatist enabled him to turn out virtually anything that was needed in the making of a comedy, a tragedy, or a tragicomedy, including a large number of things he should not have attempted to turn out.

In the end, his work as a collaborator seems not to have encouraged him to extend his range, or to make his stylistic manner more flexible. His stylistic manner served well enough for the kind of descriptive and expository work which more and more he was called on to do during these years. Only rarely, as in *The Double Marriage*, was he called on to provide a sustained examination of the changes that time and circumstances bring about in a group of characters. More typically, what Massinger was called upon to do in his Fletcherian collaborations was to show things as they were at the beginning of a play, and things as they are at its end; the representation of the forces of change that cause a given beginning to issue in a particular end is left to one or more other dramatists. Too often in his collaborative work, Massinger was called upon to provide effects while others produced the causes.

His work as a collaborator is instructive for what it tells us about the way Jacobean plays were put together, and about the implications of the process for the creative imagination. In the course of the decade that separates Massinger's fervent contribution to the high-pitched melodrama of *Thierry and Theodoret* from the routine frames that he provided for the action of plays like *The False One* or *The Elder Brother* or *The Fair Maid of the Inn*, something withered in his dramatic talents, so far at least as his work in collaboration with others is concerned. Aspiring as he evidently was during these years to establish himself as an independent playwright, his work as a collaborator must have been understandably onerous; presumably he was driven to it by financial need. In certain circumstances, one can imagine work in collaboration with other more experienced writers might provide valuable training for a young dramatist, but whatever benefits Massinger may have gained from his early association with Beaumont and Fletcher, the association with Fletcher went on too long, and Massinger's development suffered from it. Fletcher's style was too powerful and too well established in the favour of theatrical audiences to permit a collaborator any role beyond that of a subordinate assistant. Only in *The Custom of the Country* do we see the two dramatists working together as co-equals. Only in *The Double Marriage* do we see Massinger being allowed to develop at some length plot material that engaged his deeper interests. For the most part, he functions as a skilful but by no means master painter in the studio of a Titian or a Tintoretto, painting in backgrounds, supplying necessary but more or less formulaic borders designed to set off the central subject and chief exhibit.

In these circumstances, his verbal powers never really developed, and most of his dramatic efforts went into the work of reducing to some kind of order the tangled yards of romantic story material that were the inevitable sources for the plots of Jacobean plays. To handle this sort of material effectively, a dramatist needed more wit than Massinger ever displayed: he needed to take pleasure in the sheer act of dramatic contrivance, in the sheer fact of dramatic artifice, as Shakespeare can be seen doing with romance material in his last plays, and as Fletcher can be seen doing — perhaps too enthusiastically — throughout his entire career. Massinger was too earnest for this. He seems to have distrusted dramatic artifice and contrivance unless they were aimed at a specifically didactic purpose. His approach to the improbable materials of Fletcherian tragicomedy is usually a literal one. It seems inevitable that by the end of his period of collaboration with Fletcher, he had been reduced to dramatic peripheries, supplying opening and closing acts, like some operetta composer who writes only overtures and final ensembles.

NOTES

1   The body of the letter is by Field, with postscripts signed by Daborne and Massinger. Both appear to have been imprisoned with Field, and all three were presumably collaborating on the same play, though the document does not make these facts explicit. Fletcher – to judge from Daborne's postscript – seems to have had some connection with the play. See Gerald Eades Bentley, *The Jacobean and Caroline Stage* (7 vols., Oxford, Clarendon Press, 1941–68), vol. 4, p. 752; and Philip Edwards and Colin Gibson (eds.), *The Plays and Poems of Philip Massinger* (5 vols., Oxford, Clarendon Press, 1976), vol. 1, pp. xvi-xvii. The conjectural date 1613 is W. W. Greg's (*Henslowe Papers* (London, A. H. Bullen, 1907), pp. 65–6). It has sometimes been suggested that the play in question was *The Honest Man's Fortune*, the manuscript of which declares it to have been 'Plaide in the yeare 1613', but the identification is uncertain. For Massinger's share in that play, see my 'The Shares of Fletcher and his Collaborators in the Beaumont and Fletcher Canon' (IV), *Studies in Bibliography*, 12 (1959), 100–8.
2   See Cokayne's various verse epistles on the subject, extracts from which are reprinted in Bentley, vol. 4, p. 753; and Edwards and Gibson, vol. 1, pp. xix–xx. For Massinger's share in *The Fatal Dowry*, see Edwards and Gibson, vol. 1, pp. 1–2. For his share of *The Virgin Martyr*, see my *Introductions, Notes and Commentaries to texts in 'The Dramatic Works of Thomas Dekker'* (4 vols., Cambridge, Cambridge University Press, 1980), vol. 3, pp. 192–3.
3   Fletcher, Massinger and Field's *Jeweller of Amsterdam* (1616–17) is lost.
4   For a summary of the authorial divisions made by late nineteenth- and early twentieth-century scholars, see E. H. C. Oliphant, *The Plays of Beaumont and Fletcher* (New Haven, Yale University Press, 1927). For a more recent investigation, see my 'Shares of Fletcher and his Collaborators', published in seven parts in *Studies in Bibliography*, 8 (1956), 129–46; 9 (1957), 143–62; 11 (1958), 85–106; 12 (1959), 91–116; 13 (1960), 77–108; 14 (1961), 45–67; 15 (1962), 71–90.
5   This fact is noted by Maurice Chelli, *Étude sur la collaboration de Massinger avec Fletcher et son groupe* (Paris, Les Presses Universitaires de France, 1926), pp. 133–5.
6   In his revision of *Love's Cure* and *The Lovers' Progress*, Massinger has

rewritten opening and closing scenes with particular thoroughness. See my 'Shares of Fletcher and his Collaborators' (II, VI), *Studies in Bibliography*, 9 (1957), 151–2, and 14 (1961), 48–56.

7 Quotations from *The Spanish Curate* are based on R. B. McKerrow's edition of the play in the Bullen Variorum Edition (London, 1905), vol. 2. In the discussion of the play that follows, parenthetical references to act, scene and line numbers are based on this edition.

8 'A new Play, called, *The Parliament of Love*' was licensed for performance on 3 November 1624 (Joseph Quincy Adams (ed.), *The Dramatic Records of Sir Henry Herbert* (New Haven, Yale University Press, 1917), p. 30). For the relation of this play to *The Little French Lawyer*, see Bentley, vol. 3, p. 358.

9 Quotations from *The Little French Lawyer* are based on Cyril Brett's edition of the play in the Bullen Variorum Edition (London, 1912), vol. 4. Parenthetical references to act, scene and line numbers of the play in the discussion that follows are based on this edition.

10 Quotations from *The Custom of the Country* are based on R. Warwick Bond's edition of the play in the Bullen Variorum Edition (London, 1904), vol. 1. Parenthetical references to act, scene and line numbers of the play in the discussion that follows are based on this edition.

11 Massinger would rework this situation in *A Very Woman*, where the arrogant Don Martino is apparently killed in a duel with a rival, but is restored to life by a doctor, and upon his recovery, recognizing the errors of his past ways, repents and is a new man.

12 *The Double Marriage*, I.ii, Alexander Dyce (ed.), *The Works of Beaumont and Fletcher* (11 vols. London, 1843–6), vol. 6, p. 328. (Parenthetical references to act and scene numbers of the play in the discussion that follows are based on this edition. Page numbers in Dyce are given in brackets). Cf. *The Virgin Martyr*, IV.ii.90–1, ed. Fredson Bowers, in *The Dramatic Works of Thomas Dekker* (4 vols., Cambridge, Cambridge University Press, 1953–61), vol. 3, rpt. 1966.

13 *The Roman Actor*, III.ii.83ff., Edwards and Gibson, vol. 3.

14 Quotations from *The False One* are based on Morton Luce's edition of the play in the Bullen Variorum Edition (London, 1912), vol. 4. Parenthetical references to act, scene and line numbers of the play in the discussion that follows are based on this edition.

15 Quotations from *The Queen of Corinth* are based on Dyce, *The Works of Beaumont and Fletcher*, vol. 5. Parenthetical references to act and scene numbers of the play in the discussion that follows are based on this edition. Page numbers in Dyce are given in brackets.

16 Eugene M. Waith, *The Pattern of Tragicomedy in Beaumont and Fletcher* (New Haven, Yale University Press, 1952), pp. 204–7.

17 *The Fair Maid of the Inn*, III.ii.78–103, in F. L. Lucas (ed.), *The Complete Works of John Webster* (4 vols., 1927; rpt. New York, Oxford University Press, 1937), vol. 4.

18 *The Dramatic Records of Sir Henry Herbert*, p. 31, where the play is attributed to Fletcher.

19 There is not space in the present study to discuss Massinger's undoubted

revision of Beaumont and Fletcher's *Love's Cure*, of Fletcher's *The Lovers' Progress*, and of his own and Fletcher's *A Very Woman*.

20 Parenthetical references to act, scene and line numbers of *Rollo*, and quotations from that play, are based on the edition of J. D. Jump (London, University Press of Liverpool, 1948).

21 See my 'Shares of Fletcher and his Collaborators' (VI), *Studies in Bibliography*, 14 (1961), 57–8.

22 *The Dramatic Records of Sir Henry Herbert*, p. 49.

23 Quotations from *Beggars' Bush* are based on Fredson Bowers's edition in *The Dramatic Works in the Beaumont and Fletcher Canon* (5 vols. to date, Cambridge, Cambridge University Press, 1966–82), vol. 3, 1976.

24 Quotations from *Thierry and Theodoret* are based on Robert K. Turner's edition in *The Dramatic Works in the Beaumont and Fletcher Canon*, vol. 3, 1976.

25 *A King and No King*, ed. George Walton Williams, in *The Dramatic Works in the Beaumont and Fletcher Canon*, vol. 2, 1970.

26 The pattern of collaboration in Barnavelt is unlike that in any other play of Massinger and Fletcher's joint authorship. No other play of theirs exhibits so many brief, alternating scenic units. See my 'Shares of Fletcher and his Collaborators' (II), *Studies in Bibliography*, 9 (1957), 145.

27 For Massinger's repetitions, see my 'Verbal Formulae in the Plays of Philip Massinger', *Studies in Philology*, 56 (1959), 600–18.

High Seriousness and Popular Form: The Case of *The Maid of Honour*

RUSS McDONALD

HE dramas of Philip Massinger resist easy classification. Individually and collectively, the plays comprise incongruous and sometimes contradictory forms and ideas. Even the most familiar and enduring of them, *A New Way to Pay Old Debts*, is difficult to describe satisfactorily, owing to its mixture of satiric and comic elements. The canon as a whole is like that too, a gallimaufry of tragedies, satiric comedies, tragicomedies, and permutations of these kinds, and this is to consider only the surviving independent plays, not the lost works nor the collaborations. *The Maid of Honour* may serve as a reliable index to the artistic problem raised by virtually all its author's plays – the potential incongruity between the dramatic structures Massinger created and the purpose for which he created them.[1] Specifically, Massinger used popular and fashionable forms to express abiding and unfashionable ideas. Moveover, his thinking about man's condition is as difficult to label as the forms designed to convey it. A sharp sense of natural frailty co-exists with an essential faith in man's moral strength, making the playwright seem pessimistic and optimistic at once. Such disparities have puzzled critics and produced corresponding inconsistencies in the criticism of Massinger's work: one writer claims that his moral impulses invariably tyrannize his artistic sense, while another insists that he cares nothing for morality at all.[2] Finally, all these inconsistencies contribute to a larger problem, that some of Massinger's plays are artistically successful and some are not. I think that *The Maid of Honour* can be shown to be an artistic success, a play in which the dramatist's theatrical impulses and ideas function in concert.

The play's representative value is increased if we accept the proposition that *The Maid of Honour* is probably one of Massinger's earliest independent plays, perhaps his very first. Entered in the Stationers' Register in 1632 and printed in the same year, it has been variously dated from 1623 to 1631, but none of these suggestions has won general support, chiefly because the methods used (usually political allusion) have seemed unreliable.[3] Recently scholars have tended towards the opinion that *The Maid of Honour* is a very early play, its absence from Herbert's Office Book attributable perhaps to its having been staged before Sir John Astley (Herbert's predecessor) began keeping those notes in 1622. This possibility is made probable by the claim on the title page that the work was performed at the Phoenix: in 1621 Massinger is known to have been writing for Christopher Beeston's actors at that theatre, and *The Maid of Honour* may well be one of these efforts. The editors of the Clarendon edition seem certain that Massinger wrote the play quite early in his independent career – 'Dated 1621–2, *The Maid of Honour* is with *The Duke of Milan* the earliest of Massinger's ventures in writing plays on his own' – and I am persuaded by their arguments.[4]

The play thus becomes an exercise in artistic self-definition, and it is on this basis that I propose to begin examination of it. Liberated from the direct influence of John Fletcher, Massinger was free to confront the moral issues that would engage his attention throughout his career and was able to select what he considered the appropriate dramatic means for revealing the nature of these issues. It will be useful to look first at the importance of Massinger's two greatest dramatic predecessors, Shakespeare and Jonson, under whose influence he seems consciously to have composed. The next task must be to define as precisely as possible Massinger's relation to Fletcher, and this may be achieved through comparison of *The Maid of Honour* with *The Prophetess*, a tragicomedy written with Fletcher at about the same time. From such a study emerges a clear sense of Massinger's moral propensities and dramatic talents. Having established the dramatic legacy with which he began, I shall study *The Maid of Honour* with an eye for Massinger's particular thematic and technical interests, paying especial attention to their mutual effect. Massinger was concerned above all else with the human penchant for betrayal, especially self-betrayal; his previous theatrical experience had taught him how to engage an audience with surprise, shifts of direction, and irony; and in Painter's tale of the scorned Sicilian widow he found ideas and an implied structure appealing to his taste and experience. To observe his development of ideas into a harmonious and meaningful form is to recognize that Massinger was capable, in *The Maid of Honour* at least, of achieving artistic distinction.

Comprehension of Massinger's distinctive style depends upon a recognition of his artistic debts to Shakespeare and Jonson as well as to Fletcher, his immediate master. It has long been established that Massinger is a derivative writer: L. C. Knights and others have persuasively documented the imitative quality of his verse.[5] In addition, the impression remains that his *œuvre* is generally derivative, that his two most familiar plays (*A New Way* and *The City Madam*) are diluted versions of Jonsonian comedy, many characters pale re-creations of Shakespearian originals, and his numerous tragicomedies little more than exercises in the popular Fletcherian mode. Although these generalizations distort the case in allowing too little credit to Massinger's own originality and powers of synthesis, they are founded upon the truth that Massinger does seem to have worked with Shakespeare, Jonson, and Fletcher in mind. Certain historical information is helpful in sorting out questions of influence and originality. Jonson was still a potent force in the theatrical world when Massinger set up on his own. Although Shakespeare had been dead for five years when the younger dramatist began to write alone, Massinger would have been exposed constantly to the green memory of Shakespeare through his work with Fletcher and his association with the King's Men. Not only were some of the master's plays still in the repertory, but certainly by 1622 and perhaps as early as 1620 or 1621 Shakespeare's colleagues had begun to assemble the material for the Folio. Thus it is possible that Massinger was able to read in manuscript or in proof some of the plays unavailable in quarto versions. *All's Well* springs immediately to mind, for if Massinger wrote *The Maid of Honour* in 1621 or 1622, before the first publication of *All's Well* in 1623, then it is difficult to explain otherwise the frequently noted resemblances between the two plays.[6] And finally, it should be obvious that the influence of Fletcher, successor to Shakespeare, chief dramatist of the King's Men, and Massinger's past and future collaborator, would have been inescapable. But consideration of this most direct influence must wait until the less apparent debts have been mentioned.

Prompted by the awareness of theatrical history, one begins to notice in *The Maid of Honour* specific parallels and echoes of the work of Shakespeare and Jonson, and the most prominent resemblance is to *All's Well*. The likeness is not exact, of course: Helena chases Bertram from beginning to end and from France to Italy and back again, until she finally wins him, and Bertram remains an unwilling object of pursuit throughout; Camiola and Bertoldo both change their minds twice, and when Camiola finally gets her man she doesn't want him. But in outline the stories are similar: a virtuous maid loves a man who is her social superior but moral inferior; he leaves her for the wars, where he takes up with another woman; the heroine pleads her case before the court and is granted her will. Clearly the main point of identity is character. Camiola's constancy recalls Helena's virtuous persistence, and Bertoldo might have been modelled directly on Bertram. Both plays move back and forth from court to battlefield, and both attach cowardly soldiers to their protagonists. Above all, the major themes in both works proceed from the moral fortitude of their heroines. Camiola's unexpected reversal in the final scene breaks the symmetry at an important point, of course, but her cunning arrangement of the dénouement recalls other Shakespearian conclusions, such as Rosalind's oblique promises at the end of *As You Like It* and particularly Vincentio's tricks in the last act of *Measure for Measure*. The tone of *The Maid of Honour* is reminiscent of that found in *Measure for Measure* and *All's Well*, where the serious issues considered produce a relatively sombre mood broken occasionally by the nonsense of a buffoon. And the main subject of Massinger's play, man's devotion to the ideal of honour and his failure to meet that ideal, is familiar from *Troilus and Cressida*. It is important that most of the striking Shakespearian parallels are with 'the problem plays', and an awareness of this link will help to define the hybrid form of *The Maid of Honour*.

The specific influence of Jonson, although less obvious than that of Shakespeare, is also worth noticing. The play's opening encounter, in which Adorni and Astutio suffer the abuse of Fulgentio, might have been suggested by the opening of *Sejanus*, for both beginnings cover similar ground: hypocrisy, 'shifts', and the arrogance of power. The most telling case is probably Massinger's depiction of Signior Sylli, the narcissist who might have stepped from the pages of one of the humour comedies. When he refers proudly to the family of the Syllis (II.ii.101), one cannot help thinking of Sir Amorous LaFoole's disquisition on his family name in the first act of *Epicoene*: 'They all come out of our house, the LA-FOOLES o' the north, the LA-FOOLES of the west, the LA-FOOLES of the east, and south – we are as ancient a family, as any is in *Europe* –'.[7] This one specific instance is more than usually significant because it suggests that Massinger has emulated Jonson's well-known habit of thematic unification. Like many a character in Jonsonian comedy, Signior Sylli's contribution to the plot is negligible, but he extends the moral design, filling out the dramatist's portrayal of the follies of self-absorption. A related case of imitation occurs after the battle, when the two courtiers-turned-soldiers behave with all the courage of a captive Sir Epicure Mammon. Their reminiscences about the lost pleasures of life at court, 'godwits, pheasant, partridge, quales,/Larkes, wood-cocks, calverd sammon' (III.i.81–2),[8] exhibit Massinger's acquaintance with the sensual fantasies of Mammon and Volpone. Bertoldo's expression of contempt for their triviality,

> quilts fill'd high
> With gossamire and roses, cannot yeeld
> The body soft repose,   (III.i.104–6)

echoes a famous passage from *The Alchemist*. The prominence of these borrowings indicates Massinger's desire to achieve Jonson's didactic goals with Jonson's dramatic ends, his concern to expose the difference between what men are and what they think they are.

Such particular cases of imitation are less important, however, than the more general influences to which they point. Massinger seems to have assimilated certain of Shakespeare's and Jonson's dramatic tastes and habits and reproduced them in *The Maid of Honour*; and the combination of these influences helps in part to account for the curious mixture of forms and ideas in the play. The narrative from Painter's collection is the sort of story that often appealed to Shakespeare, who took the main plot of *All's Well* from Painter and regularly drew upon such tales for his comedies (as in *Much Ado*, *Measure for Measure*, and *Cymbeline*). The plot, in short, is romantic, and yet its ending might have been dictated by Jonson himself: there is no marriage, and the audience's expectations are frustrated for the sake of moral significance. As the comparison with *All's Well* has suggested, the major characters in *The Maid of Honour* remind us of Shakespearian figures, particularly the excellent heroine; but throughout the work the characters' actions are subjected to the kind of social criticism for which Jonson is best known. If we admit that we are speaking broadly, we may say that Jonson throws the emphasis on man's failing, whereas Shakespeare stresses his capacity for recovery. It seems fair to conclude that Massinger offers both, combining Jonson's sceptical streak with Shakespeare's faith in human resiliency. Like both his great forebears, Massinger takes his characters and their predicaments seriously, and the earnestness with which he approaches his material gives his work a quality that we tend to think of as Elizabethan and to associate with Shakespeare and Jonson. But Massinger's creation of a Fletcherian structure for *The Maid of Honour* marks him as a Jacobean playwright, attracting the public with theatrical turns and surprises, and close attention must be paid to his relationship with Fletcher.

To assign *The Maid of Honour* to 1621–2 is to place it in an especially interesting period of Massinger's career, the phase in which he was still collaborating with Fletcher but was beginning to write independently as well. Their collaboration lasted until Fletcher's death in 1625, but during those last five years Massinger wrote as many plays on his own as he did with his master. The tones of Massinger's artistic voice emerge most clearly when *The Maid of Honour* is studied alongside the collaborative piece that it most nearly resembles, *The Prophetess*.[9] This tragicomedy, licensed 14 May 1622, seems to have been written just after or perhaps just before the *The Maid of Honour*. One would like to know which came first. Did Massinger decide to move away from his partner gradually but in a known direction, basing much of his own play on the plot of *The Prophetess*? Or did the process work in reverse, with the two dramatists deciding that they could capitalize on the success of Massinger's play by adding a supernatural layer to the story of *The Maid of Honour*? To speculate at any length on the question of precedence would be a waste of time, but we can be reasonably certain that the two plays were written within a year of each other, and this proximity alone makes comparison instructive.

Such comparison will be worthwhile if it helps us to separate Massinger from his mentor. Massinger's efforts in the realm of tragicomedy have led some critics to identify him almost automatically with Fletcher. The most extreme statement of this failure to discriminate is found in the essay by Peter F. Mullany (see note 2), one of the only full-length articles on *The Maid of Honour*. He believes Beaumont and Fletcher to be utterly without moral conscience and, in this respect, Massinger to be their willing disciple: 'Massinger structures *The Maid of Honour* in the Beaumont and Fletcher manner; surprise, reversal, and emotional climaxes are his dramatic goals ... Massinger asks for serious responses to materials which he has not taken very seriously, for they are no more than the means to sensationalist ends.'[10] To read *The Maid of Honour* in light of *The Prophetess* is to see the impropriety of such generalizations. Insofar as the tragicomic form is geared to the astonishment of the spectator, Massinger is committed to such theatrical ends, as are Beaumont and Fletcher. But to assent to this notion is not automatically to disallow moral concern. The error in Mullany's argument is his assumption that because Massinger employs certain elements of the structural pattern developed by Beaumont and Fletcher, he therefore shares their supposed moral indifference. One might well question the justice of his generalization that 'Beaumont and Fletcher' (a phrase used rather loosely throughout) have no moral intention whatsoever. Similarity of structure there may be, but Massinger is no slavish imitator – of Beaumont and Fletcher or of Fletcher alone.

The two dramatists' shares in *The Prophetess* have been certainly identified: Fletcher wrote Act I, Act III, and the final scene; Massinger contributed the second and fourth acts and the first two scenes of Act v.[11] The assignment of parts is based on linguistic criteria, and it would be a mistake to attempt to discern either playwright's artistic predilections in the scenes he is known to have composed. For example, Massinger wrote the scene (II.iii) in which Delphia and Drusilla, seated invisibly above the capitol, observe Diocles's capitulation to Aurelia and invoke supernatural comment on the act, an episode one might be tempted to give to Fletcher if linguistic standards did not indicate otherwise.

Yet it seems safe to conclude that Fletcher was the guiding spirit behind *The Prophetess*. He was the senior of the two play-wrights, the leading writer for the King's Men, and, along with Jonson, the most important living dramatist; he wrote the beginning and the ending; and, above all, the play's affiliations with the Fletcherian canon are readily apparent. Dyce's erroneous conclusion that *The Prophetess* was 'written wholly by Flet-cher'[12] reflects the fact that the play more nearly resembles the works of Fletcher than it does anything of Massinger's.

Analysis of *The Maid of Honour* with *The Prophetess* can serve to liberate Massinger from the shadow of his more famous colleague and provide a clear sense of his artistic identity at an early stage in his career.[13] The similarities between the two plays are sufficiently numerous and significant to make the differences arresting. Both *The Prophetess* and *The Maid of Honour* tell similar stories of male inconstancy: a young woman's lover rejects her in favour of a more advantageous attachment. In *The Prophetess*, Drusilla is in love with Diocles, who has promised to marry her as soon as he is made emperor, in fulfilment of the prophecy of Delphia, Drusilla's aunt; in the second act, having killed Aper and been offered a share in the throne, he is also promised the hand of the present emperor's sister, the beautiful Aurelia, which he willingly accepts. The last three acts are given over to the faithless Diocles's efforts to marry Aurelia and Delphia's supernatural machinations to thwart that union and reclaim him for her niece. Ultimately Drusilla gets her man and Diocles retires with her to the country. Throughout the work the dramatic emphasis falls upon the love story, for which politics is merely the backdrop. *The Maid of Honour* displays a similar emphasis and balance. Although Bertoldo has courted Camiola, she has suppressed her attraction for him and refused his offer of marriage. When he is taken prisoner, however, she ransoms him and, with his willing consent, engages herself to him. Immediately thereafter, Bertoldo submits to the admiration of the Duchess Aurelia and agrees to marry her instead. In the last act Camiola presents her grievance to the court of Roberto (the half-brother of Bertoldo); thanks to her persuasive gifts, she wins Bertoldo back; and then, rejecting him finally, she retires to a convent.

It will be clear that *The Prophetess* and *The Maid of Honour* are very different plays, that one is not a reworking of the other. Still, the resemblances are compelling. The main sources of dramatic conflict are identical, the protagonist's rejection of his betrothed for a more important woman. Moreover, despite the different endings, both resolutions move in the same direction, as the errant males are made to repent their broken vows and return to their original lovers. And recognition that the shapes of these actions are parallel leads to other instances of similarity.

The chief male characters are both soldiers, ambitious men seeking worldly glory. Bertoldo, illegitimate half-brother of the King of Sicilia, seeks to make a name for himself in battle, and Diocles is a common soldier whose dreams of success are realized when he courageously seeks out and kills the wicked Aper. Both lovers accept the gifts of Fortune, in both cases the love of a high-born woman named Aurelia, and thus break the vows sworn to Drusilla and Camiola. These stories of love and infidelity take place against a military and political background. In both cases battles are fought and prisoners taken, but such events exist chiefly to complicate and illuminate the love stories. For both Diocles and Bertoldo the prospect of honours, embodied in the two Aurelias, woos them away from honour. Although courageous on the battlefield, both are weak-willed and susceptible to ambition; both blame Fortune for unhappiness that is clearly the result of their own actions. The effect of each man's perfidy upon the spectator is similarly calculated: in both cases, having been led to expect and applaud the marriages to Camiola and Drusilla, we are repelled at the sight of each man's weakness and pride. Here is Diocles's capitulation:

> Oh, you gods,
> Teach me how to be thankful! you have pour'd
> All blessings on me, that ambitious man
> Could ever fancy. – Till this happy minute
> I ne'er saw beauty, or believ'd there could be
> Perfection in a woman: I shall live
> To serve and honour you: and, so you vouchsafe it,
> This day I am doubly married, to the empire,
> And your best self.   (II.iii. (p.239))

Bertoldo's surrender is rather more hesitant, more self-conscious, but he sounds a similar theme:

> And yet who can hold out
> Against such batteries, as her power and greatnesse
> Raise up against my weake defences!   (IV.iv.161–3)

This submission is the critical point in both dramas, occurring at the moment when the protagonist is finally free to keep his original commitment, Bertoldo because he has been ransomed and Diocles because he has fulfilled the prophecy. Moreover, our response is similarly conditioned by our alliance with the two spurned women: we favour Camiola because she is the eponymous heroine, and Drusilla (although she herself is uninteresting) because she is the niece and protégée of the prophetess. Finally, the ideas that emerge from these similar conflicts are obviously comparable: we are made to contemplate the perils of human ambition and pride, the ease with which men break their vows, the pain that attends such weakness, and the distinction between superficial and genuine honour. And these acts of infidelity prepare for another similar reversal: the audience takes moral and theatrical satisfaction in each young woman's reclamation of her beloved.

Awareness of these parallels clarifies the differences between the two plays, differences that are especially telling because they reflect two distinct views of the theatre, two opposing conceptions of the function of dramatic art. The principal conflict in both plays turns upon a man's faithlessness in love, but the resolutions of the conflict are notably dissimilar, and the management of these dénouements affords us a clear understanding of the normative style of Fletcherian drama and, more importantly, of Massinger's departures from it. The major distinction is apparent in the titles of the two plays. I have described Bertoldo and Diocles as if they were protagonists, but it is more appropriate to regard them as antagonists. The main figures, the characters who have captured the imaginations of their creators and on whom the audiences concentrate, are the maid of honour and the prophetess, Camiola and Delphia. It is they who respond to the treachery of the faithless lovers and who bring about the positive endings of each play. But they do so by very different means.

In *The Prophetess*, the audience has been made acquainted in the first two acts with Delphia's prophetic skills. Her prediction is fulfilled in Diocles's triumph in Act II, his elevation to the empery, and Delphia (with Drusilla in tow) witnesses this spectacle from above and sanctions the proceedings by calling down celestial music. But Diocles's success coincides with his treachery, his sudden acceptance of Aurelia as his bride, and thus the audience is teased with the prospect of supernatural retaliation by Delphia:

> I will punish
> His perjury to the height. – Mount up, my birds! –
> Some rites I am to perform to Hecatè
> To perfect my designs; which once perform'd,
> He shall be made obedient to thy call,
> Or in his ruin I will bury all.　　　　　(II.iii. (p.240))

The remaining three acts are devoted to the chastening of Diocles – now Dioclesian – and his restoration to Drusilla. But while all these efforts are made on behalf of Drusilla, the authors pay little heed to her constancy or suffering. They concentrate instead upon the clash between Dioclesian's will and Delphia's magic. The sorceress's magical assault upon the faithless lover constitutes the major interest in the second half of the play: she causes Aurelia to reject Dioclesian in favour of Maximinian, his younger nephew; when Dioclesian apologizes to Drusilla, Aurelia is allowed to return to him, and his willingness to accept her again provokes Delphia's fury; Delphia allows the Persian army to abduct the members of the Roman court; and she then agrees to aid Dioclesian in rescuing them if he will remain faithful to Drusilla. That this contest is the focus of the second half is illustrated by the confrontation at the end of Act III, when Dioclesian turns on Delphia:

> *Delph.*　　　　　　　　I contemn thy threatenings;
> And thou shalt know I hold a power above thee. –
> We must remove Aurelia: come [*Aside to* DRUS.]. – Farewell, fool:
> When thou shalt see me next, thou shalt bow to me.
> *Dio.* Look thou appear no more to cross my pleasures.
> 　　　[*Exeunt, on one side,* DELPHIA *and* DRUSILLA;
> 　　　*on the other,* DIOCLESIAN].
> 　　　　　　　　　　　　　　　(III.iii. (p.259))

The resolution of this conflict depends upon the moral awakening of Dioclesian, and the prophetess performs her magic in order to generate such a recognition in him. The emphasis, however, is upon the reversals and thrills that arise from her hectoring the wandering lover.

This emphasis becomes even more evident when the resolution is compared to that of *The Maid of Honour*. Camiola's discovery of Bertoldo's betrayal does not occur until the first scene of the last act (the audience has seen his surrender to Aurelia in iv.iv). This difference in structure between the two plays is revealing: in *The Prophetess* the early betrayal throws the dramatic focus upon Delphia's magical reconstruction of Dioclesian, whereas in *The Maid of Honour* stress falls upon events leading up to Bertoldo's late rejection of Camiola. In *The Prophetess* the audience is promised spectacular retribution upon the faithless lover; in *The Maid of Honour* the heroine conceals her scheme, and in the event it proves far less protracted and flashy than Delphia's. Like Rosalind in *As You Like It*, she secretly undertakes a plot to win back Bertoldo:

> He shal be then against his wil my husband
> And when I have him, I'll so use him –   (v.i.112–13)

Here too we are teased by the possibility of surprise, particularly in the breaking off of her sentence, but this is nothing like the expectation of magic in *The Prophetess*; for one thing, there is little time for anything but the climax. And finally, it is part of Massinger's point that his heroine works miracles with words.

The point towards which I have been moving in this discussion of structure is that the organization of each of these two plays reflects a different theatrical bias which in turn reflects a different moral purpose. In *The Maid of Honour* Camiola is both victim and avenger, whereas in *The Prophetess* these two roles are divided between Drusilla and Delphia. Drusilla is virtually a cipher, a wronged *ingénue* who hasn't the means of taking action against her betrayer. She must rely on external agency, the magical powers of her aunt. In fact, Delphia's only connection to the plot is her connection to her niece; like the necromancy she employs, Delphia is essentially a theatrical device, a machine out of which the happy ending issues. In *The Maid of Honour*, on the other hand, Massinger's uniting of victim and avenger in Camiola attests to his interest in another kind of power, an inner strength as efficacious as Delphia's magic. Upon hearing the news of Bertoldo's apostasy, she speaks not of magical charms or supernatural threats but of her own innocence and its moral force, its power to influence others:

> I must not be
> Cruell by his example; you perhaps
> Expect I now should seeke recovery
> Of what I have lost by teares, and with bent knees
> Beg his compassion. No; my towring vertue
> From the assurance of my merit scornes
> To stoope so low. I'll take a nobler course,
> And confident in the justice of my cause,
> The king his brother, and new mistrisse, judges,
> Ravish him from her armes.   (v.i.101–10)

This is theatrically promising, to be sure, but we are led to concentrate less on the process of Bertoldo's moral awakening than on its import, less on the means of achieving justice than on justice itself.

The fundamental difference between *The Prophetess* and *The Maid of Honour* is the difference between virtuosity and virtue. Even the titles suggest this difference: the collaboration promises a medium; Massinger offers virtue in his heroine. *The Prophetess* makes its impact with theatrical machinery: invisible cars drawn by dragons, solemn music to enhance important moments, magical reversals of character (as in Aurelia's shift from Dioclesian to Maximinian and then back again), divinely ordained military victories, and thunder and lightning introducing omens ('*A hand with a bolt appears above*') (v.iii. (p.287)). These are the tools with which Delphia secures Dioclesian's return to Drusilla. In *The Maid of Honour*, on the other hand, Camiola's only weapon is her 'towring vertue' and her rhetorical gifts. The heavenly power to which Camiola appeals – 'My good Angell helpe me/In these extreamities!' (v.i.120–1) – does not appear on stage. Her victory, which consists of Bertoldo's confession, Aurelia's apology, and the general recognition of her virtue, is generated by nothing more than her moral example and her skill in expressing herself.

To make this distinction between *The Prophetess* and *The Maid of Honour* is not to retreat once again to the familiar proposition that Fletcher is interested only in theatrical gim- crackery. *The Prophetess*, like most of his other plays, does depend for its effect upon elaborate theatrical apparatus, whether it be an invisible chariot or a last-minute discovery; but to say so is not to preclude some moral concern in Fletcher and his collaborator. The magic in *The Prophetess* is put to heuristic use. The initial prophecy is designed to bring about justice in the execution of Aper, Delphia's manipulation of Dioclesian finally promotes his recognition of his weakness and cruelty, and the omens in the last act warn Maximinian and Aurelia that they have been ungrateful and wicked in their ambition:

> *Aur.* Oh, it shakes still!
> *Maxi.* And dreadfully it threatens! – We acknowledge
> Our base and foul intentions: stand between us!
>
> (v.iii. (p.288))

Such a moment implies both a serious purpose and a moral conception of man's place in the universe, although one cannot help suspecting that the moral recognition may be an excuse for the theatrical dazzlement by which it is achieved. The spectator at a performance of *The Prophetess* would no doubt have left the theatre talking about the special effects. Massinger's means are considerably simpler. He relies upon the power of words to create the final harmony. The spectator must be impressed with goodness itself. In *The Prophetess* the weak and the wicked respond to magic, whereas in *The Maid of Honour* they are moved by virtuous example. And the same is true for the audience. Bloody bolts and powerful words are both theatrical devices, but the difference between them elucidates the difference between the artistic styles of Fletcher and Massinger.

The conclusions of the two plays faithfully represent the relationship between them; that is, the endings are similar enough to make the differences instructive. In both plays major characters resolve the conflict by retreating from the world: Diocles marries Drusilla and retires to the countryside, surrendering his claim to the throne to his nephew; Camiola, proving her right to Bertoldo's hand and securing his promise to marry her after all, renounces him and enters a convent. Both of these may fairly be called surprise endings. Camiola's decision is certainly unexpected, and even though Diocles fulfils our expectations by agreeing to marry Drusilla, his yielding of power is unlooked-for. The conflict in *The Prophetess* has hinged upon the incompatibility of Diocles's promise to Drusilla and his ambition for the throne. Although we might have expected that Diocles would be able to have his cake and eat it too, the playwrights surprise us with his rejection of power, but they also tease us with the possibility that he might renege on his decision. The marriage and retirement come at the end of Act IV, and Maximinian's fears lead us to suspect that the tension might not be concluded. In a sense, the entire last act is a recapitulation of the first four: the same conflict, the danger of Diocles's ambition, is resolved by the same theatrical device, Delphia's magic, and Diocles remains married and retired. The final surprise is the removal of the protagonist from the element in which and for which he has lived through most of the play. This tactic alters the final harmony, modulating it, we might say, into another key, and clearly the ending is calculated to promote a moral point. Delphia's power awakens Diocles to the perils of infidelity and the vanity of political glory; his self-discovery creates the unexpected shape of the ending. This bit of prestidigitation would seem to call into question the commonplace that Fletcher shows no interest in moral problems, that he 'fled from' the 'consequences of moral choice'.[14] One does not wish to overstate the case or to transform Fletcher into a sober-sided didact, but this does appear to be one instance in which his famous technique is made to serve a moral end. Perhaps this effect is attributable to the influence of Fletcher's collaborator.

Massinger's choice of an ending for *The Maid of Honour* is nothing if not moral. Whereas *The Prophetess* offers the audience some comfort in the hoped-for marriage, Massinger astounds us by withholding the conventional happy ending altogether. We are made to reconsider the nature of a happy ending, to recognize that the union of Bertoldo and Camiola would not produce felicity. Love and politics (or military glory) have been the principal issues here, just as in *The Prophetess*; but Bertoldo achieves neither political nor amatory fulfilment, and Camiola comes to understand that Bertoldo is unworthy of her honourable love. I shall have a good deal more to say about the ending of *The Maid of Honour*, but it is undeniably a product of the same moral rigour that has chosen and shaped the action of the play, and this moral sense is considerably more urgent than that which guided the composition of *The Prophetess*.

Philip Edwards has argued that Massinger 'made a very determined effort to make his art both popular and moral, to present convincing theatrical action which should at the same time be the figured language of morality. Finding himself a dramatist by necessity, and being a moralist by nature, he tried to make "two distincts, division none." To watch him at work, bending an unlikely form of play to its moral mold, is perhaps to find a better artist and a more interesting moralist than has sometimes been recognized.'[15] Massinger's choice of a story to dramatize owes something to both of these considerations. To a sometime student in the school of Fletcher, Boccaccio's story of the virtuous widow, retold in William Painter's *Palace of Pleasure*, must have had a strong formal appeal. 'A Gentlewoman and Wydow called Camiola of hir owne minde Raunsomed Roland the Kyng's Sonne of Sicilia, of purpose to haue him to hir Husband, who when he was redeemed vnkindly denied hir, agaynst whom very Eloquently she Inueyed, and although the Law proued him to be hir Husband, yet for his vnkindnes, shee vtterly refused him.'[16] As even this bare preface to Painter's text exhibits, the shape of the story must have recommended itself to one who had learned to amuse an audience with unlikely turns, for this single sentence itself builds toward the unexpected reversal in the final clause. The contents of the tale must also have struck Massinger as theatrically compelling: love between a prince and a social inferior whose financial means are able to rescue him, captivity and ransom, a broken engagement, a courtroom scene in which justice is finally done, and a last-minute reversal based on higher justice. Not only the contents of Painter's story but also the omissions must have made it attractive to Massinger. There is nothing supernatural or magical about the conflict or its resolution, and the motives for the characters' actions, both the young man's denial and the widow's final refusal, are conveniently nebulous. Massinger can account for the conduct of Bertoldo and Camiola in terms consistent with his own view of natural human strength and weakness. And it seems likely that the great speech of self-defence that Painter's widow delivers before the King at the end of the story constituted the most meaningful feature of the source for the playwright. Painter's Camiola uses rhetoric founded in moral strength to make her audience see the virtue of her plea, and this, of course, is what Massinger himself hopes to do. In short, the dramatist apparently selected the Italian story both for its power to astonish and for its limitation on the means of astonishment.

Massinger's distinctive treatment of this story will occupy my attention for the remainder of this essay, and the feature that

distinguishes his work at all times is theme.[17] The choices that
Massinger makes in presenting actions and their agents are consistently determined by thematic concerns, and in this instance
his theme is honour. Noble instincts impel man towards honourable behaviour, but ignoble tendencies impede him. The story
becomes a conflict, in Sidney's terms, between the erected wit and
the infected will. Massinger has arranged and supplemented Boccaccio's story so as to reveal the moral complexity of most human
action, and the first problem he addresses is our understanding of
right action, the definition of honour. He seeks to send his audience from the theatre with a more complete comprehension of
honour than they brought with them, and thus it is appropriate
that he has invested virtually every scene with dramatic reflections of what is honourable behaviour and what is not.[18]

The first scene exemplifies this care, for we find the word
'honour' used repeatedly and in a variety of senses. Roberto informs Ferdinand's ambassador that the agreement between their
governments was created to provide aid in the event of a foreign
invasion: 'so farre in my honour I was tied' (I.i.154). The King
'would be knowne' as the guardian of his people's safety and is
determined to protect another kind of honour, his reputation.
But Bertoldo challenges his brother's refusal of aid by introducing another interpretation of the term: 'Cannot the
beames/Of honour thaw your icie feares?' (I.i.172–3). To the
fiery Bertoldo, honour consists in heroic activity:

> Let Sycophants, that feed upon your favours,
> Stile coldnesse in you caution, and preferre
> Your ease before your honour; and conclude
> To eate and sleepe supinely, is the end
> Of humane blessings: I must tell you Sir,
> Vertue, if not in action, is a vice,
> And when wee move not forward, we goe backeward.
>
> (I.i.181–7)

Bertoldo's definition of the honourable life continues at length in
the same vein and depends on similar images. Man was made to
fight; peace leads inevitably to 'sloth'; it is natural for humans to
seek 'the glory of the warre'; 'armour/Hung up' is a badge of
shame; virtue is nothing more nor less than *virtù*:

> Rowze us, Sir, from the sleepe
> Of idlenesse, and redeeme our morgag'd honours.

99

> Your birth, and justly, claimes my fathers Kingdome;
> But his Heroique minde descends to mee,
> I will confirme so much.   (I.i.235–9)

Bertoldo makes a stirring case for heroic achievement, an argument buttressed by his passionate diction as well as by the context of the court, which has been shown to be frivolous and shifty. And yet his position is qualified by his indiscriminate application of it: clearly Ferdinand is undeserving of aid. Bertoldo's honour is form without content, fighting for the sake of fighting. And earlier in the same scene Massinger has already offered, albeit briefly, a counter-example of heroism when Urbin's ambassador describes Siena's general, 'the great *Gonzaga*', as 'the honor of his Order' (I.i.134–5). The first scene, with its opposing conceptions of honour and its dense reference to the problem, forecasts the importance of the subject throughout the play.

Succeeding scenes are as abundant as the first with such examples and counter-examples, definitions and contradictions. Virtually all the main characters introduce partial and opposing conceptions of honourable conduct. For instance, Bertoldo's devotion to glorious deeds is extended into the second scene. When Camiola refuses his proposal of marriage (on the grounds that marriage would compromise his honour as a Knight of Malta), the rejected suitor resolves to 'Let the glorious light / Of noble war extinguish loves dimne taper' (I.ii.163–4). Committing himself to heroic action, he abandons thoughts of love: 'Honor, be thou my everliving Mistresse' (I.ii.166). (It might be pointed out that he will reject this new mistress also when he loses the battle.) Astutio, the King's statesman, thinks of honour as loyalty to his monarch, even if it requires the commission of disloyal action. He departs 'With the wings / Of loyalty and duty' (II.i.40–1), although his mission involves perjury. As soon as Astutio departs the court, Fulgentio also plans a journey, sending his page to advise Camiola that he will

> honour her with a visit.
> *Page.*   'Tis a favour
>   Will make her proud.
> *Fulgentio.*   I know it.   (II.i.55–6)

To this self-important courtier, honour is the dignity that accompanies high position. Trading upon pride of place in all encounters, Fulgentio arrogantly approaches Camiola, and when he is bluntly rejected, his immediate response is to defame her, to blacken her honour. This insult inflames Adorni's sense of honour, which requires that he preserve Camiola's reputation by challenging her accuser, after the fashion of a courtly lover: 'I must doe,/Not talke' (II.ii.193–4). Here he considers his challenge a gift in honour of Camiola's birthday, but she, ironically, gives gifts on that occasion rather than receive them. Aurelia regards honour as a natural feature of noble birth, and when Gonzaga questions the propriety of her advances towards Bertoldo, she invokes this definition in her reproof:

> As I am
> A Princesse, what I doe, is above censure,
> And to be imitated.   (IV.iv.126–8)

Even the absurd Sylli is pertinent to this topic, for his rampant egoism, his pride in his 'good partes', has persuaded him that marriage to him would do honour to Camiola. Pride, heroism, great place, birth, reputation – the kinds of honour I have enumerated and illustrated are related to one another in at least two ways. They are all public interpretations of honour, and they are all inadequate.

Massinger prefers, and asks his audience to endorse, a more personal construction of honourable conduct, and Camiola, of course, is his representative of private integrity. Throughout the play her strict understanding of the term is set against the loose and self-serving definitions of the other figures. Such oppositions are obvious in her original refusal of Bertoldo, her justified contempt for Fulgentio, and her exposure of Fulgentio before the offended King. This last episode (IV.v) is especially telling: Roberto warns her upon his arrival that he has come to correct her obstinacy, not to do her 'honour', but he leaves having recognized her honour and offered her his favour. Camiola's clearest statement of her principles, those convictions that justify her title as the maid of honour, appears in response to her discovery that Adorni has been wounded in the duel over her reputation. She condemns the specious kind of honour that depends upon the opinion of others:

> O how much
> Those Ladies are deceiv'd and cheated, when
> The clearnesse and integrity of their actions
> Doe not defend themselves, and stand secure

On their owne bases! (III.iii.53–7)

She tells Adorni that his defence of her has backfired:

> In this
> This your most memorable service, you beleev'd
> You did me right, but you have wrong'd mee more
> In your defence of my undoubted honour,
> Then false *Fulgentio* could. (III.iii.61–5)

A persuasive speech occurring in the very centre of the play, this serves as a guide for interpreting the various attitudes towards honour presented by all those who come in contact with the heroine.

But there is a fly in the ointment, a discrepancy between Camiola's eloquent professions and her own behaviour, and this same scene illuminates that contradiction. Having declared that she would have welcomed such a defence of her honour by Bertoldo, she condemns it in the low-born Adorni, and this inconsistency implies that her understanding of honour is tainted with considerations of pride and position. Furthermore, Massinger reinforces that impression with a clever dramatic juxtaposition: Bertoldo's followers enter forthwith to announce his imprisonment, and by the end of the scene Camiola has violated the King's interdiction, arranged to redeem Bertoldo, and offered to take him as her husband. This decision appears in a double light, as both a virtue and a fault, an ambiguity that her declaration to Adorni makes clear:

> *Camiola.* Yet I so love the gentleman (for to you
> I will confesse my weaknesses) that I purpose
> Nowe when he is forsaken by the king,
> And his owne hopes, to ransome him, and receive him
> Into my bosome as my lawfull husband,
> Why change you colour?   ADORNI *starts and seems troubl'd.*
> *Adorni.*   'Tis in wonder of
> Your vertue, Madam. (III.iii.196–202)

Camiola has persuaded herself that the ransom is a deed of honour which will erase the social difference between her and Bertoldo, and it is true that her courage leads her to penetrate and defy the King's hypocrisy. But Camiola has allowed passion to deform her worthy conception of personal honour. Discovering in herself

Som sparks of fire, which fann'd with honors breath
Might rise into a flame, and in men darken
Their usurp'd splendor, (III.iii.160–2)

she acts according to the public code that she has previously de-
cried. As Anne Barton puts it, Camiola does 'the right thing for the
wrong reason'.[19] Her act itself is honourable, but she is prompted
to it by her passion and concern for her lover's reputation. She falls
when she accepts Bertoldo's misplaced conception of honour. By
the end of the play, of course, she has recognized her error and
clarified her sense of what real honour is, but her 'weakness', as she
herself describes it, is crucial.

Massinger is too sophisticated a playwright to suggest that
Camiola is invariably right and everyone else invariably wrong.
Her stated conception of honour is admirable, but she cannot
adhere to it unfailingly. And Bertoldo's commitment to valour is
limited, to be sure, but is not utterly without merit. The presence of
Gonzaga, 'the honor of his Order', is calculated to demonstrate
as much. Gonzaga fulfils the definition of honour that Bertoldo
proclaims but fails to meet. In both the main fields of activity, love
and war, the idea of honour is defined and redefined as the characters interact with one another. As they modify, abandon, or exchange their opinions for others, so the audience is required to
compare and contrast the conflicting views and to observe the distance between belief and practice.

The theme of honour is treated in the same ironic key as are the
main events, characters, and other ideas in this play. Bertoldo
enters declaring the importance of honour in all human
endeavour, and yet in virtually every conflict, military or amatory,
he behaves shamefully; the man who devotes himself to glory finds
opprobrium, cannot meet his own exalted standards. For most of
the play the idea of honour is assumed to be the province of the
male, but its true representative is female. Camiola's path to
genuine honour, moreover, is highly ironic. She dishonours herself
in seeking honour, and it is this mistake that enlarges her
comprehension of the idea. Men pursue honour through heroic
action; she achieves it with words. Many seek honour at court; she
finds it in solitude. Heroic activity yields to contemplation. Massinger's perception of ironies and inconsistencies in the meanings
of honour reflects his view of the problem of strength and
weakness in human character generally: man is a giddy thing.

This thematic principle governs the structure of *The Maid of Honour*. The plot comprises a series of peripeties, lapses, and recoveries calculated to signify the unstable nature of all human action. The first lines of the play introduce the audience to the mutable, capricious nature of life in the Sicilian court. The scene opens with a pair of what we might call Shakespearian expositors, Adorni and Astutio, whose introductory remarks frame an encounter with Fulgentio, the fickle and corrupt member of the King's inner council. When Adorni seeks a simple piece of information from Fulgentio, that worthy replies that he never speaks without a fee: 'And yet for once, I care not if I answer/One single question, *gratis*' (1.i.16–17). Fulgentio has changed his mind, altered his normal practice. But after satisfying Adorni that the ambassador is to receive an audience that day, Fulgentio declines to name the hour –

> I promis'd not so much.
> A sillable you begg'd, my Charity gave it.
> Move me no further–   (1.i.19–21)

and promptly leaves the stage. Behaviour here is unpredictable, characters break their word and then keep their word, or vice versa, and inconsistency is the rule. When Adorni announces his incredulity at such business, Astutio declares that it is so common as to need no remark: 'This you wonder at?/With me 'tis usuall' (1.i.21–2). As for the outsider, so for the audience: we must 'wonder' at such habitual alteration.

And yet this sort of inconsistency has become usual for the audience too before many minutes of stage time have passed. Massinger has supplemented and prepared for the story of Camiola and her faithless lover by developing at some length the military struggle in which Bertoldo is captured. In so doing, he has developed minor betrayals to prepare for the main story of infidelity. In affairs of state as in affairs of the heart, man is given to the pursuit of self-interest and self-satisfaction at the expense of all other considerations. Roberto, King of Sicily, typifies this pursuit of self-interest by all available shifts. His first appearance is the interview with the ambassador from Urbin, the granting of which was in doubt in the play's opening conversation, and his unpredictable behaviour throughout the scene clarifies Massinger's purpose in developing the lengthy political introduction

to the love story. Roberto honourably refuses to honour his reciprocal agreement with the perfidious Ferdinand; but he changes
his mind and permits Bertoldo and his mates to serve 'as Adven-
turers, and Voluntiers'. After Bertoldo and his followers have
departed for the battle, however, Roberto announces his pleasure
at being rid of his ambitious brother and takes action to hide his
compromise. He sends Astutio as messenger

> To the Duchesse of *Siena*, in excuse
> Of these forces sent against her. If you spare
> An oath to give it credit, that, wee never
> Consented to it, swearing for the King,
> Though false, it is no perjury.   (II.i.29–33)

Astutio responds to this directive with a self-justifying defence of
the political lie. Massinger devotes so much attention to these
details of political strategy to press the parallel between leaders
and subjects. Roberto would behave honourably, but demands of
the moment interfere with good intentions, and this conflict per-
tains to virtually all the characters in *The Maid of Honour*.

It would be superfluous to consider in such detail the contribution of all the supplementary incidents, but it is worth
mentioning others to illustrate the care with which Massinger
has depicted human fickleness. According to Fulgentio, Bertoldo's followers

> ere they went
> Prophanely tooke the sacrament on their knees,
> To live and dye with him.
> *Roberto.*   O most impious!
> Their loyalty to us forgot?   (II.i.18–21)

Not only is their loyalty to the King forgot, but when things go
wrong at the battle of Urbin their commitment to their new
master deserts them as well: the complaints of Gasparo and
Anthonio and their unprincipled willingness to free themselves
reveal that their only loyalty is to their own comfort. In another
phase of the action, Adorni presses his amorous suit upon
Camiola and in so doing undermines his fundamental loyalty to
her. Fulgentio reverses ground and seeks revenge when Camiola
rejects his insulting attentions. Signior Sylli admits his fanatical
devotion to his own person and therefore vows to wait until
Camiola is unable to resist him, but by the last act, his oath
abandoned, he is in wild pursuit of her. Broken promises, changes

of heart, opportunism, and infirmity of purpose fortify the central conflict at every turn.

   Bertoldo's betrayal of Camiola in the fourth act is the action towards which the play moves, and from the beginning his role consists of a series of shifts and turns forecasting this reversal and representing man's natural penchant for inconstancy. Bertoldo's apparel in the first scene marks him as a Knight of Malta, a fraternity of which the dignity and moral rigour would have been well-known to the audience, and yet his very first words concern a jewel that he sends to Camiola as an earnest of his affection for her. In the discussion of war that makes up the second half of the scene, the moral fault of Ferdinand is made quite clear (is admitted even by his own diplomat), and yet Bertoldo proposes to take up arms for him against the lady, in violation of the principles of his order. In proposing marriage to Camiola in the second scene, he is equally cavalier about his oath of bachelorhood:

> *Camiola.*   you are Sir
>   A Knight of Malta, by your order bound
>   To a single life, you cannot marrie me,
>   And I assure my selfe you are too noble
>   To seek me (though my frailtie should consent)
>   In a base path.
> *Bertoldo.*   A dispensation Lady
>   Will easiely absolve me.
> *Camiola.*   O take heed Sir,
>   When, what is vow'd to heaven, is dispens'd with,
>   To serve our ends on earth, a curse must follow,
>   And not a blessing.
> *Bertoldo.*   Is there no hope left me?
>
>   (1.ii.146–55)

Camiola recognizes the spirit of these strictures; Bertoldo first proposes a legal dodge and then changes the subject. When she refuses him, he shifts his devotion to military fame.

   In this arena he is similarly inconstant: caught up in the expectations of glorious victory, he is unprepared for the consequences of defeat. After his capture and the King's refusal to ransom him, Bertoldo resolves to

>   weare
>   These fetters 'till my flesh, and they are one
>   Incorporated substance   (III.i.189–91)

and closes by invoking, à la Bussy D'Ambois, the conventional metaphor of the great cedar. By his next appearance he has changed his mind, delivering a self-pitying soliloquy in which he petulantly rejects the consolation of Stoic philosophy and tosses away his copy of Seneca. Can there be censure for

> Tearing my locks, and in defiance throwing
> Dust in the ayre? or falling on the ground, thus
> With my nayles, and teeth to digge a grave or rend
> The bowells of the earth. (IV.iii.28–31)

By the end of this scene he has been ransomed by Camiola and has agreed through Adorni to marry her; by the end of the next he has shifted his affections again:

> *Bertoldo*. I am wholly yours.
> *Aurelia*. On this booke seale it. (IV.iv.182)

This last reversal is the structural and moral pivot of *The Maid of Honour*. Bertoldo's earlier mutations have prepared for it, the ironic ending issues from it, and Massinger, aware of the dramatic and moral significance of the event, takes pains to exploit its theatrical potential and clarify its meaning. His first tactic is to shock us with Aurelia's revelation of her passion as soon as Bertoldo appears before her: 'A prisoner! nay, a princely sutor rather!' (IV.iv.52), she declares, and leads him away for private conference. Massinger reinforces our response with the astonished comments of the assembled soldiers and courtiers, and our dismay is intensified, of course, by the knowledge of Bertoldo's very recent engagement. Aurelia's attraction to Bertoldo leads her, before she snares him, to countermand the ransom just arranged. When Bertoldo complains that 'This is/Against the law of armes', she promptly rejoins, in an aside, 'But not of love' (IV.iv.74–5). Massinger then develops the moral conflict by focusing attention on the young man's sequence of responses. Bertoldo steps apart and wonders at the Princess's forward conduct ('BERTOLDO *walking by musing*'), and then he summarizes the dilemma in a series of asides:

> No, no, it cannot be, yet but *Camiola*,
> There is no stop betweene me and a crowne.
> Then my ingratitude! a sinne in which
> All sinnes are comprehended! Aide me vertue,
> Or I am lost. (IV.iv.153–7)

Two more theatrical devices attest to Massinger's command of his material. When Aurelia demands a reply, Bertoldo declares that marriage to her is out of the question: 'I am already too too much ingag'd/To the king my brothers anger' (IV.iv.171–2). The striking effect of the pun on 'ingag'd' seems to me typical of the cooperation of Massinger's theatrical and moral senses. Finally, when Aurelia promises to mollify Roberto and thus wins Bertoldo's consent, the couple's departure is delayed by a brief interruption:

> Adorni.　　Camiola.　　　　Whispers to BERTOLDO.
> Aurelia. How doe you?
> Bertoldo.　　　　Indisposed, but I attend you.　　Exeunt.
> (IV.iv.188–9)

The stage is left to Adorni, whose soliloquy, although it moves towards an expression of his own hopes, begins by summarizing the moral point of the entire episode: 'The heavie curse that waites on perjurie,/And foule ingratitude, pursue thee ever' (IV.iv.190–1). Massinger has made thematic use of this spectacular climax, illustrating the power of will and self-satisfaction to override the claims of honour and duty. His preoccupation in this scene is quite clear: Bertoldo fulfils the pattern of inconstancy established at the beginning, and Massinger's inclusion of supplementary betrayals and reversals enriches his portrayal of the topic.

In opposition to all this shiftiness stands Camiola, whose ultimate act of constancy completes this pattern of turn and counter-turn and thus gives meaning to the network of actions. But Camiola's first reversal, her redemption of Bertoldo, must be given its due. Just before her first interview with him, Camiola enunciates the theme of honour and constancy, admitting that she longs to do what her reason forbids:

> Camiola if ever, now be constant:
> This is indeed a sutor, whose sweet presence,
> Courtship and loving language would have stagger'd
> The chast Penelope.　　　　　　　　　　　　(I.ii.60–3)

Initially she resists her suitor's ardent pleas, reminding him of their social inequality and of his vow of celibacy. But despite her good intentions, she cannot escape participation in the world of weakness and self-interest. Her surrender to passion catches the heroine in the ironic net which contains all the other characters. Moreover, it generates other reversals, most importantly Bertoldo's rejection of her for Aurelia, indicating that self-betrayal begets further betrayals. There is additional irony associated with her defection from her nobly-stated principles: like Angelo in *Measure for Measure*, the saint tempted by a saint, Camiola's attempt to gain honour leads her to lose it. And, finally, her lapse prepares for the doubly ironic reversal in the final scene. Camiola's submission to desire is consistent with Massinger's mixed view of human character. The heroine is virtuous but not saintly, firm but not immovable, wise but not infallible. And her capitulation to will here is as important to the ironic design of *The Maid of Honour* as her conquest of will in the dénouement.

Camiola reclaims her title as the maid of honour by an ironic reversal, the breaking of a promise. The dramatic values of this theatrical *coup* are obvious at once. Massinger intensifies suspense in Camiola's response to the information that Bertoldo has betrayed her and arrived at the court with the intention of marrying the Princess. She denounces his infidelity – 'O false men!/Inconstant! perjur'd!' (v.i.119–20) – and sets out to state her claim upon him, but the ambiguity of her language is purposefully mystifying. I have mentioned her promise to 'so use him', and there are other nebulous promises and threats:

> If I marry, 'tis
> This day, or never.   (v.i.124–5)

> something I will doe
> That shall deserve mens prayse, and wonder too.
>   (v.i.131–2)

Camiola's auditors here interpret her words in different ways: Adorni assumes that she will reclaim Bertoldo, Sylli that she will finally agree to become his bride. Besides the parallel to Rosalind in *As You Like It*, other Shakespearian endings come to mind. Camiola behaves rather like Helena in *All's Well* towards a man who resembles Bertram, and Camiola's remarks to Adorni contain an elaborate metaphor of man as an actor for the angelic audience which is so much like Isabella's words to Angelo that the surprises in the last act of *Measure for Measure* seem pertinent. In short, the audience is given some indication that a surprise is in store, but its form is left unknown.

That the ending takes the shape it does, Camiola's winning of
Bertoldo and her immediate renunciation of him, attests not only
to Massinger's control of his theatrical means but also to his
understanding of their moral efficacy. Camiola's speech of self-
justification is Massinger's dramatic version of the feature that
seems to have attracted him to Painter's tale in the first place, the
widow's rhetorical triumph that makes up most of the story. With
this speech she awakens the stage assembly to the same sense of
justice and morality that the audience, owing to its privileged view
of Camiola's experience, has developed through the course of the
play. Roberto, Ferdinand, Gonzaga, and Aurelia serially confess
their admiration for 'the vertues of [Camiola's] minde' (v.ii.164)
and admit the necessity of her claim, and Bertoldo himself follows
their exclamations with a lengthy self-indictment. In its opening
lines he summarizes the shape of the play's moral conflict:

> Oh, how have I stray'd,
> And wilfully, out of the noble tract
> Mark'd mee by vertue! (v.ii.177–9)

and in his final reversal he contributes to the pattern that
Camiola's impending surprise will conclude. Her winning again
the hand of Bertoldo we have been led to expect; her refusing him
in favour of a religious life surely astonishes us. Here Camiola
serves as a surrogate for the playwright, employing a theatrical
gesture to clarify the moral implications of her action.

Camiola's unexpected retreat from the world is the final ironic
reversal in a work built upon such shifts. The betrayals and broken
promises up to this point have created an ironic network consistent with Massinger's critical understanding of the world, and the
heroine's refusal of her lover, taken from Painter's story, carries on
that series of ironies. In cancelling her vow to Bertoldo, Camiola
acknowledges the impossibility of human fidelity; not only has he
been false to her, but she has been false to herself. Mortality pros-
cribes constancy. But such an inconclusive ending leaves the play
thematically incomplete, and Massinger adds a final twist that
both continues the ironic pattern and, paradoxically, ends it at the
same time. Camiola commits herself to an unbreakable eternal
contract. Her retreat into religion is an ironic means of transcen-
ding the inevitable failures and disappointments inherent in
human life. As I have suggested in comparing this ending to that of

The Prophetess, Massinger's final turn is obviously a function of his moral purpose. But what needs to be emphasized here is that he achieves his moral aim by theatrically popular means. The action that changes and completes the meaning of the play is that staple of Jacobean tragicomedy, the surprise ending.

This turn significantly alters the spectator's impression of the kind of play he has been watching and raises for the critic the problem of form. Until the final moment the tragicomic outline of the action has encouraged the audience to expect a version of the conventional ending – the triumph of the heroine by surprising or mysterious means, the surmounting of obstacles, and matrimony. When Camiola refuses Bertoldo, the irony of her decision surprises the audience and frustrates their expectations. When she reveals her intention to pursue a religious life, however, the audience is confronted with a double irony. The heroine triumphs by surprising means (retreat), surmounts the chief obstacle of the play-world (natural frailty), and closes the play with a metaphoric wedding:

> This is the marriage! this the port! to which
> My vowes must steere me, fill my spreading sayles
> With the pure wind of your devotions for me,
> That I may touch the secure haven, where
> Eternall happinesse keepes her residence,
> Temptations to frailty never entring.   (v.ii.267–72)

Massinger achieves his unconventional happy ending by the same ironic means that he has used throughout. It is clear that we are to applaud Camiola's marriage to a life of prayer, that the monastic life is the only proof against temptation. And the symbolic quality of the 'marriage' gives a symbolic dimension to the actions of the play as a whole: 'eternall happinesse' is not to be found on earth.

Some may argue that the dramatist plays unfairly, that his summoning the unfamiliar friar to claim Camiola amounts to an illegitimate tactic. But Massinger makes meaning out of his theatrical trick. He goes outside the world of the play for the same reason that she does, to find a 'secure haven' free of error and weakness. Retirement is the one defence against the incontrovertible pattern of betrayal and self-betrayal. Massinger's replacement of the normal wedding with a higher kind of union indicates that he is playing with the tragicomic form, causing the

audience to reconsider the familiar conception of a happy
ending. His practice here indicates yet another possible case of
Jonson's influence. Not only is the surprising twist reminiscent of
The Silent Woman (and, to a lesser extent, *The Alchemist*), but
the denial of expectations for moral ends is typically Jonsonian.
Massinger makes his ending a critique of the world and of the
unpredictably predictable way that tragicomedy represents that
world in its ending. Life as Massinger conceives it does not afford
the cleverly arranged, happy solutions that his audience was
accustomed to seeing on the Jacobean stage, and so his
dramatization of life deprives the audience of the normal
conclusion.

It appears that Massinger himself referred to *The Maid of
Honour* as a tragicomedy, and this description needs to be reck-
oned with. On the first page of text (B1ʳ) in the 1632 quarto, just
beneath the title, the work is designated 'A Tragae-Comedy', and
the location of this label – not on the title page, where a printer
might have placed it – would seem to indicate authorial origin
(although a scribe might have been responsible). Even if Massinger called his play a tragicomedy, it seems clear that the
dramatist was using the term in a very loose sense, that such a
definition is the first in a tissue of ironies, and that the meaning of
the play depends upon its ironic relation to the tragicomic mode.
Certainly *The Maid of Honour* does not fit Fletcher's famous
definition, in the preface to *The Faithful Shepherdess*:[20] the audience is allowed to feel little sense of potential tragedy. Despite
the presence of a siege, the harsh captivity of the protagonist, and
a duel in an ancillary line of plot, Massinger does not allow the
audience to take these matters very seriously. There is no killing
here. Nor is there much mirth. The serious presentation of
characters and their predicaments is enough to make it no
comedy in the familiar sense. If it is necessary to settle for 'tragicomedy', then the term must be used in a very specialized way.
And this is especially true since by 1620 the category had become
so elastic as to reveal very little about the kind of play being
offered.

The tragicomic label applies to *The Maid of Honour* to about
the same degree that it applies to *All's Well*, *Measure for
Measure*, and perhaps *Troilus and Cressida*. That is, it will do,
but it fails to capture thoroughly our experience of the play.

These works can serve as useful guides to appreciating Massinger's distinctive combination of dramatic elements. The most obvious parallel is that Massinger, like his great predecessor, finds a way to bring some very unsavoury dramatic action to a positive conclusion. Shakespeare's endings are perhaps more straightforward in that they can usually be foreseen, but still they offer little basis for hope. Often they seem inconclusive, artificial, or ironic. Massinger's ending, although calculated to provide a sense of hopeful finality, is similarly artificial and ironic. And these endings conclude plots that expose humankind in some of its least attractive attitudes. *Measure for Measure*, to take the most apparent similarity, presents case after case in which will dominates judgement, promises are unkept, and result mocks intention. I have already outlined some of the main resemblances between *All's Well* and *The Maid of Honour*. And even *Troilus and Cressida*, despite the difference in its ending, portrays a world of insecurity, dishonour, and self-betrayal in the very arenas with which Massinger is concerned, love and war. Moreover, Massinger's play follows all these plays most faithfully in its inordinate dependence on irony throughout, particularly irony of the critical variety.

I believe that we can do justice to the form of *The Maid of Honour* if we borrow the term sometimes applied to these Shakespearian texts – dark comedy. It captures the complex mixture of tones, dubiety and hope, that is the source of the generic problem. The depiction of man that proceeds from the action is shadowy and discouraging; the methods used to create this picture are critical and sometimes even satiric; the issues raised are serious, even grave. And yet the resolution of these negative actions is, generally speaking, positive. Massinger suggests that moral victory is attainable but is available only to the strongest, most exceptional kind of individual. Camiola escapes the snares of the world, but as she sails into that 'secure haven' the rest of the cast is left to flounder in the sea of weakness and failure. Swinburne, following Leslie Stephen, worried about Massinger's tendency to overrate the power of rhetoric, a bias which seemed to those two critics dangerously sentimental.[21] But Philip Edwards is surely correct in describing the implications of the ending as 'austere and stern'.[22] That the other characters must remain in the world suggests a kind of damnation. Massinger implies that they are condemned to repeat their patterns of error. Rhetoric can illuminate but not transform.

This essay has begged certain questions, such as the quality of Massinger's verse or his skill at characterization. Although these are interesting matters demanding more attention, I have neglected them in favour of two questions that must come first in a consideration of Massinger's achievement: the problem of artistic independence, and the relationship of idea to form. In other words, it has seemed appropriate to establish first that Massinger deserves to be taken seriously as a playwright, and on this point *The Maid of Honour* is uncommonly helpful. The play gives a fair sense of its author's literary debts. These are numerous and important, but Massinger did not merely stitch together Shakespeare's and Jonson's remnants into a pattern taken from Fletcher's workbasket. The threads have been rewoven into a distinctive shape. Second, the play helps to establish certain principles that have too often been doubted – that Massinger had a brain, that he was not content to rehearse conventional ideas, that the moral questions in his plays are more than debating topics, that his approach to dramatic structure was original and suitable, that there is a right relation between morality and form. We see that he had a point of view and a plan for expressing it. Above all, *The Maid of Honour* should teach us that apparent inconsistency, here and throughout the canon, may signify complexity and not confusion.

NOTES

1 Philip Edwards, 'Massinger the Censor' in Richard Hosley (ed.), *Essays on Shakespeare and Elizabethan Drama in Honor of Hardin Craig* (Columbia, University of Missouri Press, 1962), pp.341–2, presents a brief survey of this critical consensus. Edwards's is one of the two most helpful essays on Massinger; the other is Anne Barton's 'The Distinctive Voice of Massinger', *TLS* (20 May 1977), 623–4, reprinted as an appendix in this volume.
2 T. A. Dunn supplies the clearest statement of the first position when he insists that in Massinger 'artistic conscience always succumbs to the conscience of the moralist'. See *Philip Massinger: The Man and the Playwright* (Edinburgh, Thomas Nelson, 1957), p.74. For the contrary view, that Massinger is not interested in the moral problems he seems to raise, see Peter F. Mullany, 'Religion in Massinger's *The Maid of Honour*', *Renaissance Drama*, n.s. 2 (1969), 143–56.

3 Philip Edwards and Colin Gibson, in their introductory comments on *The Maid of Honour*, discuss and dismiss these speculations. *The Plays and Poems of Philip Massinger* (5 vols., Oxford, Clarendon Press, 1976), vol. 1, pp.105–6.

4 Edwards and Gibson, vol. 1, p.106.

5 Knights, *Drama and Society in the Age of Jonson* (1937; rpt. New York, Norton, 1968), pp.270–3. T. S. Eliot, following Cruickshank, has much of interest to say about Massinger's borrowings, although not all of his generalizations are equally persuasive; see *Elizabethan Essays* (London, Faber and Faber, 1934), pp.153–63. Cyrus Hoy, 'Verbal Formulae in the Plays of Philip Massinger', *SP*, 56 (1959), 600–18, while not denying Massinger's habit of taking phrases from others, presents a thorough and impressive account of his tendency to repeat himself.

6 In her edition of *The Maid of Honour* (London, 1927), Eva A. W. Bryne considers some of the parallels with *All's Well*; since she thinks *The Maid of Honour* was written between 1623 and 1625, the problem of Massinger's access to Shakespeare's play does not occur to her. See pp.xxxiii–v. Massinger might have seen a performance of *All's Well*, although he would have been about twenty years old when it was new and nearly forty when he wrote *The Maid of Honour*.

7 Ben Jonson, *Works*, ed. C. H. Herford and Percy and Evelyn Simpson (11 vols., Oxford, Clarendon Press, 1925–52), vol. 5, (I.iv.37–40). Bryne mentions this parallel.

8 I quote throughout from the edition of Massinger's works by Edwards and Gibson, cited above.

9 I have used the edition of Alexander Dyce, *The Works of Beaumont and Fletcher* (11 vols., London, 1843–6), vol. 8, pp.207–89.

10 'Religion in Massinger's *The Maid of Honour*', pp.146–7.

11 Cyrus Hoy, 'The Shares of Fletcher and his Collaborators in the Beaumont and Fletcher Canon' (II), *Studies in Bibliography*, 9 (1957), 152.

12 See his prefatory note to the text, p.209.

13 Bryne, although she identifies a number of valuable parallels between *The Maid of Honour* and *The Prophetess*, is concerned mainly to document and emphasize the influence of Fletcher.

14 Edwards, 'Massinger the Censor', p.342.

15 'Massinger the Censor', p.341.

16 William Painter, 'The Thirty-Second Novell', in *The Palace of Pleasure*, rpt. and ed. Joseph Jacobs, (3 vols., New York, Dover, 1966), vol. 3, pp.354–62.

17 The perils and abuses of thematic criticism have been set forth recently in a series of stern warnings by Richard A. Levin and Norman Rabkin, among others. See Levin, *New Readings Versus Old Plays* (Chicago, University of Chicago Press, 1979), and Rabkin, *Shakespeare and the Problem of Meaning* (Chicago, University of Chicago Press, 1981). The method, despite its pitfalls, seems unavoidable with Massinger, particularly since here the topic at issue is his moral involvement in his works.

18 Edwards draws some similar conclusions about the importance of

honour, although his analysis is brief. See 'Massinger the Censor', pp.344–6.

19 'The Distinctive Voice of Massinger' (see p.230, below).
20 'A tragie-comedie is not so called in respect of mirth and killing, but in respect it wants deaths, which is inough to make it no tragedie, yet brings some neare it, which is inough to make it no comedie'. 'To the Reader' in Fredson Bowers (gen. ed.) *The Dramatic Works in the Beaumont and Fletcher Canon* (5 vols. to date, Cambridge, Cambridge University Press, 1966–82), vol. 3 (1976), p.497.
21 Edmund Gosse and Thomas James Wise (eds.), *The Complete Works of Charles Algernon Swinburne* (20 vols., London, William Heinemann, 1926), vol. 12, pp. 255–6.
22 'Massinger the Censor', p.346.

Massinger's Political Tragedies

DOUGLAS HOWARD

THE death of Fletcher in 1625 marked an obvious turning point in Massinger's career as a playwright, since thereafter he occupied Fletcher's place as chief dramatist for the King's Men. Massinger had been associated with this company as Fletcher's collaborator as early as 1616, but before 1625 only two of his unaided plays, *The Duke of Milan* (?1621–2) and *The Unnatural Combat* (?1624–5), were written for audiences at the Globe and indoors at Blackfriars. The remainder of his extant unaided works from the years before the death of Fletcher were undertaken for Christopher Beeston's companies at the Phoenix (or Cockpit) in Drury Lane, and they were all either tragicomedies or comedies.

After 1625, however, Massinger's name was – with the puzzling exception of *The Great Duke of Florence* (1627)[1] – associated exclusively with the King's Men. The majority of his plays continued to be tragicomedies, but those tragedies he did produce during the Caroline period follow a recognizable trend in the direction of political controversy. As early as 1619, Massinger had run into trouble with the authorities for his part in *Sir John van Olden Barnavelt*, a tragedy written in collaboration with Fletcher and based on recent political and religious conflict in the Netherlands.[2] The play was licensed by the Master of the Revels, but its performance was temporarily delayed on account of a prohibition by the Bishop of London.

Massinger was twice more to encounter resistance for the political implications of his plays. In January 1631 Sir Henry Herbert refused to license the original version of *Believe As You List* because it treated the life of Don Sebastian, King of Portugal, who died in the battle of Alcazar-el-Kebir in 1578. After Don Sebastian's defeat, when Portugal had been annexed by Philip II, a number of pretenders appeared claiming to be

Sebastian, and Herbert considered Massinger's sympathetic portrayal of one of them to be a dangerous matter in view of England's alliance with Spain. Massinger promptly set about rewriting the play, moving the scene from Portugal to Carthage and substituting the classical stories of Antiochus the Great and of Hannibal's persecution by Titus Flamininius for the Don Sebastian material.[3] Herbert licensed the revised version of the play on 6 May 1631, and it was subsequently acted by the King's Men.

Seven years later, Massinger once more ran foul of the Master of the Revels regarding the political implications of a play, now lost, called *The King and the Subject* (1638). Herbert ordered among other things that the name of the play be altered, and King Charles himself required the omission of one offending passage, noting, 'This is too insolent, and to be changed.'[4] The play was eventually allowed to be acted, 'the reformations most strictly observed, and not otherwise' (Bentley, vol. 4, p.795), but Herbert's entry does not indicate what the new title was. There being no other record of a play called *The King and the Subject*, efforts have been made to identify this work with another title. That most often suggested, by Fleay among others,[5] is the lost Massinger tragedy called *The Tyrant*, which, though its date is unknown, is conjecturally assigned to 1628 in the Harbage (rev. Schoenbaum) *Annals*.[6] The play is first mentioned in Moseley's list (1660), and it can be traced as far as Warburton's sale in November 1759 (Bentley, vol. 4, p.819), but nothing is now known of its whereabouts. Both Greg and Bentley doubt Fleay's linking of *The Tyrant* and *The King and the Subject*,[7] but even if the titles represent separate plays, both add to our impression that Massinger's later tragedies were increasingly political in nature.[8]

While changes in the political climate after the coronation of Charles no doubt helped shift Massinger's attention away from personal tragedy and towards tragedies of power,[9] this new direction was a natural and inevitable one for the dramatist. His general moral outlook was clearly more suited to social and political questions than to the kinds of internal strife that he had tried to represent in characters like Sforza in *The Duke of Milan* and Malefort senior in *The Unnatural Combat*. Among the tragedies Massinger may have written between 1625 and his death in 1640, only *The Roman Actor* (1626) and *Believe As You*

List (1631) are extant, but in both of these plays the central action is more nearly a conflict between good and evil characters than a war between reason and passion within the individual. Instead of the clash between Malefort's noble public self and his incestuous longings, we have Domitian's relentless persecution of innocent men in *The Roman Actor*. The line of battle is also clearly drawn in *Believe As You List*, where Flaminius is relieved of his duties as ambassador to Carthage in order that he may devote his full energy to the destruction of the saintly Antiochus.

The Roman Actor and *Believe As You List* are, then, departures from Massinger's previous attempts at tragedy; they are, moreover, happy departures for a dramatist whose earlier tragedies were marred by his failure to make convincing tragic protagonists out of characters – like Malefort, Sforza, even Charalois in *The Fatal Dowry* (?1617–19) – whose combination of public self-assurance and private disablement by passion seems somehow implausible. Shakespeare was able, in *Antony and Cleopatra*, for example, to turn such inconsistent behaviour as that of Malefort or Sforza into a statement about the enigmatic and paradoxical nature of the tragic personality. Chapman created similarly convincing, if contradictory, figures in Bussy D'Ambois and the Duke of Byron, and certainly Webster found tragic potential in Vittoria Corombona's inscrutable mixture of treachery and defiant individualism in *The White Devil*.[10] Massinger, however, was less comfortable with such amalgams of virtue and vice, and with the idea that their greatness in some way exempted them from judgement according to established societal norms. In both *The Roman Actor* and *Believe As You List*, Massinger moves away from such mixed characters, which, in a less exaggerated form, Aristotle himself thought best for tragedy, and towards characters whose complete goodness or thorough villainy reminds one that the influence of the Morality tradition was still to be felt in English tragedy.

Massinger was not, of course, the only seventeenth-century dramatist to write tragedy based on something approximating to a battle between virtues and vices. Jonson's *Sejanus* (1603), upon which Massinger drew heavily in *The Roman Actor*,[11] focuses upon a thoroughly evil character who kills off his betters in an effort to gain power. Chapman turned from Bussy and Byron to the innocent and pitiable hero of *The Tragedy of Chabot* (1622), and even Shakespeare set Edgar and Edmund, as well as Cordelia and her evil sisters, in unmistakable moral opposition to one another. Since Massinger was not the sole practitioner of tragedy involving such antithetical figures, the important issue is the kind of tragic effect produced by this sort of play and its difference from tragedy which results from a flaw in character. Plays like *The Roman Actor* and *Believe As You List* are, in one sense, bleaker in outlook than those where suffering results from some failure of the individual. King Lear may be more sinned against than sinning, but his ill-advised division of the kingdom and his rash banishment of Kent and Cordelia implicate him in his own downfall. More important, Lear enters into a new state of self-awareness as a result of his suffering – something that does not happen in tragedies where destruction is a result of blind chance, or of personal malice. To Antiochus in *Believe As You List*, our chief reaction is pity; we may fear, but what we fear is the hideousness of his fate, not – as in *Lear* or in *Oedipus the King* – that we might bring such an end upon ourselves. And since the persecution of Antiochus does not, like that of Dorothea in Massinger and Dekker's *The Virgin Martyr* (?1620), bring with it the promise of a heavenly reward, we are left at the end of the play with a sense of hopelessness about the protagonist's fate. We feel, as we do after reading Hardy's *Tess of the D'Urbervilles*, that an innocent individual has been made to suffer by a horrifying combination of human depravity and divine neglect.

The mood of *The Roman Actor*, on the other hand, is less nearly one of despair. Although Domitian in his reign of terror causes many noble Romans to die unjustly, he finally pays for his crimes, and his cruelty is made to seem ineffectual when men like Rusticus and Sura insist that the tyrant's rending of their bodies merely adds lustre to their souls (III.ii.95–108). The pattern of *The Roman Actor* is essentially that of all *de casibus* tragedy; it combines the vicissitudes of fortune with retribution for sin in bringing about the fall of a prince. Domitian might say with Lord Mowbray in *The Mirror for Magistrates* (1559) that Fortune did her part in his fall, but that 'Vyce onely vyce' causes the heart to incline to evil.[12]

The fact that Domitian comes to a bad end (while Flaminius, the antagonist in *Believe As You List*, does not) is only one of the important distinctions between the two plays. An even more revealing difference is that the protagonist in *The Roman Actor* is not completely innocent in the way that Antiochus is in the later, more narrowly political *Believe As You List*. Paris, unlike the exiled Asian king, has a disastrous slip from honour when he momentarily gives in to the sexual advances of Domitia, the emperor's wife. If Antiochus has ever been guilty of wrongdoing, he has atoned for his sins: we first see him as he emerges from 22 years of wandering about the world in repentance for the foolish ambition that caused him to lose 12,000 men on 'Achaias bloodie plaines' (I.i.38).

Paris is virtuous, but not in the awe-inspiring way that Antiochus is, or even in the way that Lamia and many of Domitian's other victims are in *The Roman Actor*. He is peculiar among Massinger's tragic protagonists for being a believable near-miss at perfect goodness. He does not alternate, as Massinger's earlier protagonists do, between unconvincing extremes of good and evil, nor is he a paragon of virtue like Dorothea or Antiochus; he is an essentially noble individual who in a moment of trial compromises his honour.

The difference between Massinger's treatment of Paris and Antiochus is best explained by observing that Paris's character is not the moral focus of *The Roman Actor* in the way that Antiochus's is in *Believe As You List*. In the former play our attention is largely taken up with Domitian, his crimes, and the retribution that he brings upon himself. If Antiochus's stoic fortitude is meant to move us to virtue, then Domitian's gruesome death is meant to dissuade us from vice. That makes Paris's downfall ancillary to the main action of *The Roman Actor*, even though the title of the play obviously refers to him as well as to Domitian, the 'new actor' (IV.ii.237). There is ample evidence in the commendatory verses included in the first edition (1629) of *The Roman Actor* that Massinger's contemporaries saw the play in this light. Thomas Jay, one of the work's dedicatees, praises the author for his creation of Caesar, who

> (forgetting Heavens rod)
> By His Edicts stil'd himselfe great Lord and God.

Paris, on the other hand, is mentioned only for his eloquent defence of actors. Similarly, in Robert Harvey's tribute to the play, the reader is invited to witness Domitian's tragic fall.

LONG'ST thou to see proud *Cæsar* set in State,
His Morning greatnesse, or his Euening fate?

Harvey asks, and then urges the reader to admire Massinger's setting forth of the story.

The failure to recognize that Paris's chief purpose is to defend the moral influence of the acting profession has led critics to distort the meaning of *The Roman Actor* by attributing to Paris more tragic significance than Massinger allows him. A. P. Hogan argues that Paris's ambition, and thus his willingness to serve a tyrant, brings about his 'very ironic' downfall.[13] Hogan's conclusion is based largely on Paris's very conventional remark in the first scene that

> Our aime is glorie, and to leaue our names
> To after times.   (1.i.31–2)

There is no other suggestion in the play that Paris is ambitious, and his wish to be memorialized is a harmless commonplace of poets that one finds, as Willard Farnham has observed, in Boccaccio's *De Casibus*, the *Secretum* of Petrarch, and elsewhere.[14] Moreover, Massinger goes out of his way to show Paris's favour with Domitian in the best possible light. His source for the actor's privileged position is Juvenal's *Saturae* where the political power of the *histrio* does, as Colin Gibson notes, come under attack,[15] but Massinger shows Paris consistently using his influence with Domitian to good ends. Aesopus praises Paris for his bounty to his fellows (1.i.26–30), and even Parthenius remarks that:

> many men owe you
> For Prouinces they nere hop'd for; and their liues,
> Forfeited to his anger.   (II.i.77–9)[16]

Certainly, Paris's capitulation to the lascivious Domitia is pathetic, but neither that lapse nor Domitian's subsequent killing of Paris constitutes an ironic commentary upon the actor's favour with the emperor. Perhaps David Richman puts the case most clearly when he argues that Paris's 'mistake' is never explored enough to allow us to respond tragically.[17] But if Massinger does not develop the tragic possibilities in the character of Paris, it is merely because his interests as a moralist lead him in another direction. With the example of Paris, as with that of Domitian himself, Massinger's purpose is to show us:

> what honours waite
> On good, and glorious actions, and the shame
> That treads vpon the heeles of vice.   (1.i.23–5)

The whole of *The Roman Actor* is, in fact, an elaborate illustration of the Horatian idea,[18] so often repeated by Massinger, that cold precepts cannot, like representation on the stage,

> fire
> The Bloud, or swell the veines with emulation
> To be both good, and great.   (1.iii.80–2)

Like so much else in Massinger's plays, Paris's defence of the stage is conventional. It ultimately derives from *Poetics* 4 (1448[b]) where Aristotle observes that men are better pleased when they learn by seeing. Horace further emphasized the moral significance of poetry by giving profit and delight equal billing,[19] and Sidney, following the Italians, allowed that 'the speaking picture of Poesie' might teach virtue better than either the philosopher's precepts or the historian's examples.[20]

But while Massinger's ideas about the moral function of art may be purely derivative, it is important to note that they are not treated uncritically in *The Roman Actor*. Paris takes an orthodox line in his oft-quoted defence in Act I, but his pronouncements are rigorously and methodically tested as we move through the play itself. We see them tested when Domitia decides that Paris, on the basis of his performance in 'Iphis and Anaxarete' (III.ii), must in real life be the perfect lover; we see them tested in 'The False Servant' (IV.ii) where Paris, in spite of his having played this role so often, proves that he has not learned its lesson; but most important, we see such assertions about the moral influence of art tested in the first of these plays-within-the-play, 'The Cure of Avarice' (II.i). Here Paris hopes to reform Parthenius's avaricious father, Philargus, by presenting a play in which a man is awakened from his moral stupor and made to repent of his miserliness. Philargus sees the play, is unmoved, and is sent to his death by the emperor who is displeased at his intractability. The failure to cure Philargus is a sign of Massinger's unwillingness to accept easy answers to complex questions about the relationship between life and art, and it is part of the sceptical undercurrent in this play which led Anne Barton to suggest that 'There is a sense in which *The Roman Actor* is more pessimistic about the power

of art to correct and inform its audience than any other play
written between 1580 and 1642.'[21]

The whole of *The Roman Actor* does not, however, leave one
with the sense that Massinger's essential faith in the theatre as a
tool of moral instruction is at all shaken. He maintains the hope
that Paris's good intentions, like the dramatist's own, will not be
without their impact upon the audience. Even Paris's ultimate
failure to live up to his high moral expectations of himself has its
instructive value, for Massinger clearly wants to show us that
even the best men have no easy task in always heeding the voice of
reason.

If we are looking for evidence of Massinger's convictions in
this play about the moral effectiveness of his art, we must also
look at his treatment of Domitian, the unprincipled tyrant
around whose career *The Roman Actor* is really built. Just as
Massinger altered his source in Juvenal in order to make Paris a
more appealing and sympathetic figure, so he at every turn
blackened the picture of Domitian which he found in the *De Vita
Caesarum* of Suetonius and elsewhere. Suetonius's final verdict
is, as Colin Gibson points out, that Domitian was 'one made of
an equal mixture of virtues and vices, until he turned his virtues
too into vices, being, so far as one may conjecture, greedy
through lack of money, cruel because of fear'.[22] This description
might fit Massinger's earlier tragic figures, but it does not apply
to the bloody emperor he sets before us here. Clearly Massinger
wants us to make no mistake about the enormity of Domitian's
crimes or the justice of his final punishment. 'Besides suppressing
every creditable action recorded by the historians', Gibson
writes, 'the dramatist introduces fresh crimes from other sources
hostile to Domitian, and invents further ones.'[23]

Part of the reason for Massinger's portrayal of Domitian as a
thoroughly villainous character is, as I have already indicated,
that he wants to make a conventional moral point about tyrants
and the inevitability with which retribution is visited upon them.
Such a character is less fraught with tragic potential than the
complex and divided personalities – Charalois, Sforza, Malefort
– that Massinger had earlier depicted, but Domitian, like Antiochus at the opposite end of the ethical spectrum, is far better
suited to Massinger's moral purposes. Malefort's 'Vertues so
mix'd with vices' (III.ii.34) in *The Unnatural Combat* might have

made for superb tragedy in the hands of Chapman, or Webster, or Ford, but Massinger's insistence upon clear moral example prevented him from treating internal conflict in a convincing manner. Domitian, though his character has a limited range, is more life-like than Massinger's earlier attempts at tragic complexity.

It is not merely the broad strokes of villainy with which he is painted that make Domitian interesting, however. His is the story of a despot, a man who governs by whim and whose fall marks the end of a long progress of evil. Although Ascletario's death and the emperor's fearful dream give the play a sense of the numinous, Domitian's murder is the work of human agents, and Massinger brings all his ethical scrutiny to bear upon those who conspire in his death. Of course, Massinger is also careful to give the conspirators just cause in their plot against Domitian. Both of Massinger's chief sources, Suetonius and Dio Cassius, have the murderers acting largely out of fear,[24] but Massinger himself provides nobler motives. In Suetonius's account, Stephanos is under a charge of embezzlement, but Massinger makes him a disinterested avenger, exacting punishment for Domitian's abuse of Domitilla. Similarly, Parthenius is an auxiliary to the crime in Dio's version of the story, but Massinger has him avenging the death of his father, Philargus.

The most important change in Massinger's version of the conspiracy, however, is the addition of the three women – Domitia, Julia, and Domitilla – to the list of assassins.[25] Domitia's expanded role in the plot helps to unify the play as a whole, since she seeks vengeance for the death of Paris, just as in her initial pursuit of him she sought to redress the wrongs done to Lamia, her husband. (See v.i.76–81 and v.ii.73.) Julia, Domitian's niece, seeks retribution for the emperor's incestuous involvement with her, and Domitilla, with the help of Stephanos, also exacts punishment as a victim of Caesar's lust. Massinger makes clear, in other words, that Domitian's crimes are the cause of his fall. There is no confusion here, no unexpected accusation of villainy like those by which we are surprised at the end of *The Duke of Milan* and *The Unnatural Combat*; we have witnessed Domitian's evil deeds from the outset, and now we see him called to judgement for them.

Given the fact of Domitian's tyranny, we are left to weigh the justifiability of revenge on the one hand, against the perils of regicide on the other. Massinger is quite consistent on both scores in this as in his other plays. The 'entirely hard-headed bourgeois disapproval of revenge' which Fredson Bowers observes in *The Fatal Dowry*[26] surfaces again in *The Roman Actor*, and with it comes an even deeper aversion to the killing of a king. It is not so much that Massinger had a greater sense of loyalty to the crown or a greater reluctance to countenance revenge than his fellow dramatists, but that here for the first time, as Bowers contends, 'the romantic stage conventions of personal justice are outspokenly contrasted to the legal and moral code by which the vast majority of Elizabethans lived.'[27] As with every other ethical issue, Massinger insisted upon pursuing the moral consequences of revenge, and he has no need, as Shakespeare does in *Richard III* and the *Henry IV* plays, to justify the claim to the throne of a benevolent usurper. Granted that political expediency might have required some statement about the divine right of kings, we cannot help but hear at least an echo of Massinger's own voice when Domitilla first declines Stephanos's offer to avenge her wrongs:

> The immortall powers
> Protect a Prince though sould to impious acts,
> And seeme to slumber till his roaring crimes
> Awake their iustice: but then looking downe
> And with impartiall eyes, on his contempt
> Of all religion, and morrall goodnesse,
> They in their secret iudgements doe determine
> To leaue him to his wickednesse, which sinckes him
> When he is most secure. (III.i.58–66)

Whether one demands satisfaction in a just cause, as Charalois does at the end of *The Fatal Dowry*, or whether one awaits the fall of a wicked prince, as Domitilla and the others do here, Massinger is reluctant to see the individual take the law – human or divine – into his own hands.

The first Tribune's speech at the end of *The Roman Actor* sums up Massinger's dilemma in this regard. He begins by accusing the conspirators and ordering the wicked Domitia imprisoned:

> Yet he was our Prince,
> How euer wicked, and in you 'tis murther
> Which whosoe're succeeds him will reuenge. (V.ii.77–9)

Massinger's Political Tragedies

Then, as Massinger would no doubt approve, the Tribune leaves it to the senate to censure Domitia.[28] But the speech does not end here; the same Tribune offers a final and revealing assessment of Domitian's reign:

> He in death hath payd
> For all his cruelties. Heere's the difference:
> Good Kings are mourn'd for after life, but ill
> And such as gouern'd onely by their will
> And not their reason, vnlamented fall;
> No Goodmans teare shed at their Funerall.   (v.ii.88–93)

The two sides of the argument are clear enough, and since the instance is only a hypothetical one based on ancient history, the claims both of loyalty and of justice can be honoured. But in his final extant tragedy, *Believe As You List*, Massinger turned to events which, as Sir Henry Herbert reminded him, were dangerously contemporary, and to a time when the English were already growing impatient with Charles's failure to set what they considered appropriate royal priorities.

Like *The Roman Actor*, *Believe As You List* is a tragedy about the fall of a prince, but in the latter play we pick up the story long after Antiochus's defeat; he has spent 22 years in self-imposed exile and has, under the guidance of a Stoic philosopher, reflected upon his downfall. As in Sophocles' *Oedipus at Colonus*, we have a tragic protagonist who has survived the catastrophe, but who has found no place to dwell among the living. The play is even more firmly rooted in the tradition of *The Mirror for Magistrates* than is *The Roman Actor*. Antiochus stands before us in the opening scene like the ghosts of fallen Worthies in Boccaccio, in Lydgate's *Falls of Princes*, as well as in *The Mirror* itself,[29] and like them he hopes that:

> my fall
> might not bee fruitlesse, but still liue the greate
> example of mans frayletie.   (i.i.278–80)

This theme of human vulnerability is carried through to the last lines of the play where Antiochus, cast off even by his most loyal followers, again hopes that his fate will be a lesson to those who live after him:

> may my storie
> teach potentates humilitie, and instructe
> prowde monarchs, though they governe humane thinges
> a greater power does rayse, or pull downe kinges.   (v.ii.240–3)

127

On the simplest level, then, *Believe As You List* is, like so much late medieval tragedy, a tale about mutability, and its moral is that one ought to be humble and expect the worst of this sublunary existence.

In a larger sense, however, this play represents a strikingly modern commentary upon the conflict between political expediency and the basic human values of trust and honour. We watch as Flaminius convinces Antiochus's former allies, one by one, that protection for the deposed monarch is not in their own best interest. Without exception, their conclusion is that of Carthalo, who decides:

> wee are bounde to waigh
> not what wee showlde doe in the poynt of honor,
> swayde by our pittie, but what may bee donne
> with the safetie of the state. (II.ii.9–12)

Every one of Antiochus's friends recognizes him, and they all acknowledge him as the king of Lower Asia, but none is willing to give him sanctuary or to support his claim to the throne in the face of Rome's opposition. From a modern perspective, Antiochus's rejection seems to illustrate that pusillanimity in the face of moral crisis which Hannah Arendt labels 'the banality of evil' in her report on the Eichmann trial. There can be no doubt, in fact, that Massinger's chief purpose here is to show us the overwhelming odds against which an untarnished figure like Antiochus fights in the 'labirinth/of politique windinges' (III.i.14–15) that the world has become.

But while Massinger hopes this tale

> may move
> compassion, perhaps deserve yor love,
> and approbation, (Prologue, 11–13)

he is careful not to weight the scales too heavily in favour of Antiochus. We are certain throughout the play that Antiochus is the king he declares himself to be, but the arguments of his detractors are made to seem almost equally valid. In spite of the authenticity of Antiochus's claim to the throne, the difficulty remains that his return would throw the current political order into disarray; Rome has brought peace to its Asian territories, and Flaminius urges the Bithinian king, Prusias, 'to preserue what shee hath 'conquer'd/from change, and innovation'

(III.iii.86–7). The certain political upheaval that Antiochus's return to power would bring is everywhere remarked upon in the play. Even in the final scene, after Flaminius himself has been arrested for the crooked means whereby he sought to incriminate Antiochus, Marcellus, Flaminius's accuser, places Antiochus under house arrest. Earlier in the same scene, Marcellus and his wife Cornelia have had a very moving reunion with Antiochus, but now the Proconsul tells the forlorn king:

> pray you thincke s^r
> a Roman, not your constant freinde that tells you
> you are confinde vnto the Gyaræ
> with a stronge garde vpon you.   (V.ii.233–6)

The 'necessitie of state' (II.i.126) that Flaminius pleads as justification for his determined pursuit of Antiochus is, then, more than a mask for personal vindictiveness. It is important to remember that Flaminius is alone when he urges his allegiance to Rome as an excuse for his misdeeds. He has just sent Chrysalus and Geta to their deaths because they know Antiochus's claim to the throne to be a valid one, but as the two informants are taken to what they expect to be their reward, Flaminius has an attack of conscience:

> doe I feele a stinge heere
> for what is donne to theis poore snakes?   (II.i.114–15)

he asks himself, but promptly calls upon reason to allay his fears of cruelty:

> that assures mee
> that as I am a Roman to preserue
> and propagate her empire, thowgh they were
> my fathers sonnes they must not liue to witnesse
> Antiochus is in beeinge.   (II.i.116–20)

Reason in the service of passion this may be, but it makes the case against Antiochus a difficult one to dismiss, for while the authenticity of his title and the perfection of his virtue are never in doubt, both are measured against the equally desirable good of political stability, and the better claim – at least so far as the characters in this play are able to judge – is that of political stability.

That Massinger has set up Antiochus as a kind of saviour of his

people and at the same time made the case against him so ten-
able has resulted in general confusion about the author's own
point of view in this play. Roma Gill, for example, argues that
Marcellus provides 'the only solution compatible with both
humanitarianism and policy'[30] when he has Flaminius arrested
and orders Antiochus released from the galleys and taken to
prison. While Marcellus's verdict does acknowledge both Antiochus's rightful claim and the demands of political expediency,
it can hardly have represented an acceptable solution to Massinger, any more than it does to the modern reader. The greater
likelihood is that there is no wholly satisfactory answer to be
had to the problem, that what we see here is that clash of
opposites, that 'self-division and intestinal warfare of the ethical substance'[31] of which, in Hegel's definition, tragedy is constituted. Flaminius plays Creon to Antiochus's Antigone, and if
the Roman point of view here is lent more credence than we
might expect, the explanation is that Massinger wants us to
recognize the choice between political stability and allegiance
to the deposed king as a serious dilemma.

Roma Gill goes too far, however, when she contends that
Massinger's portrayal of Flaminius shows him to be a serious
student of Machiavelli. Gill tries to prove that Massinger
ignored the stage conventions of the Machiavellian villain and
turned to *The Prince* itself as a source for Flaminius's political
acumen. She writes: 'Flaminius has the welfare of the state at
heart; it is his sole motivating force.'[32] This sort of overstate-
ment upsets the careful balance Massinger has created between
Flaminius's ambition and unscrupulousness on the one hand,
and his intermittent sense of civic duty on the other. Flaminius
exists in this play not as a purveyor of Machiavellian statecraft,
but as a reminder that the simple, untainted goodness of Antiochus is bound to be destroyed by the 'botches' that 'are made in
the shoppe of policie' (IV.i.92–3). In fact, if one were looking
for the influence of Machiavelli in *Believe As You List*, one
might better search Antiochus's character than Flaminius's.
Machiavelli foretells the doom of such idealists in Chapter xv
of *The Prince* where he observes that:

how we live is so far removed from how we ought to live, that he who
abandons what is done for what ought to be done, will rather learn to bring
about his own ruin than his preservation. A man who wishes to make a

profession of goodness in everything must necessarily come to grief among so many who are not good.[33]

A political climate in which the good man might survive was for Machiavelli a thing of the imagination; for Massinger, it was merely a thing of the past, and thus the dramatist looks with a certain nostalgia upon 'the image of a kinge' (v.i.150) as it is so gloriously represented in Antiochus. He is a holdover from a golden age of perfect virtue and unquestioning allegiance who has lived on into an age of iron; he is a larger-than-life figure who can find no niche in a society whose workings are too complex and whose goals are too mundane to tolerate his bold idealism. The tone of *Believe As You List* is an elegiac one, and if one presses too hard for a choice between Flaminius's politic man-oeuvring and the regal splendour of Antiochus, one is likely to miss the essential mood of the play. What Massinger wants us to feel is regret. His sense of political reality was too great for him to have denied the claims of empire, and his commitment to honour was too strong for him to have let Antiochus's case go unheard, but neither of these facts suggests that we can or should make a choice of opposites. We simply leave the play wishing things might be different, but knowing that they are not.

The kind of moral stalemate with which *Believe As You List* ends is, admittedly, unusual for Massinger. His preference is more often for unequivocal moral statement, even at the expense of tragic meaning. I do not mean to suggest that Massinger's own allegiances are unclear in the play: there is no doubt that his sympathy lies with Antiochus, but he does not allow himself the luxury of believing that moral victory is easily won. We are urged by the example of Antiochus to stand for honour and loyalty, but we are not made to think that that will save us from being torn apart in the political fray. As in *The Roman Actor*, Massinger here shows himself to be a dramatist who believed in the moral influence of art, but who was at the same time aware that its powers are in no way miraculous. We, like the Carthaginian nobles, have been presented with incontrovertible evidence that Antiochus's claim is authentic, but our capacity to defend that claim in the face of Flaminius's threats would, Massinger seems to say, be no greater than theirs.

This reading of the play is in general agreement with Philip Edwards's conclusion, in a more topical vein, that Flaminius (or

Philip II in the original version) was for Massinger 'a metaphor for a kind of modernism'[34] that the English found objectionable in the policies of Charles I. Edwards points out that the causes of the king's unpopularity – his autocratic efforts to raise money, his unwillingness to convene Parliament, his failure to come to the aid of the Elector Palatine – were all viewed as evidence of his would-be absolutism. His was the role of a dangerous innovator, and the negative reaction against his increasingly authoritarian rule carried with it a large measure of nostalgia. 'Those who opposed Charles wished not to advance but to return', Edwards contends, 'and the reign of Queen Elizabeth took on a quite extraordinary sentimental lustre as the golden image of all that life under the Stuarts failed to be.'[35]

Edwards's conclusions about the original version of *Believe As You List* are more difficult to accept. Since only the revised version of the play is extant, we cannot be certain how Massinger originally treated the Don Sebastian story, but C. J. Sisson's introduction to the Malone Society Reprint of the play argues convincingly that Massinger made as few changes as were required to appease the censor.[36] In fact, as Sisson was the first to observe, Massinger substituted names that were metrical equivalents of the originals (Antiochus for Sebastian, Carthage for Venice, even Demetrius Castor for Sebastian Nero) to avoid changing the verse. In spite of such evidence that Massinger's revisions were minimal, Edwards argues that Antiochus's portrayal is substantially different from the earlier one of Don Sebastian. Massinger's purpose in treating the Don Sebastian story was, Edwards believes, to bring dignity and credibility to a pretender who had, like the protagonist in Ford's *Perkin Warbeck* (1633), been discredited by history. Edwards writes:

In the rewritten story, the indispensable element of dubiety is lost. Antiochus is no longer a mysterious pretender; he is the true king returning. The earlier hero, the Portuguese pretender, was, like Warbeck, an enigma who puzzled and divided his contemporaries, a famous real pretender of modern history.[37]

There is, in fact, nothing to suggest that Massinger represented Don Sebastian as having a more dubious claim to the throne than Antiochus does in the revised *Believe As You List*, or that his hero in the first version was more enigmatic. While Ford's treatment of Warbeck does suggest one possible method of development, he and Massinger were very different writers and they would not

have been likely to treat the subject in exactly the same way. Moreover, had Massinger's Don Sebastian been so enigmatic a figure or
so dubious a claimant as Edwards asserts, it is just possible that
Herbert would have found nothing objectionable in the play.

In comparing Massinger's play with *Perkin Warbeck*, Edwards
says that 'it is essential to keep Massinger's original purpose in
mind',[38] but that purpose appears not to have changed perceptibly
in the course of revision. Although Edwards does not say so
himself, his insistence upon the distinction between Sebastian, the
pretender, and Antiochus, the returning king, appears to be a way
of accounting for the puzzling fact that Massinger allows the case
against Antiochus such validity. Had Antiochus been a mere pretender, like the one claiming to be Don Sebastian, then Flaminius's
merciless routing of him in the name of policy would not be nearly
so appalling, and the desertion by his supporters would be seen as
an astute political manoeuvre rather than the unconscionable display of cowardice that it is in the later version of the play.

The difficult ethical question Massinger poses in pitting Antiochus's claim against Flaminius's plea for political stability need
not be explained away either by Edward's hypothetical reconstruction of the original play or by Roma Gill's contention that
Massinger is defending Machiavellian statecraft. Clearly, Massinger was not so naive as to expect that the stoic wisdom acquired
by Antiochus in the desert was something that a fallen world
would either tolerate or share in. But like Spenser before him and
Milton after, Massinger believed that virtue is a meaningful quality only if it is persistently tested in the everyday world. Thus, the
Stoic tells Antiochus in the opening scene of *Believe As You List*:

> you must now forget
> the contemplations of a private man
> and put in action that w^{c}h may complie
> with the maiestie of a monarch.   (I.i.7–10)

Antiochus is not like ambitious men, of the sort described by Marcellus, who seek 'the golden fetters of imployment' (v.i.45), but
who,

> when they haue tri'ed
> by a sad experience the burthen of 'em,
> when 'tis not in their power at any rate
> ... woulde redeeme their calm securitie
> morgagd in wantonesse.   (v.i.47–51)

Such politic creatures always seek a permanent escape when they discover, as Dioclesian does in Fletcher and Massinger's *The Prophetess*, that the glories of empire cannot save them from 'a shaking fever', or 'the uncorrupted dart of Death'.[39] For Antiochus, the call to the active life is a call to duty, and even if the end is defeat, the obligation cannot be ignored.

Antiochus does lose in the end, but his defeat is, as Edwards has observed, a practical not a moral one.[40] His regal bearing and his unfaltering virtue strike wonder in everyone who encounters him, and no one is able to deny his right to the crown, even if it is kept from him as a matter of political expediency. There can be no doubt about the play's austerity or the sense of hopelessness with which it ends. Its spirit is not, however, one of resignation: Massinger was too much a product of English humanism ever to have submitted to the view of the Stoics or, much later, of Schopenhauer, 'that the world, that life cannot grant any true satisfaction, and hence they do not deserve our attachment'.[41]

A mood of despair may well inform *Believe As You List*, just as a kind of scepticism about the moral influence of art underlies *The Roman Actor*, but in both instances we are seeing only a part of Massinger's broad range of dramatic expression. In assessing the Massinger canon as a whole, the grim verdict of these two plays – that the virtuous will be devoured by the fallen world they inhabit – is a useful corrective to the impression of Massinger left by his numerous tragicomedies, where the capacity of virtue to arouse wonder and the power of example to alter character often seem too easily granted.

NOTES

I should like to thank Professor Colin Gibson and Dr Martin Butler for their helpful comments on an earlier draft of this essay.

1 Malone's note that '*The Great Duke* was licensed for the Queen's Servants, July 5, 1627' is difficult to explain in light of Massinger's otherwise exclusive association with the King's Men after 1625. Philip Edwards's suggestion that 'Massinger had in earlier times undertaken to produce the play for Beeston, had been paid for it, but was very slow in delivering the copy' seems the most likely answer to the problem. See Joseph Q. Adams (ed.), *The Dramatic Records of Sir Henry Herbert* (New Haven, Yale University Press, 1917), p.31, and Philip Edwards and Colin Gibson (ed.), *The Plays and Poems of Philip Massinger* (5 vols., Oxford, Clarendon Press, 1976), vol. 3, p.95.

2 See G. E. Bentley's account of the play's prohibition in *The Profession of Dramatist in Shakespeare's Time* (Princeton, Princeton University Press, 1971), pp.178–9.

3 Colin Gibson provides a convenient summary of Massinger's alterations in Edwards and Gibson, vol. 3, pp.294–8. For a more elaborate discussion see P. M. Smith, 'Massinger's Use of Sources, with special reference to *The Duke of Milan* and *Believe As You List*' (Unpublished Ph.D. thesis, University of Birmingham, 1963). The findings of Gibson and Smith are supplemented by David Bradley's discovery that Massinger's principal source for the first version of *Believe As You List* was almost certainly Edward Grimestone's translation and continuation of Louis de Mayerne Turquet, *The Generall Historie of Spaine*, London, 1612. See Bradley's 'A Major Source of Massinger's *Believe As You List* (1631)', *Notes and Queries*, 29 (1982), 20–2.

4 G. E. Bentley, *The Jacobean and Caroline Stage* (7 vols., Oxford, Clarendon Press, 1941–68), vol. 4, p.795.

5 F. G. Fleay, *A Biographical Chronicle of the English Drama, 1559–1642* (2 vols., London, 1891), vol. 1, p.229. See also Edmond Malone (ed.) *Shakespeare: Plays and Poems*, Variorum edn. (21 vols., London, 1821) vol. 3, pp.230, 240; and Adams, *The Dramatic Records*, p.22, n.3.

6 Alfred Harbage (rev. S. Schoenbaum), *Annals of English Drama, 975–1700*, 2nd edn (Philadelphia, University of Pennsylvania Press, 1964), p.124.

7 Bentley, *Jacobean and Caroline Stage*, vol. 4, p.795, and W. W. Greg, *A Bibliography of the English Printed Drama to the Restoration* (4 vols., London, Oxford University Press, 1939–51), vol. 2, p.1003.

8 Among Massinger's lost plays are two which seem to represent tragedies of a non-political nature, *The Forced Lady* (date unknown) and *The Unfortunate Piety* (1631).

9 The attempt of S. R. Gardiner, 'The Political Element in Massinger', *The Contemporary Review*, 28 (1876), 495–507, to read Massinger's plays as political allegories has been much disputed, but Philip Edwards argues convincingly about the topical nature of *Believe As You List*, in 'The Royal Pretenders in Massinger and Ford', *Essays and Studies*, 27 (1974), 18–36. See also Allen Gross, 'Contemporary Politics in Massinger', *SEL*, 6 (1966), 279–90.

10 See Willard Farnham's study of the deeply flawed heroes of Shakespeare's later tragedies, *Shakespeare's Tragic Frontier* (Berkeley, University of California Press, 1950). Timon, Macbeth, Antony, and Coriolanus, Farnham argues, 'draw from us reactions that vary widely between profound antipathy and profound sympathy. Along with sympathy they can inspire admiration' (p.9).

11 See Colin Gibson, 'Massinger's Use of his Sources for *The Roman Actor*', *AUMLA*, 15 (1961), 60–72.

12 Lily B. Campbell (ed.), *The Mirror for Magistrates* (Cambridge, Cambridge University Press, 1938), p.102.

13 A. P. Hogan, 'Imagery of Acting in *The Roman Actor*', *MLR*, 66 (1971), 273–81.

Douglas Howard

14 Willard Farnham, *The Medieval Heritage of Elizabethan Tragedy* (Berkeley, University of California Press, 1936), p.83. The desire of poets to be immortalized is often mentioned by Dante, and Horace, *Odes* III.30, might also be added to Farnham's list.

15 Gibson, 'Massinger's Use of his Sources', p.64.

16 Gibson cites these two passages in order to illustrate Massinger's sympathetic portrayal of Paris. See 'Massinger's Use of his Sources', pp.63–4.

17 David Richman, 'Dramatic Craftsmanship in Jacobean Tragedy' (Unpublished Ph.D. thesis, Stanford University, 1978), p.338.

18 Gibson notes (Edwards and Gibson, vol. 5, p.184) Gifford's suggestion that Massinger here expands upon Horace, *Ars Poetica*, 179–82.

19 Horace, *Ars Poetica*, 343–4.

20 Sir Philip Sidney, 'An Apology for Poetry', in G. Gregory Smith (ed.), *Elizabethan Critical Essays* (2 vols., Oxford, Oxford University Press, 1904), vol. 1, pp.163–5. See also Marvin T. Herrick, *The Fusion of Horatian and Aristotelian Literary Criticism, 1531–1555* (Urbana, University of Illinois Press, 1946), pp.39–47.

21 Anne Barton, 'The Distinctive Voice of Massinger', *TLS* (20 May 1977), reprinted as an appendix in this volume (see p.231).

22 Suetonius, *De Vita Caesarum*, VIII.3, cited by Gibson in 'Massinger's Use of his Sources', p.71.

23 Gibson, 'Massinger's Use of his Sources', p.71.

24 Gibson, 'Massinger's Use of his Sources', p.67.

25 Domitia's compliance in the plot is clear from the historians, but Massinger's inclusion of her among the actual assassins was his own invention.

26 Fredson Bowers, *Elizabethan Revenge Tragedy, 1587–1642* (Princeton, Princeton University Press, 1940), p.190.

27 Bowers, p.192.

28 It is difficult to tell in lines 86–7 whether the Tribune continues to address Domitia, or if, having sent her to her punishment, he now turns and speaks to the other conspirators. In either case, he is allowing the law to take its course. The first Tribune's recognition that punishment for regicide is inevitable, even though Domitian was a tyrant, is also the substance of Lysippus's final pronouncement in Beaumont and Fletcher's *The Maid's Tragedy* (1610).

29 See Howard Baker, *Induction to Tragedy: A Study in a Development of Form in 'Gorboduc', 'The Spanish Tragedy' and 'Titus Andronicus'* (1939; rpt. New York, Russell and Russell, 1965), p.111.

30 Roma Gill, '"Necessitie of State": Massinger's *Believe As You List*', *English Studies*, 46 (1965), 415.

31 A. C. Bradley, 'Hegel's Theory of Tragedy', in his *Oxford Lectures on Poetry*, 2nd edn (1909; rpt. London, Macmillan, 1923), p.71.

32 Gill, '"Necessitie of State"', p.410.

33 Niccolò Machiavelli, *The Prince* and *The Discourses*, intro. Max Lerner (New York, The Modern Library, 1950), p.56.

34 Edwards, 'The Royal Pretenders', pp.34–5.

35 Edwards, 'The Royal Pretenders', p.33. Anne Barton has recently studied Jonson's similar recollection of the bygone age of Elizabeth in 'Harking Back to Elizabeth: Ben Jonson and Caroline Nostalgia', *ELH*, 48 (1981), 706–31.
36 C. J. Sisson (ed.), '*Believe As You List* by Philip Massinger, 1631' (Oxford, Oxford University Press, for the Malone Society, 1927), pp.xix–xx.
37 Edwards, 'The Royal Pretenders', p.20.
38 Edwards, 'The Royal Pretenders', p.20.
39 Alexander Dyce (ed.), *The Works of Beaumont and Fletcher* (11 vols., London, 1843–6), vol. 8, p.272.
40 Edwards, 'The Royal Pretenders', p.29.
41 Walter Kaufmann, *Tragedy and Philosophy* (1968: rpt. Garden City, NY, Anchor-Doubleday, 1969), p.342.

Romans in Britain:
The Roman Actor and the Early Stuart Classical Play

MARTIN BUTLER

WHEN Massinger dramatised the downfall of the tyrannical emperor Domitian in *The Roman Actor*, he was
not the only playwright of his time turning to first-
century imperial Rome for inspiration, yet, oddly, his tragedy has
never been considered in relation to that group of similar and
near-contemporary plays with which it so obviously belongs.
The late Jacobean–Caroline period produced, within only a
dozen years, not just *The Roman Actor* (1626) but also the
anonymous *Nero* (before 1623), Thomas May's *Julia Agrippina*
(1628) and Nathanael Richards's popular melodrama *Messallina*
(c. 1635), a flourishing of classical plays all the more remarkable
since the classical history was a genre which, despite several
major achievements (principally Shakespeare's), had not had any
great or lasting vogue on the English stage at its height and had
all but disappeared after *Catiline* (1611). It is as though Jonson's
Sejanus (1603), to which, as a common dramatic original, each of
these four plays implicitly or explicitly refers its audience,[1] had
suddenly and very belatedly brought forth its expected progeny.
They form a striking and distinctive group. If we include *Sejanus*,
the playgoer of the 1620s and 1630s could have seen almost all
the first-century despots: Tiberius, Caligula (in the induction to
Julia Agrippina), Claudius, Nero, Otho and Domitian. Galba is
in the wings at the end of *Nero*; the antitype, Augustus, is conspicuous by his absence. The panorama is impressive both for its
comprehensiveness and for its sudden and deliberate concentra-
tion on this period of classical history, and in this last respect
these plays stand in marked contrast to their counterparts of
twenty or thirty years earlier. We can sum up broadly by saying
that there is a shift from Livy and Plutarch to Tacitus,[2] among the
reasons for which are the preoccupations, particularly about
politics, of England (and Europe at large) in these decades. This

narrowing of range and alteration of focus within the genre identifies for us the changed relationships Massinger and his contemporaries were sensing with the classical past, the new and distinctive significances they were finding there for their generation. I believe we may illuminate *The Roman Actor*, and perhaps explain some of its anomalies, by attending to its classicism not merely as an archaeologizing tendency, but as part of an urgent need to re-create the past in terms of the anxieties of the present; it manifests a shared consciousness of the real and dynamic tensions working to transform Massinger's age.

I

Massinger was born into a world rediscovering the relevance of Tacitus. The *editio princeps* appeared in 1575, and the following century saw a massive explosion of commentary, citation and exposition of Tacitus and his ethic. There were over one hundred European editions, and Savile and Grenewey's English translation reached its sixth printing in 1640.[3] Partly his popularity was as a stylistic model – of curtness and even obscurity – but it really rested on his reputation as a political anatomist, 'a seminary of morall, and a magazine of politique discourses, for the provision and ornament of those, that possesse some place in the managing of the world' (as Montaigne said).[4] He was regarded as a shrewd and useful compendium of political wisdom and behaviour, whose value lay in his realism and his penetration into the motives and influences underlying history, and in the fact that he narrated not only the mere sequence of events but their hidden springs and causes; it is entirely characteristic that his most enthusiastic English reader was Francis Bacon. Ben Jonson complained of the inflation of vulgar curiosity into public affairs, that London swarmed with 'ripe statesmen' who 'carry in their pockets Tacitus,/ And the *Gazetti*, or *Gallo-Belgicus*' (*Epigrams*, xcii).

So Tacitus was valued, firstly, for his mastery of statecraft or *realpolitik*, the modern arts of manipulation and accommodation, governed by laws of prudence, expediency and pragmatism. His speciality was the secret ways of politics, the *arcana imperii* of 'false doublenesse; and the treacherous Art to doe that which a man saies not, and to say that which one meaneth not'.[5] By dramatizing Tiberius, Jonson had chosen the prince who had come down through Tacitus as the arch-despot, the perfect tactician and dissembler. It was even said that all 'the now present Reason of State' originated in Tacitus, that he demonstrated how princely power cleverly wielded could override all the safeguards of custom, law, property and liberty. This made him an ideal sounding-board for the concerns of early Stuart England but also a dangerous ally. Tacitism – the vogue for Tacitus – could be red or black, exposing the strategies of tyrants or actually being of use to those princes 'that desire to learne the skill and knowledge absolutely to command'.[6] This ambivalence is echoed in the English Tacitean tragedies; their despots are horrific, but they also exude a certain glamour.

On the other hand, Tacitus always placed 'reason of state' in a perspective that was profoundly, even passionately moral, and his portraits of noble Romans of conscience endeavouring to maintain their integrity and self-respect under a burgeoning and intolerant state power would have spoken for the experience of many living under the modern and ambitious European monarchies. In a lecture on Tacitus, the French academic Marc-Antoine Muret commented, somewhat cautiously:

Although by the blessing of God we have no Tiberiuses, Caligulas, and Neros, yet it is profitable for us to know how good and prudent men managed their lives under them, how and how far they tolerated and dissimulated their vices: how, on the one hand, by avoiding an unseasonable frankness they saved their own lives when they would have served no public end by bringing them into danger, and on the other hand showed that baseness was not pleasing to them by not praising things in the conduct of princes which a good man cannot praise, but which he can cover up, or pass by in silence.[7]

Muret is probably thinking of Tacitus's reflections on the senator Lepidus who managed to serve Tiberius without incurring personal moral blame (*Annals* IV.xx), and certainly of the futility and dangerousness of Thrasea Paetus's protests against Nero (XIV.xii). The problem of compromise and acquiescence in an objectionable regime is a leading issue in *The Roman Actor*. Massinger's senators reluctantly agree to

>   obey the time, it is in vaine
> To striue against the torrent.
> *Rusticus.*   Lets to the Curia
> And though vnwillingly, gieue our suffrages
> Before we are compeld.
> *Lamia.*   And since we cannot

With safetie vse the actiue, lets make vse of
The passiue fortitude.   (I.i.113–18)[8]

Paris and even the unattractive Philargus are sympathetically
portrayed in unintended collision with a power demanding the
assent of their minds as well as bodies (II.i.429–30, IV.ii.72–3).[9]
The dying words of Thrasea Paetus were cited to similar effect by
Muret's friend and the great editor of Tacitus, Justus Lipsius:
'Young Man, consider well . . . you are born in those times that
require the well fixing your mind by Examples of Constancy'[10]
(cf. *Annals* XVI.xxxv). Lipsius, typically, led the Renaissance recovery of Seneca and his stoicism.

Tacitus clearly found a sensitive nerve of early modern Europe.
He was up-to-date: he dealt with courts and the corridors of
power, and he enabled a sceptical, unillusioned, 'political' view
of politics to be canvassed at a time when his admirer,
Machiavelli, was regarded with suspicion and hostility. His depiction of good men suffering in bad times and of the relentless
consolidation of power by ruthless and uncontrolled despots was
highly pertinent to a Europe destabilized by civil and religious
conflicts and in which the great nation-state firmly established
under the rule of the absolute and autocratic monarch was
coming to be the order of the day. Montaigne commented: 'His
service is more proper to a crazed troubled state, as ours is at this
present: you would often say, he pourtrayeth and toucheth us to
the quicke.'[11] Moreover, he was potentially subversive: he was
said to have made it 'no longer possible for Princes . . . to cast
dust into their subjects eyes', for through him they had learned
the realities of power and 'that they are cheated, cozened and
deceiued'.[12] With his deep, aristocratic nostalgia for better and
freer days he was a powerful ally against tyranny. The fifteenth-
century Italian republics had invoked his authority in defence of
their civic liberty against princely despotism, and the Caesars
were execrated in the famous radical tract *Vindiciae Contra
Tyrannos* (1579); later, Tacitus would appeal to the American
revolutionaries as a great hater of tyrants.[13] Of course, these last
implications were not yet available in the England of the 1620s
and 1630s where a political alternative which excluded the
princely element was barely conceivable, at least in English
terms. Nevertheless, within these limits there existed plenty of
English pessimism and anxiety about the progressive tendencies

of early Stuart government. There was a sense that under James and Charles, with their expensive courts, personal style of rule and (in Charles's case, at least) pursuit of bureaucratic efficiency, England seemed to be heading the way of the rest of Europe. In 1625, the MP Sir Robert Phelips saw England's problems in relation to a continent where parliaments were everywhere going down: 'We are the last monarchy in Christendom that yet retain our original rights and constitutions.'[14] In the history of Rome under the ambitious Caesars, such anxieties found an appropriate and obvious fictional expression.

II

In England, Tacitus first caused trouble in 1600 when Sir John Hayward was hauled before the Privy Council for incorporating suspect quotations from him in his *Life of Henry IV*; he also seems to have been in vogue with the Essex circle.[15] But Roman parallels really came into their own in the 1620s, notably in a famous Commons speech of 1626 in which Sir John Eliot denounced Buckingham as England's Sejanus, citing Tacitus's account of his boldness, secrecy, pride, ambition and engrossing of power; Charles retorted, 'he must intend me for Tiberius', and sent Eliot to the Tower.[16] There were many other instances. Buckingham was lampooned as Sejanus who 'Doth bestowe/ what euer offices Doe fall' as early as 1621. Less appropriately, his client Mompesson was anathematized in the 1621 parliament as a Tiberius; Arthur Wilson said James was a peaceful prince like Augustus, yet 'Some *Parallel'd* him to *Tiberius* for *Dissimulation*'.[17] Eliot cited Tacitean aphorisms about corrupt magistrates at Middlesex's impeachment (1624) and against Buckingham's agents; another aphorism warned subjects to deny a prince's wishes only with care. In the 1625 parliament, Sir Robert Phelips complained Rome had declined when one man monopolized all business, while Eliot called Charles's chosen ambassadors Petroniuses rather than statesmen.[18] In a scandalous episode of 1627, the Dutch historian Isaac Dorislaus, lecturing on Tacitus at Cambridge, 'was conceived of by some, to speak too much for the defence of the liberties of the People', using 'dangerous passages ... so appliable to these villainous times', and had to be stopped. The same year, Buckingham, returning from disastrous failure at Rochelle, was twitted with comparisons out of Tacitus.[19] Eliot quoted Tacitus in a 1628 speech on religion and liberty, and in an anonymous poem on this parliament he and Selden were hailed as new Catos, 'who durst bee good,/When Caesar durst bee badd'.[20] Conversely, when the Buckinghamite Edmund Bolton wrote his *Nero Caesar, or Monarchy Depraved* (1624) at royal command, he carefully debunked the pretensions of Seneca, Lucan and the other participants in Piso's conspiracy, and drew the moral that even a Nero should be obeyed for the state's safety; Tacitus was that bad man 'so zealous for *Tyrannicides*', 'the most irreligious of historians'. It was suggested in 1637 that Charles should have the *Annals* suppressed.[21]

The parliaments of Charles I were perhaps the best educated assemblies England has known.[22] The minds of statesmen such as Eliot and many like him were steeped in and pervasively shaped by classical history and political philosophy, conferring a civilizing depth and discrimination on their political consciousness. Kevin Sharpe has described how the political practice of a leading statesman like the Earl of Arundel was reinforced by his cultural preferences.[23] Arundel was Jacobean England's foremost collector of antiquities and patron of cognoscenti; his collections and life-style inculcated a classically-founded ideal of gravity, personal honour and solid *virtù* which his political career exemplified. These were aristocratic values, but the point is that for all its pretensions to be a new Rome the English court under the unheroic James and *arriviste* Buckingham fell miserably short in the scale. Arundel's sentiments, cast in the mould of a nobler age, fitted him to emerge as the critic of England's decline from its 'vital spirit' and 'gallant ancient composition'.[24]

We may safely suppose that plays such as *The Roman Actor* found an appreciative audience among circles where cultivation of the classics accompanied a practical involvement in politics. For example, Arundel's allies included John Selden and Sir Robert Cotton, leading intellectuals and friends of poets and playwrights, but one a sponsor of the Petition of Right and the other founder of a library which functioned increasingly as a focus for opinion hostile to Buckingham. Cotton's librarian, Richard James, told Eliot that even Augustus was a villain, and was questioned in 1628 for verses on Buckingham's assassin called *Felton Commended* which attacked the Duke as the nation's enslaver who had debased its honours and lavished its wealth on 'pandors, minions, pimpes, and whores'. As for Felton,

> Nor [Jewry], nor Rome, nor Greece did euer see
> A greater glorie. To the neighbour flood
> Then sinke all fables of old Brute and Ludd,
> And give thy statues place; in spite of charme
> Of witch or wizard, thy most mightie arme
> With zeale and justice arm'd hath in truth wonne
> The prize of patriott to a Brittish sonne.[25]

'Patriott' carries strongly Roman connotations; James is following the mythologizing lead of other anonymous versifiers who praised Felton as the heroic saviour of his *patria*, whose 'valour great did proue a Roman spirit, / And by their lawes a thousand heavens meritt':

> hearke! they call
> Him, noble Roman; second Curtius;
> Undaunted Scaevola; that dared thus
> T'expose himself to torment, shame, and death,
> To spoile his countries spoiler of his breath.[26]

Another member of Arundel's circle was Ben Jonson, who also ran into trouble in 1628 over seditious verses he had seen at Cotton's house.[27] Only the previous year he had joined with the MP John Vaughan, a friend of Selden and Edward Hyde who was disposed 'to least reverence to the Crown, and most to popular authority ... yet without inclination to any change in government',[28] in contributing commendatory verses to Thomas May's translation of Lucan's *Pharsalia*, which recounted the fall of Roman liberty before the ambition of Julius Caesar from the perspective of a witness of Nero's atrocities. May brought Lucan's unfinished story down to Caesar's triumph over his own people, and to his nemesis at the hands of Brutus and the senate. He dedicated the poem to the king, and included a compliment to him as Augustus, but his title page depicts Lucan's execution for his part in Piso's conspiracy, and verses praise him as the

> lofty *genius* great *Apollo* chose
> When Roman liberty opprest should dy,
> To sing her sad, and solemne obsequy
> In stately number, high, as *Rome* was great.

This is a long way from Edmund Bolton's attitude to Lucan; and Ben Jonson had found words from Lucan appropriate for the mouth of his Sejanus (*Sejanus*, II.178–89).[29]

III

In so far as Jonson understands the political problem as a problem of morality, *Sejanus* is optimistic. The times are decayed because men are (1.86–9); if Tiberius could be bettered, the state would improve (1.400–9); Fortune would not rule if men were wise (v.733–4). But the play remains pessimistic because it holds out no prospect of virtue being found except among those who are politically ineffective or marginal, passive sufferers rather than actors, commentators, not participants. Virtue, in short, has no *virtù*; its proper sphere is history, which alone redeems politics by handing down testimonies to posterity. This is why the historian Cordus is so important to Jonson, but it offers cold comfort to those actually involved in politics. Their justification, precisely, is with history; it belongs to the future, not to the present.

With the anonymous *Nero* (London, 1624), we are at once in a much more militant, sanguine world. The author carefully mobilizes feeling against Nero, organizing disgust at him into two prongs. First there is the romantic gentleman, Antonius, who is in love with Nero's queen, Poppea, and backed by his friend, the *bon viveur* Petronius. Poppea scorns him haughtily, yet is secretly serviced by the court favourite, Nimphidius. Poppea's scornful ways are Nero's ('Feare, is the Loue that's due to Gods, and Princes' she freezingly retorts to Antonius (sig. C1ʳ)) and Nero is damned by association with her, while Nimphidius is the typical new courtier, a contemptible parasite and upstart, and no comparison with the worthy Antonius. Petronius advises Antonius to love honest country wenches rather than proud and shallow court ladies. Secondly, there are the serious and sober aristocrats, Seneca, Lucan and others, who participate in Piso's conspiracy, which makes up the main action of the play. Their motivation is detestation for the shame that Nero brings to Rome. He has been gallivanting through Greece performing at theatrical festivals (but avoiding austere Athens and Sparta) and returns with the spoils of fiddlers and minstrels, a triumph won not with weapons but 'vaine showes' and 'foolish things' (sig.

B1^r). His Rome is full of 'Souldyers to th' shadow traynd, and not the field' (sig. B3^r) and 'purple Fellowes' (sig. C3^v) who flatter him to the hilt and ridicule him behind his back. When the poet Cornutus is honest about Nero's verses he is banished, and truth and sincerity with him. Rome labours under dishonourable policies and mean and dishonourable men; it is the tawdry and superficial England of James I.

The conspirators are conceived as dignified heroes, who look back to the virtuous days of Brutus and Cassius (sigs. C4^v, E4^v); their second meeting is based on the corresponding scene in *Julius Caesar* (II.i) but with the ominous undercurrents removed. They aim to restore Rome's lost greatness by removing its corruptor and oppressor. As Lucan says,

> I hate him that he is Romes enemie,
> An enemie to Vertue; sits on high
> To shame the seate; And in that hate, my life,
> And blood, Ile mingle on the earth with yours.   (sig. B4^r)

They act in 'loue to th'Common-wealth' and without 'licence', intending to restore 'Law, and publique Iudgement' (sigs. D1^v–2^r), a glorious deed the gods have left to them to do (sig. B4^r). The plot is betrayed only by a slave, one of Rome's 'seruile mindes' (sig. D1^r), but in defeat they become models of noble, virtuous suffering, and everyone sees that all 'worth of earth' approves of them:

> There's not a soule that claimes Nobilitie
> Either by his, or his fore-fathers merit,
> But is with vs; with vs the gallant youth
> Whom passed dangers or hote bloud makes bould:
> Staid men suspect their wisedome, or their faith,
> To whom our counsels we haue not reueald.   (sigs. F3^{r-v})

Lucan and Scaevinus, being led to execution, speak a great and formal indictment of the corrupt state with its cruel peace, unjust laws and oppression of good men: 'A happy state, where *Decius* is a traytor,/*Narcissus* true' (sig. G1^v). Nero's position all along is a version of the Stuart credo, that

> Kings must vpon the Peoples headlesse courses
> Walke to security, and ease of minde . . .
> Where right is scand, Authority is orethrowne,
> We haue a high prerogatiue aboue it;
> Slaues may doe what is lust, we, what we please . . .
> (sigs. C2^v–3^r)

But as soon as his rule collapses he wishes he had been a 'Iudge of measures, and of corne,/Then the adored Monarke of the world' (sig. F3ʳ). The play's Victorian editor complained that the dying Nero lacked the majesty he possessed in Suetonius's narrative, but that is just the point – Nero ends a slavish, snivelling coward, shrivelled, like a punctured balloon.

May's *Julia Agrippina*, on the other hand, is more concerned with analysing 'Reason of state' (1.489).[30] It presents a terrifying world of power, cruelty and inhumanity, heralded by the rise of Caligula's ghost to prophesy a new reign in which men will *'suffer more / Then they could feare, or ere was felt before'* (Prologue, line 79). Nero attains rule by brilliant underhand stratagems. His faction arrange events, displace officials, exile opponents and, most subtly, patronize good men like Seneca to give plausibility to their bad cause. The opposing faction rest their faith in the integrity of the senate (1.267), but led by Seneca the senators greet Nero as emperor with 'free consent' (III.268). The old emperor, Claudius, is spineless and totally swayed by his wife Agrippina's servants, who insidiously twist his will to their purposes (1.504–636) while the honest servant Narcissus desperately pleads with him to awaken to the dangerousness of those who are profiting from his leniency, even if it means attacking men in highest places:

> You have already, *Caesar*, shew'd your sword,
> And if you strike not now, you do not right
> Your selfe at all, but only arme your foes
> With plots of mischiefe to prevent their owne,
> And hasten on your quicke destruction.
>
> (II.474–8)

May was writing only months after the attempted impeachment of Buckingham.

The most active intriguer for Agrippina and Nero is the ex-slave Pallas:

> What though my birth be humble, and my stile
> But one of *Caesars* freed-men, though I boast not
> Patritian blood, nor in my galleries
> Display old ranks of nose-lesse ancestours,
> Or eare-cropt images, if I enjoy
> What ever high Nobility can give

> Respect and power: The state can witnesse it.
> The Senate feare mee, and in flattery
> Have su'd to *Caesar* to conferre on mee
> Praetorian and Quaestorian ornaments.
> Which I at last vouchsafed to accept.
> When my command alone has doomed to death
> The noblest of that order, men whose names
> Old *Rome* has boasted of, whose vertues rais'd
> Her to that envi'd height that now she holds.
> Their murders stupid *Caesar* rather chose
> To take upon himselfe, then question mee.
> Let dull Patricians boast their aëry titles.
> And count me base . . .
>
> (I.83–101)

Pallas is clearly a Buckingham seen in Arundellian perspective, a new man, contemptuous of birth, breeding or prestige, dislodging worthier men and scorning their attainments; the galleries of statuary are irresistibly Arundellian. He is a pluralist like Buckingham, dangerous and efficient. Caesar shoulders his crimes exactly as Charles told parliament his ministers' acts were his own and above question.[31] There is a terrible feeling that such men are rising to power everywhere. Unlike the other Roman plays, which concentrate on a single emperor, *Julia Agrippina* shows a change of rulers, but Nero is not the legitimate heir. The play laments the loss of the true, virtuous and symbolically named prince Britannicus, and down with him go all the old nobility, while Nero promotes his drinking and whoring companions; it is Falstaff's rejection in reverse ('Now my mad shavers,' says his favourite, Otho, 'do you know me yet?' (III.355)). Narcissus's insight is that in a politic world virtue must learn the methods of survival. He tells Claudius not to 'beleeve the Gods by miracle/Will worke for you, whilest you neglect your selfe' (II.440–1) – statecraft can only be defeated by superior statecraft. Increasingly, the play focuses on the need for resolution: if only Narcissus had acted sooner Nero's ascendancy could have been prevented, but now he is in and all hope for the future lies quashed (II.244–5, 271, 484–5, 534–6; IV.36–9). These, I suggest, are the sentiments of 1628, with Charles still a relatively new king but the extent of his disagreements with parliament only gradually and shockingly becoming apparent.

IV

There is much in these two plays which illuminates *The Roman Actor* (Massinger quoted *Nero* twice, perhaps three times;[32] the printed text carried commendatory verses from May). Domitian is notable for cruelty, but also meanness of spirit. His rule is hostile to merit, 'to deserue too well [is]/Held Capitall treason' (I.i.74–5). This is based on Tacitus's *Agricola*, but the analysis is already familiar: Domitian's critics are 'Bookemen' and 'popular Senators' (III.ii.13, 15), but also men of birth and title. His freeman 'Scorne the Nobilitie' and 'to be nobly borne/Is now a crime' (I.i.96, 73), while his black book is packed with 'men of rancke' (V.i.100). Massinger introduces 'Princesses of the bloud' (III.i.83) and, unhistorically, Vespasian's mistress Caenis, in order to show Domitian reducing them to menials to his own proud paramour (I.iv.1–13, II.i.249–53, III.i.48–51). Observers are amazed at his disparagement of 'Ladies/Of such high birth and rancke' (I.iv.60–1). Under Domitian, the ancient *virtù* has withered:

> they doe conclude there was
> A *Lucrece* once, a *Collatine*, and a *Brutus*,
> But nothing Roman left now, but in you
> The lust of *Tarquin*. (II.i.132–5)

The good senators contrast him regretfully with the worth of his dead brother Titus ('tis my wonder/That two sonnes of so different a nature,/Should spring from good *Vespatian*' (I.i.81–3)). This is historically true, but gains force if we recall the unfavourable contrasts drawn between Charles I and *his* dead brother, Henry.

But the comparison with the other plays enables Massinger's more particular concerns to emerge with clarity. Interested less in the degeneracy of the corrupt court and the Machiavellian stratagems that underpin rule than in the idea, we might almost say the theory, of absolutism itself, he draws a world dominated entirely by the single, monstrous figure of Domitian, elaborated as the archetypal absolute ruler whose single, arbitrary will is utterly paramount and supreme. Domitian's is the only authority in the state, and he wields power as if it were his personal property. A monarch he defines quite simply as one who can obtain without let or hindrance his own least desire, a man who

'can command all, but is aw'd by none' (i.iv.85). Roman government really is *at the prince's pleasure*:

> The world confesses one *Rome*, and one *Caesar*,
> And as his rule is infinite, his pleasures
> Are vnconfin'd; this sillable, his will,
> Stands for a thousand reasons. (i.ii.45–8)

Domitian turns a hackneyed metaphor into reality; the phrase is
often used (i.ii.75–6; ii.i.65, 259, 280; iii.ii.3, 46) but with increasingly sinister connotations as it becomes apparent that his
'pleasures' lie in deliberate cruelties or other men's wives (i.i.100,
iii.i.109). Consequently obedience must be immediate and un-
conditional, Caesar speaks and it is done (e.g. iii.ii.46); conversely, any disapproval or contradiction, no matter how slight,
strikes at the very root of his authority – its uniqueness and
absoluteness – and must be inhibited. Domitian's most characteristic command is to doom men to silence (ii.i.238–9, 443–5;
iv.ii.164–5), his weakest moment his failure to silence the Stoics
who boast insensibility to his tortures (iii.ii.108). It is a remorseless and convincing account of life under a stifling arbitrary
power, absolutism taken to its logical extreme.

   Domitian's autocracy rests squarely on his belief in the intrin-
sic superiority of his princely will, his inherent difference from
ordinary men. He dramatizes himself as set apart, and first
appears (typically) at 'the height of humane glorie,/Riding in
triumph to the Capitoll' (i.iv.14–15). He himself congratulates
the Romans on having such a prince, forced to be his own self-
praiser because

> I am aboue
> All honours you can giue me. And the stile
> Of Lord, and God, which thankefull subiects giue me
> (Not my ambition) is deseru'd. (i.iv.34–7)

Being a prince, his every act is sanctioned by the gods (or by his
particular goddess, Minerva). Indeed, he asserts that the gods
themselves wait on princes and were created only for their convenience, not vice versa, and that he can override the people's
complaints with impunity since the gods take no account of
them. Can the gods

> haue vacant houres to take into
> Their serious protection, or care,
> This many headed monster? mankind liues

In few, as potent Monarchs, and their Peeres;
And all those glorious constellations
That doe adorne the firmament, [are] appointed
Like groomes with their bright influence to attend
The actions of Kings, and Emperours.   (III.ii.32–9)

This brings us virtually into the world of the Caroline masque.
Charles was to make gods and constellations dance attendance
on him in court entertainments, most notably in Carew's
Coelum Britannicum (1634) in which the heavens are reformed
after the superior model of the English court. Massinger
anticipates Carew's linguistic strategies with deadly accuracy:
Domitian tells the noble ladies that are forced to wait on his
mistress that to

> be slaues
> To her, is more true liberty then to liue
> *Parthian* or *Asian* Queenes,   (II.i.251–3)

a view of obedience exactly reproduced in elegant verse by
Carew for Charles and Henrietta Maria:

> So just, so gentle is their sway
> As it seemes Empire to obay.[33]

In 1626 Charles was already beginning to build a collection of
art and sculpture which asserted his sovereign authority in exactly these imperial terms; six years later he himself appeared as
Caesar leading captive kings in Townshend's Roman masque
Albion's Triumph. Massinger's mirror for tyranny stands in
radical opposition to the contemporary court culture both aes-
thetically and politically.

Furthermore, Massinger makes quite clear what the
ostentatious claims made for kingship in the Stuart masque
mean for practical politics, as may readily be gathered from the
episode in which Parthenius brazenly commandeers Lamia's
wife for Caesar's use, a scene clearly designed to speak for the
disquiets of the 1620s. Lamia, a member of the senatorial class
suspicious of the court, is bullied and intimidated in the most
high-handed way imaginable by the slick courtier Parthenius
('Not to loose time,/She's *Caesars* choice' (I.ii.61–2)). Lamia
conceptualizes the dispute in language that would have rung
immediately familiar in 1626:

> Cannot a man be master of his wife
> Because she's young, and faire, without a pattent?
> I in mine owne house am an Emperour,
> And will defend whats mine, where are my knaues?
> If such an insolence escape vnpunish'd –　　　(1.ii.65–9)

To Lamia, the rape is a shocking violation of his security of property. A 'pattent' suggests a grant held by gift *from* the prince; Lamia believes he holds his goods independently of the prince, that they cannot be disposed of save by his own consent. This right of property is a basic safeguard of his freedom and a bulwark against tyranny: in his personal liberties, guaranteed by law and custom immemorial, he is Caesar's equal, an emperor in his own home. Caesar simply overrides these fundamental, inalienable rights, denying Lamia anything which is 'his'. When Lamia appeals to law, Parthenius retorts:

> Monarkes that dare not doe vnlawfull things,
> Yet bare them out, are Constables, not Kings.　　(1.ii.85–6)

The sentiment is Seneca's (*Thyestes*, 214–15) but the application is entirely Stuart. Lamia, like the English 'senators', is concerned for the authority of fundamental law, by which even the prince is bound, but Parthenius sees law as given *by* the prince, and the prince as *lex loquens*,[34] the law's master, not mastered by it. As he pithily puts it, 'When power puts in its Plea the lawes are silenc'd' (1.ii.44), a position Domitian later angrily retorts against Lamia for thinking 'that our vnlimited power / Can be confin'd' (11.i.136–7):

> Shall we be circumscrib'd? let such as cannot
> By force make good their actions, though wicked,
> Conceale, excuse or qualifie their crimes:
> What our desires grant leaue, and priuiledge to
> Though contradicting all diuine decrees,
> Or lawes confirm'd by *Romulus*, and *Numa*,
> Shall be held sacred.　　　(11.i.143–9)

Domitian has deeply confounded authority with power. Romulus and Numa were Rome's original legislators, but their successor has elevated his will into the force of law, so that it is neither controllable nor accountable:

> 　　　　　　yeeld an accompt
> Of whats our pleasure to a priuate man?
> *Rome* perish first, and *Atlas* shoulders shrinke,

> Heav'ns fabrique fall; the Sunne, the Moone, the Stars
> Loosing their light, and comfortable heate,
> Ere I confesse, that any fault of mine
> May be disputed. (II.i.153–9)

Here is Carew's iconography again – Atlas, the ruins of Rome and even the extinguishing heavens would witness to the glory of Stuart rule in *Coelum Britannicum*. Moreover, Domitian deliberately seeks to obliterate even the memory of subsidiary rights and liberties. Lamia must not

> pretend
> An interest to that which I call mine ...
> [nor] remember, she was euer his
> That's now in our possession, (II.i.137–40)

and when he does so he earns only Caesar's derision. Domitian is indeed a cruel and wayward prince, but the crucial principle at stake is that his conception of his power exhibits exactly that challenge to the fundamental freedoms of the subject which was feared from Stuart government. Charles's parliaments returned obsessively to the disregard demonstrated by his impositions, forced loans, monopolies and arbitrary imprisonments for the constraints of law and the essential, unimpeachable liberties of person and property which law should guarantee for the subject, and the Lamia episode focuses on just this issue in precisely the same terms. Lamia, who knows that if he cannot secure his wife all his other rights are worthless, exemplifies that early Stuart nightmare, that men's goods and liberties will all fall into the power of the prince, leaving him the only 'freedman' left. At Domitian's triumph, while his people grovel, Rusticus pointedly contemns them as a nation of free men made slaves:

> *Sura.*   All we possesse.
> *Lamia.*   Our liberties.
> *Fulcinius.*   Our children.
> *Parthenius.*   Wealth.
> *Aretinus.*   And throates
>   Fall willingly beneath his feete.
> *Rusticus.*   Base flattery.
>   What Roman could indure this? (I.iv.49–52)

So it entirely misses Massinger's point, it seems to me, to describe Domitian as living in a fantasy world which collapses when it meets reality.[35] Domitian's power is not in the least illusory (after all, the senate lacks the will and the ability to oppose him, and the tribunes are happy to serve his tyranny); rather, Massinger dramatizes a style of government which was all too real a possibility to his contemporaries. The 'reality' which defeats Domitian is the very specific reality of political dissent, which is quite a different thing altogether. The conspirators who plot against Domitian are moved, like those in *Nero*, by a desire to vindicate the ancient Roman freedom and *virtù* from the slavery into which they have fallen:

> there is something more in *Rome* expected
> From *Titus* daughter, and his vncles heyre,
> Then womanish complaints after such wrongs
> Which mercie cannot pardon.   (III.i.23–6)

The orthodox view, that the gods protect princes, no matter how bad, is voiced by Domitilla (III.i.58–9) and, later, by the tribunes (v.ii.213–15; ii.77–9), but the plot is praised, equally strongly, as a 'noble vndertaking' suitable to the 'births and honours' of its actors (III.i.53, 48), and the glory of which will 'endure/To all posteritie' (v.ii.13–14):

> I am confident he deserues much more
> That vindicates his countrie from a tyranne,
> Then he that saues a citizen.   (III.i.76–8)

These are entirely pragmatic and credible reasons for Domitian's overthrow. His rule is flawed not by any lack of realism but because internally his 'dotage' on Domitia weakens him (v.i.87) and externally he alienates men sufficiently to cause them to desire to take independent political action. It is Domitian's own insupportable acts which finally create, as they inevitably must do, an opposition determined to destroy him.

V

The oddity is that Massinger does not explain Domitian's fall in political terms alone, but continually counterpoints political criticism with a pattern of disapproval we can only call 'religious'. There are repeated references to Domitian's impieties, especially that he lays claim to be a deity:

> in his edicts
> He does not blush, or start to stile himselfe
> (As if the name of Emperour were base)
> Great Lord, and God *Domitian*.   (I.i.105–8)

He is welcomed as a god at his triumph, and the heavens are said to envy his happiness (II.i.207–10); any opposition is a kind of blasphemy to him. These matters come to a preliminary head in III.ii, in which he tortures the Stoics, Rusticus and Sura, an incident bringing strongly to mind those scenes in popular martyr-plays, such as Henry Shirley's *The Martyred Soldier* (*c.* 1619) or Massinger's own *The Virgin Martyr* (*c.* 1620), in which heathen persecutors fail to convert or even to hurt Christian captives who remain serenely impervious to their torments. The philosophy of the Stoics is transcendental, almost a religion calling them to a higher, unearthly sainthood:

> In my thought I see
> The substance of that pure vntainted soule,
> Of *Thraseas* our master made a starre,
> That with melodious harmonie invites vs
> . . .
> To trace his heauenly steps, and fill a Spheare
> Aboue yon Chrystall Canopie.
>
> (III.ii.62–5, 67–8)

Domitian scorns their 'sanctitie of life' as a powerless aid, and accuses them of blasphemy against *his* deity, 'The power of Princes, that are Gods on earth' (III.ii.69, 57). However, their philosophy has turned them to pure soul, 'Aeriall spirits' (III.ii.86), and renders them insensible to the tortures Domitian tries to inflict on them, much to his discomfort since he measures his power over them according to the harm he can do them. Something miraculous is at work here. Very like the martyr-plays, the Stoics' superhuman endurance refutes Domitian's merely earthly divinity and proves the existence of superior powers which will ultimately judge him; he may destroy Rusticus's body but

> when the sandie building of thy greatnes,
> Shall with its owne weight totter; looke to see me
> As I was yesterday, in my perfect shape,
> For I'll appeare in horror. (III.ii.113–16)

Already, Lamia and Stephanos have appealed to the gods to vindicate their sufferings (I.ii.102–9, III.i.106–7), and when vengeance does fall it is prefaced by divine portents and the rise of the Stoics' sword-waving ghosts, almost as a battle between

the gods and an atheist who has blasphemed them and claimed
their power for himself. Domitian scoffs at auguries ('Perish
all/Predictions, I grow constant they are false/And built vpon
vncertainties' (v.ii.37–9)) and even attempts to thwart them by
killing Ascletario who has prophesied the manner of his own
death, but the gods fulfil their own predictions despite his
resistance and cast him down for 'presumption' that he 'would be
stilde a God' (v.i.276). Exactly as had been prophesied, Domitian
sinks 'with mine owne waight' (v.i.279; compare III.i.65–6,
ii.114).

The divine revenge is obviously important to Massinger; it was
a major factor in his choice of subject since he sticks closely to his
source throughout Act v, whereas Acts I–IV elaborate freely on
only a few historical suggestions. But as I have argued, Massinger
has already made the political causes alone entirely sufficient to
account for Domitian's fall. Apart from undermining Domitian's
confidence, the anger of the heavens actually achieves nothing
which the assassins do not themselves bring about by purely
secular means. The portents do not cause but merely announce a
vengeance which will happen anyway without their assistance;
the authority of the heavens is vindicated but Domitian is still
overthrown in a largely pragmatic manner. Furthermore, there is
remarkably little interaction between the two aspects of the revenge, which run parallel but never really interact. Massinger, it
seems, is deliberately overplotting; he supplies a gratuitous redun-
dancy of causation.

The comparison with *Sejanus* is instructive. Jonson's Rome is
wholly pragmatic, the political forces operate impersonally and
amorally. Massinger, though, restores exactly that element of
Providence which Jonson went to Tacitus to escape, and so, coinci-
dentally, does the author of *Nero*, whose emperor explicitly repu-
diates heavenly constraints ('Let meane men cry to haue Law, and
Iustice done/And tell their griefes to Heauen, that heares them
not' (sig. C2ᵛ)), only to have his subjects call on heaven indeed
(sig. E3ᵛ) and turn his words against him at the last, the extraordinary conclusion being:

> Thus great bad men aboue them finde a rod:
> People depart, and say there is a God.   (sig. I3ʳ)

It is difficult not to ascribe this development to the changing political tone of the 1620s. *Nero* and *The Roman Actor* were written for spectators for some of whom hostility to the policies of Stuart government was coming to be reinforced by religious worries, as well as a concern for law and liberty. They are putting God back into politics but according to a very different scheme from that of the Tudor histories of the 1590s – their view of tyrants as answerable to a divine power which champions the interests of the good or pious-minded subject would have been highly gratifying to those godly men who are more usually thought of as opponents of the stage in this period. In fact Massinger could readily have found the Roman emperors discussed in precisely these terms by contemporary puritan moralists, who used them as horrific examples of persecutors of the saints, and as examples of people who despised God and tried blasphemously to usurp His power. Cromwell's schoolmaster Thomas Beard, for example, used Domitian as an example of God's terrible vengeance on a man 'so puft vp and swolne with pride, that he would needs ascribe vnto himselfe the name of God'.[36] There was an inherently dramatic side to such godly moralists, who liked to speak of the world as God's great theatre of justice in which His judgements on sinners and great men were acted out to the astonishment of earthly audiences, which finds some fulfilment in *Nero* and *The Roman Actor*. The conspirators in *Nero* plan to kill the prince when he is acting on the stage,

> And so too truely make't a Tragedy:
> When all the people cannot chuse but clap
> So sweet a close,   (sig. D2ʳ)

an idea closely matching the kind of 'true tragedy' of which the puritan moralists so frequently thought of themselves as being the presenters.

This may suggest some reasons why Massinger devotes so much attention to the Roman *actor*, Paris. In a Rome where actors are so favoured and Caesar stages spectacles of cruelty, Domitian finds himself to be only another actor on the great world-stage (1.iii.49–51) in a play scripted by God. Moreover, if these plays are going beyond the range of sympathies normally associated with the Stuart theatre, then we may be alerted to some anomalies in Massinger's treatment of the actors. It has already been remarked that after Paris's famous defence of the stage in I.iii the 'Cure of Avarice' playlet (II.i) signally fails to effect the moral reform he has claimed for the drama,[37] but I do not think that the quite astounding way that Massinger concedes points to critics of the stage all down the line has been noticed. Not only does Philargus resist being cured of his avarice by the playlet, he completely mistakes the fiction for reality and calls on Caesar to intervene (II.i.337), and instead of sympathizing with the 'approved' characters, he praises only the villain of the piece. This last is a plain confession of the inherent ambivalence of the drama, that its imitation of reality is always complex and ironic – puritans complained that even the most moral plays had to include bawdry and vice and had to make them attractive. The fiction–reality confusion is another pervasive ambiguity. Puritanism was horrified at the falsity of play-acting, that the actor endeavours to be what he is not, and to arouse real feelings in his audience. This is Domitia's mistake, too, that Paris really is the gamesome lover he impersonates (IV.ii.30–9). Throughout the 'Iphis and Anaxerete' playlet (III.ii) she misinterprets imitation as truth, and is finally overwhelmed by the genuine passion it has artificially generated in her (III.ii.281–4). She is that puritan bugbear, the female spectator in love with the actors, intoxicated by the delightful falsehood of the stage. The third playlet, in which Caesar kills Paris (IV.ii.) is another drama which incites and liberates passion instead of controlling it, now with murderous effect. Here indeed are the violent effects of playing which Gosson feared, jest made earnest with a vengeance, and which prove that in merely acting a bad deed the actor, and his audience who enjoy it, participate in the guilt as if it were real. Far from being the noble defence of theatre it was long taken to be, *The Roman Actor* surely achieves the exact opposite. Paris's apology takes up the traditional humanist justifications, based on the drama's power to involve its spectators, that the theatre improves people morally by purging, changing and reforming, but this honoured defence is entirely discredited by subsequent events. The theatre does indeed change people but, as the puritans with some reason objected, this does not make it moral; if it has power to improve it may also corrupt, and the effects of play-acting as Massinger shows them are disruptive, mischievous and downright subversive. It is hard to understand the plays-in-the-play in any other way than as a demonstration of the speciousness, danger even, of the arguments of I.iii, especially since the

players themselves are so obviously men of substance and sobri-
ety – it is not they, but play-acting itself which is suspect. Massinger is deliberately writing the most anti-theatrical play of the
English Renaissance, presenting Paris and his fellows in a light
that is powerfully 'puritan'.

This anti-theatricalism is not found in *Julia Agrippina* but is
strongly present again in *Nero*, whose author is *so* obsessed with
the damage that Nero's love of the theatre does to Rome. Nero is
a player-king, besotted with the stage, who herds his people into
the theatres to watch him perform and who chooses to play
murderous roles which ingrain his personal propensities to real
violence (sigs. C3^r, D3^v). The mob follow him mindlessly into his
shallow and disgusting pleasures; there is a real horror about the
description of how Rome is being overrun with players which is
quite familiar from the puritan anti-theatrical pamphlets:

> But to throw downe the walls, and Gates of Rome,
> To make an entrance for a Hobby-horse;
> To vaunt toth'people his rediculous spoyles;
> To come with Lawrell, and with Olyues crown'd,
> For hauing beene the worst of all the Singers,
> Is beyond Patience.   (sig. B3^r)

The author could scarcely have been ignorant that Nero (and the
other emperors) had been grist to the mill of the anti-theatrical
polemicists, who seized on them as vivid proof of the infamy of
stage-playing. These princes had learned their cruelty from
tragedies and their dissoluteness from comedies; only the worst
emperors had enjoyed the theatre ('the most bloody, mercilesse,
and cruell Villaines breath'd; *Fit to make Actors, though fit for
nothing else*'); their patronage of the drama ruined the Romans'
virtù and made them idle, lascivious and servile, for with the
building of theatres 'was the *Romane* Common-wealth changed
into a Monarchie, and the Monarchie afterwards into Tyran-
nicall government'.[38] There is obvious continuity here with the
outlook of radical political pamphleteers, such as John Reynolds
and Thomas Scott, who saw the same national degradation recurring in Stuart England, and ascribed England's political and
religious apostasy – her failure to oppose Spain and the Pope, and
to support the European Protestant cause – to the national corruption of morality and manners, and the neglect of the old

Elizabethan martial spirit for the sake of 'Stage-Playes, Maskes, Reuels and Carousing':

> We have gone to the *Silke-worme*, and learned there to vvaste and spin out our owne bowels, to make our backes brave; To consume all in flourishes, Banquets, Maskes, Revels, and merriments; vvhilest our brethren in one faith … sit mourning and weeping by the vvaters of *Babylon*.[39]

In *Nero*, the tyrant is plunging his people into moral, social and political bankruptcy just as James and Charles seemed to their puritan critics to be doing to England, and in both cases society's degeneration from its past greatness is signified in its abandonment of serious pursuits for plays and frivolous pleasures.

The author of *Nero*, writing a play which reprehends a society's excessive indulgence in playing, is taking a calculated risk. He reproduces the social and political attitudes of the antitheatrical pamphleteers, but from within the theatre itself, and something similar seems to be at work in *The Roman Actor*. Paris's presence subtly deflates Domitian's dignity, who appears as a Caesar who spends as much time patronizing players as ruling, whose mistress prefers a player to him, and who himself finally becomes only a player, another Nero (IV.ii.224). The effect is strongest in I.iv where Domitian enters Rome in triumph but, like Nero, brings players in his wake; he compares himself with Plautus's braggart, and gives Paris his hand (I.iv.27, 75). Moreover, Paris too, for all his nobleness, seems obscurely tainted by his association with Domitian and by the undercurrent of doubt about his profession, that even when he is most himself he may still only be acting.[40] But these suggestions fail to rise to a coherent, controlling pattern. Is Paris a noble tragedian or a practitioner of an art which seduces its audience? How does he reconcile his friendship with the virtuous senators (I.i.65–6) with his studied deference to Caesar? Is Caesar a patron of the arts or a despicable butcher? The play seems to pull simultaneously in contradictory directions, articulating points of view which are radically incompatible and which, rather than enriching, ultimately obscure Massinger's intentions.[41] There are tensions in the play which Massinger never really resolves but which remain troubling and point to the difficulty of writing such a play as this at this time. The problem with a ruler like Charles was to articulate political dissent without finding oneself forced into a position of total intransigence to the regime, to express anxiety about the status quo without seeming to be repudiating it in its entirety. Massinger's dilemma is that of being at least partially committed to the society whose values, nevertheless, he largely opposes, and he places himself in an uneasy alliance with more radical government critics with whom, under a more acceptable king, he might not associate so readily. Unlike the author of *Nero*, who clearly is fully committed to the attitudes he espouses, Massinger remains equivocal even while carrying through the implications of the position he has adopted. We are left with a play which seems incompletely integrated, in which Caesar is killed justly yet always receives, from the sympathetic title-character, unqualified respect.

VI

Whatever Massinger's personal reservations, subsequent events only increased the acuteness of the disquiets to which the classical play was giving voice, and this renewed urgency is clearly indicated ten years on in the heightened tensions of Richards's *Messallina*, a vigorous and popular polemic against all aspects of court life and luxury. Richards's Messallina, revelling in the absence of her husband Claudius, is an insatiable whore whose courtiers are her pimps and studs. She seduces three more victims in the course of the play, including, typically, an actor she has seen playing the lover Troilus; when he will not consent, she has him racked out of his scruples. Court life is a never-ending provocation of the senses. Messallina drinks, dances (!) and eats 'stirring meates' (line 1522),[42] her 'incensed blood' runs in 'a violent Tyde' (lines 550, 575), she is in a 'Plurisie of lust' (line 850), her dancing 'apts my blood for dalliance' (line 1013), one lover, Silius, is 'all Flame' (line 871), she is 'on fire' for another (line 1477), his blood takes a 'hot combustion' (line 1534), and so on. The climax is a 'rich stirring Maske' (line 1876) arranged for her bigamous union with Silius, who has displaced Claudius sexually and politically. While revellers and whores dressed as queens dance below, Messallina and Silius appear in a cloud as Venus and Mars, interchangeably describing their adulterous love:

> *Emp.* Natures wonder, my delight, my pleasure.
> *Sil.* Let me suck Nectar, kisse, kisse, O kisse me.

> *Emp.* Soule to my lips, embrace, hug, hug me.
> *Sil.* Leap heart.
> *Emp.* Mount blood.
> *Sil.* Thus rellish all my blisse.
> *Emp.* Agen the pressure of that melting kisse. (lines 2214–20)

It is almost the final duet of *L'Incoronazione di Poppea* (1642), but a tolerance and moral indulgence like Monteverdi's is totally absent.

Against this popular idea of what happens in courts is placed a range of sympathetic, puritanical characters, who criticize the courtly values. Silius begins the play as a puritan indeed, 'a man of precise abstinence' (line 425) who believes 'Vertue is [the] onely true nobilitie' (line 240), quoting Seneca for what is actually an impeccably levelling sentiment. He attacks the vices of great men and the times, and before Messallina corrupts him he is a veritable Prynne among the prostitutes, visiting 'the divels vaulting schoole' (line 438) to rail against whores and their practices. His wife is sober and saintly, a model of married chastity, who ends the play urging her dying husband to repent and hope for heavenly life. Messallina's well-intentioned mother prays to the 'all-seeing power / Prostrate on bended knees' (lines 1972–3) for help and annoys the courtiers with her 'superstitious lecturing' (line 1055); she finds her vocation encouraging virgins to suicide in preference to rape with arguments that might have come straight from *Comus*:

> Is it not better die then live at court?
> Rackt, torne and tost on proud dishonours wheele,
> There to be whoor'd, your excellence defil'd,
> Rather be free, be free rare spirits for
> Succeeding times to wonder at
> . . .
> *To die for vertue is a glorious life.*   (lines 738–42, 744)

'Not unto me *Vibidia* but to heaven', she tells one of the saved vestals who has knelt to her in thanks (line 2125). Finally, Richards introduces Seneca's brother, Annaeus Mela, who passes his time in divine contemplation and lecturing

> Of that high Majestie puissant *Ens*
> From which we have our being, life, and soule,
> Which should dull flintie inconsiderate man,
> When with black deeds 'ith myrie bog of sinne,
> Beast like he wallows; consider right
> . . .

> he then no more
> Would dare t'offend his Maker, but with teares,
> Lament his soules pollution.
>
> (lines 1456–60, 1463–5)

He too sees virtue Miltonically as 'meerely adjective' unless it actively 'directs/The mind to honest Actions' (lines 1351–3). With 'divine assistance' (line 1579) he recovers Montanus, whom Messallina has seduced, to virtue, and together they fly Rome for a safe place to 'practise/*Mans sole perfection* [–] *to be heavenly wise*' (lines 1643–4).

Claudius's return brings Messallina's inevitable nemesis, but he has little stature except as the agent of the heavens' revenge, turning Messallina's squalid pomps into a real and terrible '*Tragedy*' (line 2251). The world-stage haunts the play's language: the courtiers have acted follies but are now 'scourg'd by the Tragedian death' (line 2363), and Messallina revels oblivious to the torch of vengeance literally set up above her (line 2250). In this play, the heavens really *do* intervene: the earth swallows up Messallina's panders, and an angel strikes down the courtier Saufellus with a thunderbolt. The conflict is almost an eschatological one. Messallina has invoked the furies and they really have come, dancing round her 'To fire thy mind' with arrows of lust, pride and murder (line 841); in the last scene, two dreadful spirits appear, telling her to despair, while the ghosts of her victims surround her, brandishing torches. Moreover, she is another Circe (lines 817, 2400), carrying a cup of poison to enchant men (line 489) – Richards surely expected his audience to associate her with the Whore of Babylon herself, who intoxicates the reprobate nations with her wine in Revelation (18.3), and who was identified by militant Protestantism with the corruptions of the Church of Rome. This was certainly how one spectator saw it: '*Romes* mightie Whore by thee adornes the Stage:/For to convert not to corrupt this *Age*' (lines 165–6). The same friend praised Richards as '*that happy wit whose veines can stirre*/Religious thoughts, *though in a* Theater' (lines 173–4).

This extraordinary play, then, demonstrates that even in 1635 political, social and religious radicalism could be reconciled with dramatic performance at the Salisbury Court theatre; nor was this the only example.[43] Richards's combination of distrust of the ways of courts, hostility to the rich and powerful, sainthood for the pious and expectations of Providential justification shows the defensive anxieties of these years metamorphosing towards a much more militant and defiant persuasion which would later make an enormous contribution to the political crisis that was to produce the challenge to the king and eventually cause *his* overthrow. The same themes continued to reverberate in classicizing drama down to the civil war. In Webster's *Appius and Virginia*[44] the unjust judge attempts to have his wicked way with the senatorial lady, Virginia, by having her declared a slave, her freedom forfeit. The setting is Rome's republican period, but at the play's centre is the outrage of a citizen who, like Lamia or Charles's subjects, finds her liberty being turned to serfdom by a tyrannous power:

> Ignoble villaine,
> I am as free as the best King or Consull
> Since *Romulus*. What dost thou meane? Unhand me.
> Give notice to my uncle and *Icilius*,
> What violence is offer'd me. (III.ii.110–14)

In a pamphlet play of 1641, Richard Brathwaite's *Mercurius Britannicus*, the Ship Money judges who had aided Charles's illegal exactions are tried and condemned by the English parliament, dramatized as a Roman senate whose members are 'Consuls of true piety'.[45] And three years before, Massinger, in a play of which only one speech survives, presented a despotic king tyrannizing over his people in the belief that

> The Caesars
> In Rome were wise, acknowledginge no lawes
> But what their swords did ratifye, the wives
> And daughters of the senators bowinge to
> Their wills, as deities.[46]

But the best documented example is Thomas May, who pursued the implications of the classical parallel the furthest, and in a truly revolutionary direction. *Julia Agrippina* is the one imperial play which takes some account of the values of the republic; in the induction, the fury Megaera prophesies the decline of Rome under the poisonous and ambitious imperial dynasty:

> What though the Gods and Vertue first did raise
> *Rome* to that height it holds? they did but make
> An Empire large enough for us to take,

And build a strength for us to manage now[.]
Though Vertue made the Romane greatnesse grow:
Shee now forsakes it at the height: the Powers,
And fruits of all her diligence are ours.   (lines 12–18)

Here, and elsewhere,[47] May seems to be arguing that though the decline of republican Rome from her *virtù* in her last years made the transition to empire inevitable, as much was lost by it as was gained; although the empire produced Augustus, the Roman *virtù* was at a pitch during the republic which would not be sustained under the Caesars (and in the banquet scene in *Julia Agrippina* Nero praises Petronius, who has recited a poem on the decline of Rome and the end of the republic, for having written a satire while being himself 'No *Scaurus*, *Curius*, or *Fabritius*' (IV.506) – all austere republican patriots far removed from Nero's drinking companions). This was a point hotly championed by the fifteenth-century Florentine republicans, and as hotly denied by good monarchists such as England's Sir Robert Filmer whose *Patriarcha* (before 1642) argued that Rome was perfect under the emperors, but bloody and unstable as a republic. Twenty years after *Julia Agrippina*, this issue suddenly opened out again in an entirely new and timely way, and May, who already in 1640 had revised his continuation of Lucan to darken the character of Caesar and make his opponents more heroic,[48] and two years later had published his *Discourse Concerning the Success of Former Parliaments*, an argument to prove the necessity of kings ruling with their subjects' support, achieved new fame with his *History of the Parliament of England* (London, 1647), the official account of the Long Parliament. May retells the misrule of the Stuarts, but dignifies his views by citations from the classical historians: Strafford is compared with the apostate Curio (out of Lucan), Eliot with Thrasea Paetus, Marie di Medici with Agrippina. Under Charles, the English 'became of that temper, which the Historian speakes of his Romans, *ut nec mala, nec remedia ferre possent*, they could neither suffer those pressures patiently, nor quietly endure the cure of them' (I, p. 19); the parliamentary armies are like those of Brutus, who fought for freedom, the royalists' like Caesar's who fought for tyranny and gain (III, pp. 30–1). In his last years, May was moving in free-thinking circles among such men as Thomas Chaloner the regicide and Henry Marten the republican; his *Breviary of the*

History of the Parliament of England (1650), which brings events down to Charles's execution, sided firmly with the Independents against the Presbyterians.[49]

Massinger, of course, did not live to see the civil war, but I have been trying to suggest that *The Roman Actor* was profoundly engaged with the intellectual and political currents that helped create the crisis. Later, John Aubrey would say that May had learned his political principles from translating Lucan, and Thomas Hobbes, looking back onto the conflict, affirmed that an over-educated gentry was one of its seven main causes:

> that in their youth having read the Books written by famous men of the Ancient *Grecian* and *Roman* Commonwealths, concerning their Policy and great Actions, in which Book[s] the Popular Government was extol'd by that glorious Name of Liberty, and Monarchy disgraced by the Name of Tyranny: they became thereby in love with their form of Government: And out of these men were chosen the greatest part of the *HOUSE OF COMMONS*: Or if they were not the greatest part, yet by advantage of their Eloquence were always able to sway the rest.[50]

One gentleman of this type, though not an MP, was Milton, who called Tacitus 'the greatest possible enemy to tyrants', and compared the king with Caligula and Domitian, who had also thought themselves gods.[51] Another was John Bradshaw, the president of the judges at Charles's trial, who defended parliament's actions by reference to the senate of Rome that had sat in judgement on Nero. Milton was a lover of the theatre, and Bradshaw had not been above patronizing players in the past.[52] It could well be that they too had sat among audiences of the 1620s and '30s who had thrilled to the overthrowing of Messallina, Nero and Domitian.

NOTES

I am very grateful to Dr Howard Erskine-Hill for reading and commenting on an earlier version of this essay.

1 W. D. Briggs, 'The influence of Jonson's Tragedy in the Seventeenth Century', *Anglia*, 35 (1911–12), 277–337.
2 Tacitus is the principal source for *Sejanus*, *Nero*, *Julia Agrippina* and *Messallina*. Massinger took his material from Suetonius, but his analysis of the character of Domitian and of his rule is clearly deeply indebted to Tacitus's *Agricola*, i–ii, xxxix–xlv.
3 P. Burke, 'Tacitism', in T. A. Dorey (ed.), *Tacitus* (London, Routledge and K. Paul, 1969), pp.149–71; see p.150. See also K. C. Schellhase,

Tacitus in Renaissance Political Thought (Chicago, University of Chicago Press, 1976); M. F. Tenney, 'Tacitus in the Politics of Early Stuart England', *The Classical Journal*, 37 (1941–2), 151–63; E. B. Benjamin, 'Bacon and Tacitus', *Classical Philology*, 60 (1965), 102–10; and Leonard F. Dean, 'Sir Francis Bacon's Theory of Civil History Writing', *ELH*, 8 (1941), 161–83.

4   Montaigne, *Essays*, tr. John Florio (3 vols., London, 1910), vol. 3, p.180.

5   Traiano Boccalini, *The New-Found Politicke*, tr. John Florio and William Vaughan (London, 1626), p.18.

6   Boccalini, *New-Found Politicke*, pp.17, 27.

7   M. W. Croll, *'Attic' and Baroque Prose Style*, ed. J. Max Patrick, *et al.* (Princeton, Princeton University Press, 1969), p.152.

8   I cite from Philip Edwards and Colin Gibson (eds.), *The Plays and Poems of Philip Massinger* (5 vols., Oxford, Clarendon Press, 1976), vol. 3.

9   Massinger may well have been influenced here by the *Agricola*, ii: 'We should have lost memory itself as well as voice, had forgetfulness been as easy as silence' (Loeb edition).

10 Degory Wheare, *The Method and Order of Reading . . . Histories*, 2nd edn (London, 1694), p.107 (first published in 1637). *The Roman Actor* mentions Thrasea Paetus, unhistorically, as a victim of Domitian (II.i.120).

11 *Essays*, vol. 3, p.180. See also Burke, 'Tacitism', pp.168–9.

12 Boccalini, *New-Found Politicke*, p.31.

13 See, for example, J. W. Lever, *The Tragedy of State* (London, Methuen, 1971), pp.59–61; Hans Baron, *The Crisis of the Early Italian Renaissance* (Princeton, Princeton University Press, 1966), pp.47–78; D. J. Gordon, *The Renaissance Imagination*, ed. Stephen Orgel (Berkeley, University of California Press, 1975), pp.233–45; Schellhase, *Tacitus in Political Thought*, pp.17–25, 167; and C. F. Mullett, 'Classical Influences on the American Revolution', *The Classical Journal*, 35 (1939–40), 92–104.

14 Conrad Russell, *Parliaments and English Politics 1621–1629* (Oxford, Clarendon Press, 1979), p.56.

15 E. B. Benjamin, 'Sir John Hayward and Tacitus', *RES*, n.s. 8 (1957), 275–6.

16 John Forster, *Sir John Eliot: A Biography* (2 vols., London, 1864), vol. 1, pp.548, 552.

17 D. B. J. Randall, *Jonson's Gipsies Unmasked* (Durham, NC, Duke University Press, 1975), p.28; Burke, 'Tacitism', p.161; Arthur Wilson, *The History of Great Britain* (London, 1653), p.289.

18 Forster, *Eliot*, vol. 1, pp.163, 319, 367–8; Eliot, *An Apology for Socrates and Negotium Posterorum*, ed. A. B. Grosart (2 vols., London, 1881), vol. 2, pp.12, 96.

19 J. B. Mullinger, *The University of Cambridge* (3 vols., Cambridge, Cambridge University Press, 1873–1911), vol. 3, p.87 and note; Hamon L'Estrange, *The Reign of King Charles*, 2nd edn (London, 1656), p.69.

20 Eliot, *Negotium Posterorum*, vol. 1, p.169; F. W. Fairholt (ed.), *Poems and Songs Relating to George Villiers, Duke of Buckingham* (London, 1850), p.24.

21 Bolton, 'Hypercritica' in Joseph Haslewood (ed.), *Ancient Critical Essays*, vol. 2 (London, 1815), p.224; *Nero Caesar* (London, 1624), p.240; Tenney, 'Tacitus in Stuart Politics', p.158.

22 Lawrence Stone, 'The Educational Revolution in England 1560–1640', *Past and Present* 28 (1964), 78–9.

23 Kevin Sharpe, *Faction and Parliament* (Oxford, Clarendon Press, 1978), pp.237–43; Sharpe, *Sir Robert Cotton 1586–1631* (Oxford, Clarendon Press, 1979), pp.208–10.

24 Sharpe, *Faction and Parliament*, p.237.

25 Forster, *Eliot*, vol. 2, p.660; Richard James, *The Poems*, ed. A. B. Grosart (privately printed, 1880), pp.198–9.

26 Fairholt, *Poems and Songs*, pp.45, 77.

27 Jonson, *Works*, ed. C. H. Herford and Percy and Evelyn Simpson (11 vols., Oxford, Clarendon Press, 1923–52), vol. 1, pp.242–3.

28 Edward Hyde, *The Life of Edward, Earl of Clarendon* (2 vols., Oxford, 1817), vol. 1, p.28.

29 References are to the text in *Works*, vol. 4. To Jonson's acquaintance William Drummond of Hawthornden, Nero's judicial murders of Lucan and Seneca brought to mind the plight of the dissatisfied intellectual under James. He commented on Tacitus, 'it seldom falls out that learned princes aduance learned men. . . . I must call these tymes abject, in which it is a more worthye exercise to be a ballader, studye to paint the face, or follow some wild beast, then have the most noble facultyes of wit' (D. Laing, 'A Brief Account of the Hawthornden Manuscripts', *Archaeologia Scotica*, 4 (1857), 57–116; see p.88.

30 References are to the edition of F. E. Schmid (Louvain, 1914).

31 See S. R. Gardiner, *History of England ... 1603–1642* (10 vols., London, 1883–4), vol. 5, pp.400–1; vol. 6, pp.78–9, 108.

32 I.iv.28, 30. See E. M. Hill (ed.), *The Tragedy of Nero* (New York, Garland Publishing, 1979), p.xvii; also perhaps I.iv. 64–8 recalls *Nero* (sig. B2^r).

33 Thomas Carew, *The Poems*, ed. Rhodes Dunlap (Oxford, Clarendon Press, 1949), p.184.

34 James I's view; see J. R. Tanner, *Constitutional Documents of the Reign of James I* (Cambridge, Cambridge University Press, 1930), pp.9–10.

35 As does A. P. Hogan, 'Imagery of Acting in *The Roman Actor*', *MLR*, 66 (1971), 281.

36 Beard, *The Theatre of God's Judgments* 3rd edn (London, 1631), p.31.

37 Philip Edwards, 'Massinger the Censor', in Richard Hosley (ed.), *Essays on Shakespeare and Elizabethan Drama* (London, Routledge and K. Paul, 1963), p.343; Patricia Thomson, 'World Stage and Stage in Massinger's *Roman Actor*', *Neophilologus*, 64 (1970), 423.

38 I. G., *A Refutation of the Apology for Actors* (London, 1614), pp.14, 28. See also John Rainolds, *Th'Overthrow of Stage Plays* (Middleburgh, 1599), pp.6–8; and William Prynne, *Histriomastix* (London, 1633), pp.451–65, 544–5, 848–53 and many other references *passim*.

39 John Reynolds, *Vox Coeli* ('Elisium', 1624), p.36; Thomas Scott, *The Belgic Pismire* (London, 1622), p.48.

40 Even Paris's defence of playing is suspect. Does he mean what he says, or does he only 'Act an Orators part' (1.iii.144)?

41 One might argue, I suppose, that the murder of Paris by Domitian is both politically and dramatically necessary to Massinger, for the assassination of Domitian is possible or laudable only in a world which has lost its Parises. But this still leaves untouched the central tension between the corruption which Paris perceives in the imperial regime and his acquiescence in that regime.

42 I quote from the edition of A. R. Skemp (Louvain, 1910).

43 Trouble with the authorities was caused by a play on ceremonialism at the Salisbury Court in 1634, and by *The Cardinal's Conspiracy* at the Fortune in 1639. (See G. E. Bentley, *The Jacobean and Caroline Stage* (7 vols., Oxford, Clarendon Press, 1941–68), vol. 1, pp.278, 294. It seems highly likely that these were staged as anti-Laudian pieces.

44 This probably dates from 1624, but was still in the Phoenix repertoire in 1639. See Bentley, *The Jacobean and Caroline Stage*, vol. 1, p.331. I quote from the edition of F. L. Lucas (4 vols., London, Chatto and Windus, 1927), vol. 3.

45 I quote from a copy of the third (?) edition, BL pressmark 644.d.29, sig. a2^r.

46 Edwards and Gibson, vol. 1, p.xxxix.

47 May's opinions may be pieced together from his statements in *Julia Agrippina*, IV.454–97; in *A Continuation of Lucan's Historical Poem* (London, 1630), sigs. H6^{r-v}; 15^{r-v}; and in the important dedicatory epistle to *Lucan's Pharsalia*, 2nd edn (London, 1631), sigs. a4^r–5^v.

48 R. T. Bruère, 'The Latin and English versions of Thomas May's *Supplementum Lucani*', *Classical Philology*, 44 (1949), 145–63.

49 May's connections with the political circle of 'classical republicans' of 1649–53 have been authoritatively described by Blair Worden in 'Classical Republicanism and the Puritan Revolution', in H. Lloyd-Jones, V. Pearl and B. Worden (eds.), *History and Imagination* (London, Duckworth, 1981), pp.182–200. I am sorry not to have discovered Worden's fine article until after my own essay was complete.

50 Hobbes, *Behemoth* (London, 1679), p.3; see also pp.22, 42, 54; and *Leviathan*, II.xxi.

51 Milton, *Complete Prose Works* (8 vols., New Haven, Yale University Press, 1953–82), vol. 3, ed. Merritt Y. Hughes, pp.467, 546; Burke, 'Tacitism', p.164.

52 See William Beamont, *A History of the House of Lyme* (Warrington, 1876), pp.122–3; J. G. Muddiman, *The Trial of King Charles the First* (Edinburgh, n.d.), pp.118, 119.

Overreach at Bay: Massinger's *A New Way to Pay Old Debts*

NANCY S. LEONARD

P HILIP MASSINGER'S *A New Way to Pay Old Debts*, reputedly his best play, has long been honoured by a series of troubled and even negative appraisals. Though T. S. Eliot exempted *A New Way to Pay Old Debts* and *The City Madam* from his charge that Massinger's plays reflect 'cerebral anaemia', his well-known comments about *A New Way* are largely confined to the vitality of the play's comic villain, Sir Giles Overreach, and since Eliot's time some critics have found the play's 'theatricality', by which they chiefly mean the great part of Sir Giles, enough to guarantee the play's interest as drama.[1] One fine part is not enough to interest most critics, of course, so there has been even more attention paid to the 'moral' element of the play, to a gravely presented aristocratic ethos, and here the judgements have been quite mixed. To some, Massinger's morality in *A New Way to Pay Old Debts* is the source of the play's virtue and his mark as a dramatist;[2] to others, this 'morality' is fraudulent, an assumption behind Robert Fothergill's description of the play as 'the spectacle of the loathsome pursuing the contemptible'.[3] Still other critics find the play to be a problematic realization of Massinger's moral ideas, to betray a lack of fit between the play's doctrines and its action or feeling.[4] Alexander Leggatt, for example, points to a problem inherent in Massinger's use of comic form in *A New Way*; the 'dangers' of 'embedding an intrigue comedy in a serious moral drama'.[5] It seems to be hard for many critics to read the play sympathetically as an intrigue comedy in which a monstrous villain is undone by a conspiracy of virtuous nobles.

One recent route through the difficulties has been the attempt to revalue the play as a social document, as Michael Neill and others, following Patricia Thomson's earlier path, have done. According to this line of argument, the play can be valued as a coherent reflection of the patriarchal and aristocratic values of its time, as Massinger's defence of birth and blood against the social and economic challenges of the middle class.[6] Such a view can invigorate the play by reanimating its social doctrines. Yet the historical imagination here does seek to elicit sympathy, as humanist inquiry often does, for the dominant ideology of the play: for the nobles' view of the conflict of classes as a moral struggle. 'To fully understand the parameters of Welborne's situation', Neill tells us, 'and to sympathize with the melancholy rage which it inspires in him, one must be sensitive to the nuances of social address by which the play sets so much store'.[7] Or consider Thomson's argument about the match between Lord Lovell and Lady Alworth, the play's senior aristocrats: 'Lovell's own marriage to Lady Allworth, a rich and noble widow, is a perfect example of [aristocratic] wisdom ... put into action ... It is here that Massinger is strong. He can interpret and make valuable the aristocratic way of life'.[8] Yet Lord Lovell and Lady Alworth are characters whose 'moral' claims on our judgement, and dramatic claims on our sympathy, must be mediated through a language that does not suggest wisdom, nobility, or a sensitivity to nuances. A marriage between an aristocrat and a wealthy bourgeois, to Lady Alworth, 'is but as rubbage powr'd into a riuer ... Rendring the water that was pure before,/ Polluted, and vnwholsome' (IV.i.196–99).[9] And Lord Lovell, in reply, is reassuring: 'I would not so adulterate my blood/By marrying *Margaret*, and so leaue my issue/Made vp of seuerall peeces' (IV.i.223–5). That critics have quoted this dialogue before as an instance of the ineffective dramatization of social issues does not change the fact that any critic must deal with it, and recognize that it is perfectly consistent with the social ideas articulated in the remainder of the play. We can recognize the dialogue impartially as the natural talk of a tribe under siege without granting it the sanction of a social theory, a 'moral judgement', or a resource for our dramatic 'sympathy' or 'sensitivity'. As the negative criticism of the play may imply, the values expressed by the play's aristocratic characters may not sustain our sympathy, nor may the dramatic realization of their ideology be free of tension and ambivalence. But dynamic, even dissonant relations between rhetorical assertions, moral implications, and affective responses need not point to weakness or failure in the play. On the contrary: such dissonance can be the basis for a positive reappraisal of the effectiveness of the play as a whole.

To put the matter in broad strokes, the action of *A New Way to Pay Old Debts* combines the intrigue of the young prodigal Welborne to recover the lands held by his usurer-uncle Overreach with the romantic plot in which Overreach's daughter Margaret is successfully courted by Tom Alworth, an impoverished gentleman. But both plots are defined almost as a single action – the breaking down of Overreach's power, his holdings in land, and his effort to marry Margaret into the aristocracy. The help of Lord Lovell and Lady Alworth, who themselves contract to marry late in the play, is critical to the intrigue's success and its social definition. The traditional view of this action takes it as a Jonsonian comedy: the nobles cleanse their society by outfoxing a cunning and dangerous immoralist. But a cool-headed look at the play shows something quite different. Sir Giles Overreach, ostentatiously flanked by his creatures, Marrall and Justice Greedy, looks formidable, but he has even less effect in the play than they do, and they end up serving Welborne's purpose. Overreach, whose gargantuan ambition and avarice are well-established by the play's early exposition, actually accomplishes very little, and certainly very little that is dangerous. He talks a good game: and that, his talk, his vivid, irreverent, sinewy language, is where both his force in the plot and his dramatic attractiveness lie. The nobles, by contrast, think of themselves as great talkers, and are always giving voice to their convictions. But the main thing they do is act, and the way they act is not unlike the communal conspiracy of rogues in a comedy by Middleton or Jonson. As Gāmini Salgādo puts it, 'they cheat, lie and brazen their way through the plot'.[10] Salgādo also says that Massinger seems to admire them for this, which may well be so, but Massinger's play clearly exposes the problems in what it appears to endorse.

In what follows I will examine the rhetorical discontinuities in the play, then build on that basis to frame an analysis of the values embodied by the nobles *as these are dramatically realized*. With this in hand, I will be able to re-engage the character of Sir Giles Overreach, and by exploring his relationship to his antagonists will be able to identify the play's comic form.

A New Way to Pay Old Debts is notable for a striking gap between rhetoric and action, a gap that makes us aware of the ideas expressed in the play as shapes of thought responding to occasions, as 'arguments' or rhetorical gestures, rather than as expressive articulations in close accord with individual psychology, immediate feeling, particular events. What is distinctive about Massinger's rhetoric seems to be the degree to which it is discontinuous with action or feeling, an idea that recalls not only Eliot's charge but the comments of those who have closely studied Massinger's rhetorical style. To Cyrus Hoy, 'the Massingerian method of meeting the dramatic occasion with a rhetorical formula, somewhat in the manner of a conditioned response, will not admit of nice adjustment to the demands of the particular moment'.[11] To Eugene Waith, Massinger 'relies on the structure of argument even when the emphasis of the speech is clearly emotional ... [and Massinger's style] lacks the more direct emotional appeal which the situation seems to call for'.[12] The interest of Massinger's rhetorical arguments, however, is less in their 'sincerity' than in their function in the play's dramatic form.

The aristocratic characters in *A New Way*, Welborne, Lord Lovell, Lady Alworth and Tom Alworth, use language in ways that are as much at odds with the dramatic moment as consonant with it, and their 'characters' seem to shift during the play as their language does. Lady Alworth, for example, momentarily appears as a stepmotherly moralist when she warns young Tom against Welborne's 'manners so debauch'd' and 'vitious courses' (1.ii.117–26). This is one of the rare instances in the play in which ethical scrutiny is given to someone other than Overreach. (The other is the scene in which Lord Lovell and Lady Alworth excuse their participation in deception.) Little is made by the play of the ill-doing of prodigals, and even less of possible character defects in the pious young Tom. Lady Alworth's language does sketch Welborne's lack of respectability, but it is at odds with her character, with Tom's situation, and with any larger moral argument. When Welborne arrives at her home, she is again indignant, but this time about the offence to her dignity as a great lady. After two short speeches in which Welborne flatters her late husband (which are hard to take as a 'serious' appeal to an old friendship since the servants stand by cheering her on), Lady

Alworth, turning to her servant, states pragmatically and even
flatly 'for what's past, excuse me,/I will redeeme it. *Order* giue
the Gentleman/A hundred pounds' (I.iii.118–20). Like Fletcher,
Massinger seems to adjust rhetoric to the need of the moment,
but the consequence is less to concentrate the emotional effect, as
in Fletcher, than to disperse it. 'Personality' is built by gestures
that are not necessarily coherent, a technique plausible enough in
a dramatic world where the nature of role is at stake.

Lord Lovell, who has been called Massinger's mouthpiece,[13]
speaks an equally shifting language. When Tom Alworth uses
extravagant military and mythical imagery to convey the qualities of his love for Margaret Overreach, Lovell replies bluntly:
'speake your doubts, and fears,/Since you will nourish 'em, in
plainer language' (III.i.55–6). His comment does not stop Tom's
speechifying, so Lovell is wry again: 'Loue hath made
you/Poeticall, *Alworth*' (III.i.80–1). Lovell's suggestion of the
blunt soldier adds wit to the scene, but the wit succumbs to the
weight of Tom's pathos and the apparent gravity with which
Lovell intends to assist him. Lord Lovell's breeziness comes and
is gone. Later, when Sir Giles Overreach leaves Lovell's presence
while tossing off a cynical remark about religion, Lovell gasps out
talk of a pathos and conventionality that remind us of young Tom:

> Hee's gone, I wonder how the Earth can beare
> Such a portent! I, that haue liu'd a Souldier,
> And stood the enemies violent charge vndaunted,
> To heare this blasphemous beast, am bath'd all ouer
> In a cold sweat.   (IV.i.149–53)

Lovell reacts strongly to language that seems inappropriate, but
his own language is unstable and we know little of who he is.

Massinger's aristocrats, then, assume that their language is
stable, reasonable, and a reliable embodiment of social truth. But
the play itself shows their speech fluctuating in an insecure social
world, so that the dramatization of their moral and social values
prohibits an acceptance of the nobles as normative or even consistent characters. The language that we hear from these four
characters – and from Margaret and even the servants when they
wish to appeal to the nobles by imitation – is slippery and uncertain, easily adaptable to the purposes of rationalization,
manipulation, and bullying. Ironically, the villain Overreach is
far more of a plain speaker, or at least a truer hyperbolist. His

idiom is consistently his own, and it is in harmony with his actions and desires.

The curious emptiness of the nobles' language, its somewhat disembodied quality, is only a symptom of a larger negativity that characterizes them at every point. This negativity is central to an understanding of *A New Way*. If we recognize it, the aristocratic values that the play affirms and rewards – while dramatizing their volatile status as assertions – take on a certain fascination; without that recognition, they seem little more than devalued currency, as the tradition of negative appraisal demonstrates. If the play is to have for readers the vitality it has had for theatre-goers, its power must be located elsewhere than in social doctrines already discarded in the nineteenth century, not to mention our own. The play itself deploys its power elsewhere: in representing the drives behind ideology, drives that alter or circumvent the institutional or legal forms of justice, of marriage, and of the distribution of money. The dramatic conflict between the nobles and Sir Giles Overreach shows both sides to be victims and villains.

The first two scenes in the play effectively establish an imaginative location for the action, less in the geographical terms of a Nottinghamshire setting than in the temporal ones of a quickly receding past. The real subject of the first scene is the relation between the present and the past.[14] The scene dramatizes a contrast between the aggressive pragmatism of Tapwell, a kind of extension of Overreach's own power, and the bitter nostalgia of Welborne, who is more concerned with the elevation of his former 'under-butler' than with the ills of tavern life or even with getting something to eat. Tapwell's long story of Welborne's past – the virtues of his father, old Sir John Welborne, Welborne's dissipation of his inheritance, Tapwell's parallel rise in fortunes – earns taunts, curses, and finally a beating from Welborne. The odd power of Tapwell's narrative has something to do with its momentary evocation of an older order in which positive moral values were indissolubly connected with rank, in contrast to the present one in which incomes and titles tell more. As Tapwell reminds Welborne:

> Your dead father,
> My *quondam* master, was a man of worship,
> Old Sir *John Wellborne*, Iustice of peace
> . . .

Bare the whole sway of the shire; kep't a great house;
Relieu'd the poore, and so forth; but Hee dying,
And the twelue hundred a yeare comming to you,
Late Master *Francis*, but now forlorne *Welborne*.

(I.i.32–4, 36–9)

The civic justice and charity of old Sir John, traditionally the
responsibilities of the aristocracy, are absent from Lady Alworth's household and from the general conduct of the noble
characters (though they offer loans and counsel to their own
young). Justice and charity in the present day are represented by
the grotesquely comic Justice Greedy, Overreach's creature,
whose lean body gobbles up both the law and the 'charity' of
aristocratic meals with equal enthusiasm. Greedy is symbolically
a kind of deformed authority or 'father' – something that Overreach literally is. Yet Welborne's hypocrisy makes him a false
son; he beats Tapwell for forgetting the past, meaning
Welborne's forty-pound loan, but he himself forgets a much
larger obligation to his dead father. Tapwell's story makes it
clear that Welborne's own extravagance made him vulnerable to
exploitation by Overreach, but Welborne, here and until the
play's end, deflects responsibility for his shame to Overreach. To
do so he sometimes lies, unconsciously or not. For instance,
Welborne tells Tom Alworth, who loves Margaret Overreach,
that her father 'ruin'd' Tom's state as well as his own. This
statement is contradicted two scenes later (in I.iii) by Welborne's
story about Tom Alworth's father, which clarifies the real
reasons for Tom's poverty. The story tells that Alworth's father
was impoverished by 'debts and quarrels', and only improved his
position by marrying the wealthy Lady Alworth. The same Lady
Alworth is apparently not liberal enough with her wealth to keep
her stepson from the necessity of serving Lord Lovell. For
Welborne, the villainy of Overreach serves to efface any
economic and moral responsibility that the aristocrats themselves may have for the present period of decline.

Massinger's presentation of Tom Alworth is also influenced by
an evocation of a lost father, and in this case the dominant mood
is nostalgia rather than bitterness. The Alworth household is one
of mourning, since its dominant figure, Lady Alworth, achieves
her renown as a mourning widow who refuses to visit or receive
company. Her mourning is significant, since Welborne's appeal

to it enlists her cooperation in his plot to regain his lands from Overreach. And her self-image as a mourner helps to shape her relations with young Alworth and with Lord Lovell. Tom Alworth is characterized by the household servants as 'his fathers picture in little' (1.ii.50), and Tom takes 'comfort' from the idea. A little later, Lady Alworth refers to Tom as 'virgin parchement capable of any/Inscription, vitious, or honorable' (1.ii.78–9) – in effect as a blank or negation. And Tom himself explicitly seeks in Lord Lovell a father he can honour. While this language of fathers and sons is familiar in Renaissance comedy, in *A New Way* its use is distinctively sombre, shadowing Tom's character with nostalgia and mourning, with an orphaned quality. (We are reminded in the final scene of the portraits of Welborne and Tom as orphans, and of Lady Alworth as a widow, when Sir Giles imagines widows and orphans keeping his hand from his sword.) The nostalgia of Tom Alworth and Welborne, the young generation in *A New Way*, specifies a mood of social decline rather than vital continuity. Compare either character with the unmelancholy orphans Orlando in *As You Like It* or Sebastian in *Twelfth Night*, or recall the indecorous laughter, in *Twelfth Night*, through which the mourning Olivia is brought to herself.

If nostalgia is one aspect of the negativity of the aristocratic characters, their explicit assertions about values in the play are even more dramatically negative. Positive affirmations are rare at best; in the world of *A New Way*, virtue is represented by the noble characters as renunciation, sacrifice and suffering. An early cue to this mood is Welborne's advice to the lovesick Tom Alworth: 'where impossibilities are apparent,/'Tis indiscretion to nourish hopes' (1.i.156–7). More than 'indiscretion' is at stake; hope rarely appears in the play, either as the spring behind Welborne's attempt to regain his legacy or as the motive of the play's two betrothals. Tom Alworth's pursuit of Margaret Overreach, and indeed the larger *rite de passage* through which Lady Alworth and Lord Lovell lead him, involves not hope but the ability to endure pain – even though the Alworth plot is usually recognized as the play's most 'romantic' element.

When Lady Alworth is expressing her concern for Tom in the second scene of the play, she speaks from the ties that bound her to his dead father. She goes on, using his 'fathers words'

(I.ii.99–114), to urge him to pursue the career of a soldier. The virtue of a soldier's name, to Lady Alworth, consists in the renunciation of 'lusts' and 'riots', the readiness to 'runne vpon the cannons mouth vndaunted', and to endure heat, cold and hunger. She concludes by recommending a parallel renunciation, the avoidance of the 'debauch'd' Welborne. Alworth's reply is to repeat submissiveness; the second time he does it, saying 'I am still your creature' (I.ii.129), we hear in his language a virtue atrophied by too much courtesy and renunciation, and that quality characterizes what he says to every character in the play, including Overreach.[15]

Tom Alworth twice gives an extended declaration of his love for Margaret Overreach, the first time to Lord Lovell and the second to Margaret herself. Tom uses conventional romantic hyperbole in both scenes (the 'poetical' part, as we have seen Lord Lovell remind us), but the passages are striking for their one-sided Petrarchanism, their exclusive stress on the negative emotions of love, jealousy and suffering. Act III, Scene i proposes the values of Alworth's love which the marriage will later affirm. Tom talks so much of his jealousy of Lovell as a potential rival for Margaret that it baffles even Lovell; Tom's martial imagery is almost comic, in fact, as when he sees Lovell's 'wealth' and Margaret's 'beauty' as 'two such potent enemies ... [that are] too great for *Hercules*' (III.i.52–5). Lovell is no danger, as he keeps telling Alworth, but Tom's conventional jealousy is so elaborate and extended that it trivializes any affirmation in his passion. In the context of Lovell's paternal concern, Alworth's negations miniaturize him in a caricature of withdrawal and abstinence:

> I here release your trust.
> 'Tis happinesse, enough, for me to serue you,
> And sometimes with chast eyes to looke vpon her.
>
> (III.i.91–3)

Just as there is almost no talk of the pleasures of love, which might link Tom Alworth to the protagonists of Elizabethan romantic comedy, so here Tom's abjection before Lovell makes his deferential counterpart in *Much Ado About Nothing*, Claudio, look positively self-assertive by comparison.

Tom Alworth needs others to witness the value of his renunciations, as Lady Alworth and Margaret do for theirs. Tom and Margaret, just before the deception of Overreach is concluded, vow their love – but talk about danger and suffering. Though the characters, like the audience, are already reasonably confident of the lovers' success, Alworth speaks of his weakness, doubt, of the treachery of lovers, of his fear of her father, then offers a wish – 'faintly' – that she keep loving him. Margaret's commitment to suffering is even more imaginative, as she supposes the rage of Overreach to strike her: 'with lingring torments/In mind, and body, I must wast to ayre,/In pouerty, ioyn'd with banishment' (IV.iii.38–40). The relish of this language underscores Margaret's emulation of the aristocratic mode of virtue: suffering, abstinence, renunciation, in any order, so long as it rejects pleasure.

But renunciation and negation sweep in even more by the play's close. Marrall's trick that defeats Overreach, a chemical potion that manages to 'raze out' the deed to Welborne's lands (V.i.328), is a powerful image of erasure. Like the bare sketch of a note which gets Margaret married to young Alworth – the fewer words the better ('Marry her to this Gentleman', IV.iii.126) – this erased deed imagines victory by reduction and elimination. Tom himself, we recall, has been named 'virgin parchement' – and this second blank parchment will help him to a portion of Overreach's estate, through his marriage to Margaret and Lord Lovell's adjudication of Margaret's claims with Welborne's. Thus property will be redistributed without spilling of ink; a good part of Sir Giles's assets will, as he puts it, be 'made nothing!' (V.i.194). Made nothing, too, is the chalk register of Tapwell (which did not record a debt to Welborne), since his licence is withdrawn and his tavern closed. Tom Alworth is released from Lovell's service, and he is characterized not as a happy husband but as a gentleman relieved of the humility of his role as page. Finally, Welborne – now dressed in a new way and with his claims to his legacy restored – expresses his intention to undertake military service, specifically as the act of completing his 'halfe made vp' reformation (V.i.394). All victories in the play, with the exception of the marriage of convenience between Lord Lovell and Lady Alworth, are defined as erasures and negations.

Yet this is not all that needs to be said about the ways in which the play's aristocratic characters define values in negative terms. The other side of the coin represented by nostalgia and renunciation is downright aggressiveness. Sir Giles Overreach's egregious indifference to the means that achieve his ends has a dark, more covert parallel in the joyless and morally troublesome tactics of Welborne. The verbal abuse that attaches itself to Welborne in the first two acts of the play is transferred to Overreach in the remaining acts. Finally, Welborne is the catalyst for an intrigue by the noble characters which effectively concentrates and completes a process of objectification. Aggressive power changes from the motivation of a social outcast to the meaning behind the theatrical symbol of the usurer gone mad. While critics have noticed moral ambiguities surrounding the figure of Welborne, they identify them as weaknesses or 'problems' in the play,[16] rather than perceiving their fundamental relevance to the play's power and meaning.

The character of Welborne gives a grim tone to the play as a whole, as D. J. Enright notes:

> Much of the grimness is connected with Wellborn, who is distinguished from the conventional needy and dissolute gallant of Jacobean comedy by the bitter urgency behind his tirades and the way in which his ragged viciousness is interspersed with the remnants of good breeding.[17]

If anything, Enright does not go far enough, for Welborne embodies a *surplus* of aggression throughout *A New Way*. Though the protagonist of a Jacobean comedy may often employ aggressive or manipulative tactics, the moral questions raised by this are usually weighed in the context of some dominant satiric value, such as cleverness and wit in *The Alchemist*. But Welborne lacks such positive attributes, even the good-humoured and energetic cynicism of his counterpart, Witt-good, in the source play, Middleton's *A Trick to Catch the Old One*. Massinger makes little attempt in *A New Way* to present Welborne sympathetically on the grounds of wit. For instance, he prevents the audience from sharing the pleasure of intrigue by concealing Welborne's agreement with Lady Alworth – the crux of the plot – when it is formed. Welborne's intrigue is not really Jonsonian, as it is commonly described, nor does it closely resemble that of other Jacobean comedies. But this is not because Welborne is more serious and his intrigue more grave and decorous. Massinger has rather defined his own form of intrigue in which the bitter gallant is chiefly important for his feelings.[18]

Welborne's passion is social rather than sexual or intellectual, and it shapes our response to the play by taking the initiative in the remarkable first scene. Welborne's taut replies to Tapwell's story about the prodigal's past and Tapwell's own prosperous present have already been observed, but what needs emphasis is the way Welborne's incremental anger moves from threats to kicking and beating. The drubbing of Tapwell, accompanied by a rain of abuse for Tapwell as 'hell-hound', 'viper' and 'bawde' (I.i.72–89), is symbolic of Welborne's aggressiveness, here and throughout the play. Nothing in Tapwell's accurate story warrants it, except a tone of smugness – or warrants it in the thoroughly prepared way that a punitive drubbing does in a typical satiric comedy. We know little yet about either character; the punishment seems personal, intense. Moreover, the immediate turn in the talk between Welborne and Alworth, just afterwards, to matters of reputation seems to use decorum merely to succeed violence rather than to absorb or interpret it. The effect of the violence remains. Perhaps the most striking feature of the scene is the repetition of Welborne's aggression and rage at the scene's close, in a way that is radically discontinuous with its context. Welborne and Alworth have been talking intimately of Alworth's love for Margaret and of Welborne's ill fortune, when Alworth offers Welborne a loan of eight pieces. This is Welborne's reply:

> Money from thee?
> From a boy? a stipendary? one that liues
> At the deuotion of a stepmother,
> And the vncertaine fauour of a Lord?
> Ile eate my armes first. Howsoe're blind fortune
> Hath spent the vtmost of her malice on mee;
> Though I am vomited out of an Alehouse,
> And thus accoutred; know not where to eate,
> Or drinke, or sleepe, but vnderneath this Canopie;
> Although I thanke thee, I despise thy offer.   (I.i.172–81)

Welborne's imagery of eating and vomiting aligns his aggressive impulses with the obsession of Justice Greedy, and suggests that the two are equally self-absorbed and extravagant.

Welborne's aggressiveness is mirrored by the antagonism that he provokes in the other characters before Lady Alworth consents to help him. Recoil, revulsion, and disgust encircle the figure of the prodigal in rags. In the early scenes of the play the disdain of Tapwell and the taunts of Marrall, prompted by Overreach, are paralleled by the revulsion expressed by Lady Alworth, her servants, Sir Giles Overreach, and even Tom Alworth. It is not surprising that Overreach, on his first sight of Welborne, threatens to have him caged, thus unwittingly prefiguring his own fate, but even the much-admired Lady Alworth takes on a distinctly ungenteel tone in her reproof of Welborne's presence in her home, calling him a 'Sonne of infamie' and 'an eye-sore' (I.iii.80, 84). The obedient Tom Alworth, obliging his step-mother, cuts Welborne dead when he appears at her home, some-thing to which Welborne replies cynically: 'Better, and better. He contemnes mee too?' (I.iii.52). Though Tom later apologizes, the moment undercuts the play's only friendship among equals – ironically confirming Sir Giles Overreach's 'wicked' viewpoint, spoken about Greedy: 'let him hang, or damne, I care not./ Friend-ship is but a word' (II.i.21–2).

Lady Alworth's servants display most economically the vag-aries of regard to which the tattered prodigal is subject. Order, Furnace, and the maidservants provide comic business as they ridicule Welborne's smell and want to banish him to privy and pig-sty (I.iii.48, 53–5). Their ridicule stresses Welborne's humili-ation, and Welborne is clearly motivated by his angry humili-ation when he links his request for Lady Alworth's critical help (in deceiving Overreach) to an apparently equivalent matter, a request that her servants treat him with more respect. And they do the next time he appears, so fulsomely as to suggest that in Lady Alworth's world excessive decorum is not only compensa-tion for humiliation but its other face.

Furnace is linked with Welborne with particular closeness. The second scene of the play parallels the first one; it ironically projects Welborne's rage into the unexpected tirade of the cook Furnace, who complains that Lady Alworth ignores his culinary miracles while Greedy devours them. Like Welborne, Furnace shows pride of place: 'Twit me with the Authority of the kitchin?/At all houres, and all places Ile be angrie' (I.ii.13–14). Furnace's extravagant expressions of outraged dignity comically duplicate Welborne's serious ones. The portrait of Greedy's gar-gantuan hunger, which draws on the conventional view of gross appetite (and sets off the nobles' abstemiousness), is less inter-esting than the play's treatment of Furnace and his culinary imagery. In a significant moment, immediately after Lady Al-worth signals Welborne's respectability by graciously receiving him, Furnace directs his contempt elsewhere. Furnace's speech clarifies what happens to the general revulsion once Welborne begins his intrigue:

> Would I had
> The roasting of his heart, that cheated him,
> And forces the poore gentleman to these shiftes.
> By Fire (for Cookes are *Persians*, and sweare by it)
> Of all the griping, and extorting tyrants
> I euer heard, or read of, I ne're met
> A match to Sir *Giles Ouerreach*.   (II.ii.97–103)

Overreach becomes everyone's object of recoil, and Welborne the 'poor gentleman'.

As the play proceeds, Welborne's aggression is integrated into the nobles' intrigue plot, and apparently mitigated by it. But Welborne's language suggests otherwise; he keeps up a running commentary that interprets that intrigue in terms of aggression, contempt, and cruelty. When Welborne, dressed in a 'rich habit', receives the petitions of his creditors (IV.ii), he is contemptuous and self-serving. He bribes Marrall with promises of advancement and Justice Greedy with a yoke of oxen, then bribes the surgeon and Lady Alworth's servants to keep quiet about his sexual disease. He calls Tapwell and his former associates 'the scumme that grew rich by my riots' (IV.ii.55). Having used Marrall and Greedy as Overreach does, to serve his own ends, he brutally rejects Marrall when finished with him: 'Thanke my pittie/If thou keep thy eares, how e're I will take order/Your practise shall be silenc'd' (V.i.342–4). Welborne relishes threatening the 'false servant' that he himself has helped to create. Again, in the ensembles of nobles around the mad Overreach, who is frozen in his place, Welborne calls for Overreach to be disarmed and bound, and seems to enjoy, along with Lovell, a certain *frisson* of revulsion:

> *Lovell.*   How he fomes!
> *Welborne.* And bites the earth.
>
>   (V.i.375–6)

If Welborne's ravenous anger projects this image, it seems also to be behind Marrall's climactic rage at Overreach for exploiting him. Welborne has used Marrall too, and now cheers him on – 'to him again' – as if Marrall, like Furnace previously, rages for him. The meaning of the play's intrigue against Overreach, initiated by Welborne and interpreted by him, is clarified by an anger which only utter humiliation will satisfy.

From this point of view, the play has provided a worthy antagonist for Overreach, in the form of every other major character in the play, as combined in the two intrigues. Though the plot in which Margaret Overreach and Tom Alworth conspire to marry is interpolated with Welborne's plot against Overreach, the two actions appear to be a single, concentrated intrigue. The presentation of the aristocrats is one reason for this; the powerful portrait of the usurer is the other. It is the vitality of his language more than the effectiveness of his actions which makes Sir Giles Overreach a comic villain of such scope. As the play seeks to control him, it labours against our sympathy for one – evil as he is – who renounces nothing, and celebrates everything there is to desire.

As a comic villain, Sir Giles is an original and important derivation from the line of Marlovian and Jonsonian rogues.[19] The scope of his assertions thus functions in a Jonsonian way, dynamically, to subvert him by ironic reduction while it heightens him by imaginative enlargement.[20] If to one reader he is 'a great force, a small mind', to another he is 'a force of nature' and 'not mean-souled', because 'the aristocratic lustre on which his eyes are fixed' is the 'earthly crown of Tamburlaine's desire in a new setting'.[21] A critic who would resolve these divergent responses, in order to see the single, coherent figure that actors have admired, needs to look at this language, at the dazzling, self-absorbed speeches that seem like monologues even when other characters are present.

Sir Giles Overreach is a consistent character, not an ambiguous one. He candidly publishes his own callousness and tyranny, and beneath his bragging is an acuteness which is much more precise about his spiritual and psychological perversion than are the horrified intimations of the other characters. In the scene between Lovell and Overreach, for example, Lovell responds to Overreach's tirades by asking if he is not 'frighted with the imprecations,/And curses, of whole families made wretched/By your sinister practises' (IV.i.111–13). Overreach's cosy reply is deservedly notorious: 'Yes as rocks are/When foamie billowes split themselues against/Their flinty ribbes' (IV.i.113–15), but one should give equal time to the act of self-recognition in the conclusion of his speech. When widows' cries and orphans' tears come close, he says,

> I only thinke what 'tis to haue my daughter
> Right honorable; and 'tis a powerfull charme
> Makes me insensible of remorse, or pitty,
> Or the least sting of Conscience.   (IV.i.128–31)

Lovell's conventional view of the wages of sin is juxtaposed with Overreach's unorthodox illumination; to Overreach, 'right honorable' is a kind of superstitious defence that clears the horizon of desire of its dangers of regret, scruple, and pity. Overreach's singularity is more aptly defined by himself than by others, and it expresses a continuously conscious isolation.

Overreach's isolation is too spirited to be pitiable. At the height of his self-deception, when Tom Alworth and Margaret Overreach run off to marry, with Overreach's approval in their pockets, and he seems to have Lady Alworth's lands within reach, Sir Giles irrepressibly speaks from that longing for respectability and its forms which marks every major character in the play:

> Farewell; now all's cocke-sure:
> Me thinkes I heare already, Knights, and Ladies,
> Say Sir *Giles Ouerreach*, how is it with
> Your Honourable daughter? has her Honour
> Slept well to night? or will her Honour please
> To accept this Monkey? Dog? or Paraquit?
> (This is state in Ladies) or my eldest sonne
> To be her page, and wait vpon her trencher?
> My ends! my ends are compass'd! then for *Welborne*
> And the lands; were he once married to the widdow,
> I haue him here, I can scarce containe my selfe,
> I am so full of ioy; nay ioy all ouer.   (IV.iii.130–41)

By reducing the status he seeks for his daughter to this droll miniature, Sir Giles goads and teases his own imagination. Yet the passage is not exclusively ironic. Overreach's view of the ritual courtesies, gifts and forms of service proper to the noble rank is an attractively silly contrast to the grim decorums of Welborne or the pale Alworth, and the value he places on privilege is of course the same. But it is the climactic stress on *joy* which most engages our sympathy. Sir Giles Overreach pursues his aims for the pleasures of enjoyment, not of renunciation. Given the forces of negation and denial around him, with which we are hard put to identify, Overreach easily becomes the focus of our dramatic sympathy, a figure pushed inevitably forward by his need for joy.

Overreach does live up to his name. But this is not because Massinger dramatizes horrific abuses by Overreach in the play. Though we hear, from Overreach, of a sequence of wicked strategies designed to attain the lands of the farmer Frugal, these are plots, not actions, and the limit of Overreach's real power has been attained by the play's opening. His pragmatism is associated with spiritual perversion, however, in Marrall's failed attempt to counsel Welborne to commit suicide, and in Overreach's own effort to persuade his daughter to prostitute herself as a means to marrying Lovell. Yet both scenes are almost comic in their effects. Welborne, calling Marrall's arguments the 'fiend's' rhetoric, answers his challenge to despair by asserting his confidence in 'what respect I am entertain'd' (II.i.137–8), as if respectability were sufficient spiritual consolation. And Overreach's attempts to urge Margaret to win Lovell by kiss and tell, though a powerful instance of the blind solipsism of his rhetoric, are undercut through Margaret's own pious decorum ('In your house?' and 'This is but Diuelish doctrine', III.ii.126, 122), and through the constant interruptions of the food-obsessed Greedy. This instance of Overreach's malevolence, the most vivid in the play, is another major failure for Overreach, and the play busily suppresses the potential engagement of an audience in his oratory.

Overreach, in seeking to marry Margaret to Lord Lovell, does not really initiate a new 'adulteration' of blood, to use Lovell's word, since Welborne himself is the product of a marriage between Overreach and Welborne's aunt. And the lands of Welborne are simply one part of Overreach's existing economic power. In point of fact, Overreach falls in readily with the deceptions of Welborne, and is easily duped by what the play itself admits is the 'simplicity' of the intrigue to marry Margaret to Alworth (v.i.37). Overreach, as the facts of the play indicate, is not the devilish agent who threatens the overthrow of established society, as the nobles see it, but a long-established economic and social power in the county who is himself threatened by overthrow.

But we cannot see him entirely as a victim; like the aristocratic characters, he will embrace any available means to pursue his self-interest. In the course of the play, such means are primarily reducible to his vital language. Unlike the aristocratic characters or their imitator, Margaret, whose rhetoric is steadily discontinuous with action and feeling, Sir Giles *is* what he says. And if what he says emerges as a grotesque overvaluation of language, as when he tells Margaret 'Virgin me no Virgins' (III.ii.112) – seeing Margaret's mind and body, like friendship, only as a word – our judgement of him is qualified by a dramatic sympathy which overrides condemnation. Overreach, as the name suggests, always wants more than he can do, and in *A New Way to Pay Old Debts*, he is at bay.

It is time to return to the question of what this reading implies about the nature of the play's comic form. Though *A New Way* does allude to its predecessors in Renaissance comedy, it is much more than a late hybrid. Its debts are clear enough: to the romance and pathos of Fletcher, to the rogues and humour characters of Jonsonian satiric comedy, and to an occasionally Shakespearian touch in its language, especially at the close. Even Morality elements may be present, if problematically realized.[22] If we seek not a troublesome mixture of satire and romance but a single form, we might nominate, as some have, the citizen or city comedy of early Jacobean England. But this identification may be equally difficult, given the play's lack of a London setting, its ostensible rejection of a middle-class point of view, and the scale and complexity of its portrait of the usurer.[23] *A New Way* is probably closer to the tradition of problem comedy, and to those tragedies adjacent to problem comedy which similarly explore the borders between tragic and comic genres. In plays like *Measure for Measure*, *The Merchant of Venice*, *The Changeling*, and *The Duchess of Malfi*, there is a continuous displacement of feeling by language. This displacement, whether activated in tragic events or in dark, often stagy comic displays, evokes a world of social and philosophical uncertainty, which it centres and examines through a powerful and ambiguous central figure, such as Duke Vincentio, Shylock, Beatrice, or Bosola.[24] *A New Way* shares these general features with its tradition but it is a significantly later play. Its playwright Massinger is one who looks back, as he evokes current tension and uncertainty, to the moral authority of an earlier day and a simpler form: revenge tragedy. *A New Way to Pay Old Debts* is – what else? – Massinger's revenge comedy.

The play is formed, as I have shown, as a concentrated intrigue which pits Sir Giles Overreach against a conspiracy of noble characters, who use ideology to rationalize an aggressive power that matches his own. The eloquence of Sir Giles makes him a formidable antagonist, and the play's handling of its central scenes seeks to curtail the comic villain's power over audience sympathy and imagination. But the dramatic values of the play do not deliver either a satiric measure of justice or a romantic figuration of affirmation. What they offer is the theatrical liveliness of a revenge play, with its donnée in a revenger's justification, its parallel intrigues, its grand speeches, and its terrible and ironic climax.[25] The odd and fascinating thing about *A New Way* as a revenge comedy is that Massinger does not succeed in giving to Welborne the automatic moral authority of the revenger, and because he does not the play is enormously vital.

The ending of the play, when Sir Giles Overreach, defeated and maddened, seeks to override through the sheer force of his heroic language the intriguers arrayed against him, is neither ambiguous nor disturbing. Sir Giles, surrounded and still desiring, carries away the play, as actors who have played him in this scene have carried away their audiences. This ending is no random theatrical opportunity: it is the inevitable closure of the play. The nostalgia for a surer social order, the commitment to abstinence and renunciation, and the sheer aggressiveness which combine in Welborne's intrigue have succeeded in undoing the power of Overreach, and his own self-deception and evil have played their part. But like the prospect of Volpone cramped with irons, the image of Sir Giles caged in Bedlam ironically emphasizes his sheer size, his hold over our imaginations. In defeat he is still like himself:

> shall I then fall
> Ingloriously, and yeeld? no, spite of fate
> I will be forc'd to hell like to my selfe;
> Though you were legions of accursed spiritts,
> Thus would I flie among you.   (v.i.369–73)

There are finally two Sir Giles Overreaches. The first is the consistent character envisioned by Overreach himself, with his anti-social, egotistical values and the terrific energy that comes from the largeness of his designs. The other is the inconsistent compendium of vices and follies seen by everyone else in the play

189

– the Sir Giles that Welborne wants to see bite the earth. The noble characters, embodied in Welborne, treat Overreach as a cipher for all of the features of social life – many of which they unintentionally embody themselves – that they would like to repudiate or deny. He is a scapegoat for their repressions, and the play itself represses him by deferring his entrance and overdoing his final exit, as if to punish him by a parody of Tamburlainian aggressiveness that is finally unpersuasive.

The play achieves a far richer illumination of the social and economic uncertainties of its age than that supplied by the social doctrines of its noble characters. At least one part of Massinger may agree with those characters. But the dramatist created a play about its 'decadent' age, one in which conservative Tudor attitudes are belied by the presentation of aristocratic values as tactics. The play's dramatization of class conflict is far more complex than a simple and morally clear opposition between a bourgeois usurer and a threatened gentry; it is an emphatically current representation of the insecurities and tensions of the close of James's reign.[26] *A New Way to Pay Old Debts* is, at last, an example of the vitality of comic form in the Renaissance and Massinger's contribution to it.

NOTES

1   T. S. Eliot, 'Philip Massinger', in *The Sacred Wood* (1920), rpt. *Elizabethan Essays* (London, Faber and Faber, 1934), pp.153–76. See also M. St Clare Byrne, 'Introduction' to her edn of *A New Way to Pay Old Debts* (1956; rpt. Westport, Ct., Greenwood Press, 1976), pp.5–16; and Robert Hamilton Ball, *The Amazing Career of Sir Giles Overreach* (Princeton, Princeton University Press, 1939), especially pp.383–6.

2   See G. Wilson Knight, *The Golden Labyrinth: A Study of British Drama* (New York, Norton, 1962), pp.117–20; and Philip Edwards, 'Massinger the Censor', in *Essays on Shakespeare and Elizabethan Drama in Honor of Hardin Craig*, ed. Richard Hosley (Columbia, University of Missouri Press, 1962), pp.341–50.

3   Robert A. Fothergill, 'The Dramatic Experience of Massinger's *The City Madam* and *A New Way to Pay Old Debts*', *University of Toronto Quarterly*, 43 (1973), 68–86; see p.77.

4   After Eliot's essay, see, for example, Alexander Leggatt, *Citizen Comedy in the Age of Shakespeare* (Toronto, University of Toronto Press, 1973), especially pp.65–70; and D. J. Enright, 'Poetic Satire and Satire in Verse: A Consideration of Jonson and Massinger', *Scrutiny*, 18 (1951),

211–23. Enright's article contains a brief but very acute treatment of *A New Way*, and I am indebted to it.

5   Leggatt, *Citizen Comedy*, p.70.

6   Patricia Thomson, 'The Old Way and the New Way in Dekker and Massinger', *Modern Language Review*, 51 (1956), 168–78; Alan Gerald Gross, 'Social Change and Philip Massinger', *Studies in English Literature, 1500–1900*, 7 (1967), 329–42; Allen Gross, 'Contemporary Politics in Massinger', *Studies in English Literature, 1500–1900*, 6 (1966), 279–90; Frederick M. Burelbach, Jr, '*A New Way to Pay Old Debts*: Jacobean Morality', *CLA Journal*, 12 (1969), 205–13. The most effective recent statement of this position is Michael Neill's, in his 'Massinger's Patriarchy: The Social Vision of *A New Way to Pay Old Debts*', *Renaissance Drama*, n.s. 10 (1979), 185–213.

7   Neill, 'Massinger's Patriarchy', pp.195–6.

8   Thomson, 'The Old Way and the New Way', pp.175–6.

9   All citations of Massinger's *A New Way to Pay Old Debts* are made from the edition of Philip Edwards and Colin Gibson, *The Plays and Poems of Philip Massinger* (5 vols., Oxford, Clarendon Press, 1976), vol. 2.

10 Gāmini Salgādo, Introduction to his edn of *Four Jacobean City Comedies* (Harmondsworth, Middlesex, Penguin Books, 1975), p.26.

11 Cyrus Hoy, 'Verbal Formulae in the Plays of Philip Massinger', *Studies in Philology*, 56 (1959), 600–18; see p.601.

12 Eugene M. Waith, *The Pattern of Tragicomedy in Beaumont and Fletcher* (New Haven, Yale University Press, 1952), pp.187–9.

13 Thomson, 'The Old Way and the New Way', p.175.

14 Neill notes the contrast between present and past in this scene while interpreting it differently; 'Massinger's Patriarchy', pp.196–9.

15 When Overreach marks this quality in Alworth and Margaret – 'I like this obedience' (v.iii.66) – he is being misled by them, but he is right to see it as a passivity that can be used, not as a stoic endurance. The play does not dramatize a stoical view of virtue, as Benjamin T. Spencer would have it in 'Philip Massinger', in *Seventeenth Century Studies*, ed. Robert Shafer (Princeton, Princeton University Press, 1933), pp.3–119.

16 Enright, 'Poetic Satire and Satire in Verse'; Fothergill, 'The Dramatic Experience of Massinger's *The City Madam* and *A New Way to Pay Old Debts*'; and for the fullest statement of this point of view, Leggatt, *Citizen Comedy*, pp.66–9. Leggatt points particularly to Welborne's ruthless use of Marrall, and to Welborne's evasiveness about his debauchery until the end of the play.

17 Enright, 'Poetic Satire and Satire in Verse', pp.220–1.

18 Unlike T. S. Eliot (pp.168–9) and M. St Clare Byrne (p.12), I would not connect this stress on feeling to eighteenth-century sentimental drama, but to Massinger's response to earlier forms of Renaissance drama.

19 In my view, this is the proper historical context for Sir Giles, as opposed to the idea that he represents a topical satire on Sir Giles Mompesson. L. C. Knights, comparing Overreach to Barabas, Volpone, and Sir Epicure Mammon, anticipates me in this point; see his *Drama and Society in*

the Age of Jonson (1937; rpt. New York, Norton, 1968), pp.274–6. That Overreach is intended as a specific parallel to Mompesson seems even less probable if you accept, as I do, the convincing arguments of Philip Edwards and Colin Gibson for a 1625 date of first performance of the play, several years after the exposure of Mompesson; see the introduction to their edition of *A New Way to Pay Old Debts* in Edwards and Gibson, vol. 2, pp.273–9.

20 The complex interplay between romantic sympathy and satiric judgement in responses to the rogue should be seen as central to Jonson's form of comedy, and I find it in Overreach; see my 'Shakespeare and Jonson Again: The Comic Forms', in *Renaissance Drama*, n.s. 10 (1979), 45–69.

21 The first reader is T. S. Eliot in 'Philip Massinger' (p.23), and the second, G. Wilson Knight in *The Golden Labyrinth* (p.120).

22 On Morality elements, see Neill, 'Massinger's Patriarchy', pp.208–13.

23 On citizen comedy and *A New Way*'s relation to it, see Leggatt, *Citizen Comedy*, pp.3–13, 28–32, 65–70; on city comedy, see Brian Gibbons's *Jacobean City Comedy*, 2nd edn (London and New York, Methuen, 1980), which is especially helpful in relating city comedy to its social and economic context, though Gibbons himself dismisses Massinger's work in passing (p.159).

24 Such a form seems even more obvious in *The City Madam*, though I cannot argue the point here; the depiction of Luke Frugal, the handling of rhetoric and the energies behind the play all seem similar to their counterparts in *A New Way*.

25 Remarkably enough, *A New Way* adapts, in ways appropriate to comedy, all twelve characteristics of the revenge play as Fredson Bowers has defined them. Here they are, with necessary explanations in parenthesis: the fundamental motive of the play is revenge; the revenge is called forth by revenge upon a son (Giles's exploitation of Welborne's lands); supernatural elements are present (dead fathers and the erased letter); the revenger's hesitation is justifiable, given the failure of legal justice; madness is important; the intrigue is used by and against the revenger; the action is bloody and deaths abound (adapted for comedy: violent, aggressive language and drubbings on both sides); parallels provide contrast and enforcement of the main situation; the accomplices on both sides are killed (comically, are rewarded and punished); the villain is Machiavellian; the revenge is accomplished 'terribly, fittingly, with irony and deceit'; and there are minor devices such as the wearing of black (the wearing of tatters) or a bloody letter (the marriage letter). Bowers, *Elizabethan Revenge Tragedy, 1587–1642* (1940; rpt. Princeton, Princeton University Press, 1966), pp.71–3.

26 For a good treatment of the social and economic insecurities that I see reflected by the play, see Gibbons, *Jacobean City Comedy*, especially the first three chapters, and note 23 above for his position on Massinger. Gibbons cites G. R. Elton's warning against imposing on the Tudor period theories of class derived from nineteenth-century sociology, which create oversimplified readings of plays as enactments of a conflict between the capitalist new man and the landed gentry (pp.32–3).

'The Tongues of Angels': Charity and the Social Order in *The City Madam*

MICHAEL NEILL

'THOUGH you spake with the tongues of Angels to me,/I am not to be alter'd'[1]: when Luke Frugal dismisses the appeals of his desperate creditors for 'patience' and 'charity' in this sardonic parody of St Paul, he signals what has become the ruling theme of Massinger's comedy of City manners – 'Though I speak with the tongues of men and of angels, and have not charity, I am become as sounding brass or a tinkling cymbal.'[2] The episode, like many others in the play, is contrived as a formal tableau, illustrating with comic patness Luke's profession of his new faith in the preceding scene:

> Religion, conscience, charity, farewell.
> To me you are words onely, and no more,
> All humane happinesse consists in store. (IV.ii.131–3)[3]

In charity, Massinger suggests, is the proof of religion and conscience; and the very words in which Luke rejects it – 'like the Adder [I] stop mine ears' (IV.iii.45) – mark him as one of the Psalmist's 'ungodly' who are 'as venemous as the poison of a serpent: even like the deaf adder that stoppeth her ears'.[4] The refusal of charity is more than a mere sin of omission; it becomes, as these perversions of scripture wittily suggest, a sign of diabolic inspiration, for Luke is the apostle of an idolatrous Pentecost, filled with the powerful language of the only 'angels' this world recognizes – gold coins.[5] These are not casual touches but characteristic devices of a comedy whose argument, like that of Massinger's earlier *A New Way to Pay Old Debts*,[6] hangs upon an elaboration of familiar scriptural texts. Underlying the entire action is St Matthew's parable of the Unjust Debtor (Matthew 18.21–35): a certain servant owed a vast debt, to meet which 'his lord commanded him to be sold, and his wife, and children, and all that he had'; upon the servant's prostrate appeal for patience, the master, 'moved with compassion', forgave him the debt; the servant responded to this gesture by dunning one of his fellows for a trifling sum, denying his appeal for patience and throwing him into prison; the master, learning of this ingratitude, 'delivered him to the tormentors, till he should pay all that was due unto him'.

The parable answers a question about the nature of charity – 'how oft shall my brother sin against me, and I forgive him?' – in terms of a financial fable directly applicable to Massinger's world of City merchants; and the play repeats its pattern in Sir John Frugal's redemption of his younger brother from the bonds of debt, in Luke's merciless treatment of Fortune, Penurie and Hoyst, and in the ingrate's condemnation to the final torment of exile in the 'desert' of Virginia until he repents. Visually this parable is further echoed in a series of striking tableaux of appeal, culminating in the mute eloquence of the 'magic' spectacle which follows the Masque of Orpheus in Act v, Scene iii ('*They all kneel to* Luke, *heaving up their hands for mercy*' line 59 SD), and in the penitent prostration of Sir John's household at the end of the same scene (v.iii.81–125).[7] Combined with the Unjust Debtor is a second parable, St Luke's Waiting Servants, in which a Lord, having made his 'faithful and wise steward . . . ruler over his household to give them their portion of meat in due season', returns to find him abusing his authority:

if that servant say in his heart, My Lord delayeth his coming; and shall begin to beat the menservants and maidens, and to eat and drink, and to be drunken; the lord of that servant will come in a day when he looketh not for him, and at an hour when he is not aware . . . and will appoint him his portion with the unbelievers. (Luke 12.45–6)

In like manner, Sir John, having ostensibly retired into a monastery and given his brother power over his household as 'A faithful steward to his wife and daughters' (III.iii.67), returns when least expected to uncover Luke's iniquitous mistreatment of his family, and to 'appoint him his portion' amongst the pagan unbelievers of Virginia. This latter parable belongs to a passage in which Christ warns his disciples against the sin of covetousness:

But God said unto him, Thou fool, this night thy soul shall be required of thee: then whose shall those things be, which thou hast provided? So is he that layeth up treasure for himself, and is not rich toward God.
. . .

Sell that ye have, and give alms; provide yourselves bags which wax not old, a treasure in the heavens that faileth not, where no thief approacheth, neither moth corrupteth. For where your treasure is, there will your heart be also.

(Luke 12.20–1, 33–4)

This sermon sets covetousness against the charity of alms-giving with an image that Massinger deliberately evokes in the tableau of Luke emerging from his counting house – a 'sacred room' (III.iii.19) which he sees as 'Heaven's abstract, or Epitome' (line 31), the treasury of his own 'heart' (line 17) which his fevered imagination makes the helpless prey of 'thievs' (line 45).

Properly speaking, of course, charity (*caritas*) is by no means confined to alms-giving. Indeed, though alms may be a fit expression of Christian love, the one does not necessarily imply the other, as St Paul insisted: 'though I bestow all my goods to feed the poor ... and have not charity, it profiteth me nothing' (1 Corinthians 13.3). In the seventeenth century, however, one can detect an appreciable narrowing of the word's meaning; increasingly it tends to refer to expressions of material generosity – and, more than that, to those forms of institutionalized benevolence which the word principally describes in our own day. The late sixteenth and early seventeenth centuries were marked, as the historian of philanthropy, W. K. Jordan, has shown, by 'an immense outpouring of charitable wealth',[8] a phenomenon which had significant political and social, as well as religious implications. On the one hand it reflected the ideology of the Elizabethan Poor Law, the 'almost obsessive preoccupation of [the Tudor] rulers with the question of public order' – an order which seemed to them dangerously threatened by the growing masses of vagrant poor;[9] on the other hand, financed as it principally was by the new class of wealthy City merchants, it answered both to this group's enhanced sense of social prestige, and to its broadly Puritan commitment to the doctrine of the stewardship of wealth.[10]

While Calvinists repudiated the Catholic belief in justification by works, they acknowledged that good works remained a fruit of grace demanded by God of his saints; wealth, though it might be a sign of divine favour, was lent rather than given; the rich were accountable to God for its use, and the obligation of mercy required that they distribute their surplus to the poor: 'the rich man,' declared one preacher, 'is no more than Gods steward and the poore mans treasurer', so that (in the words of Henry Smith) the wealthy must reckon 'the overplus of their riches none of theirs, but the poores, whom they slay and murther, asmuch as in them lieth, when they detaine it.'[11] Charity, the Puritan divines insisted, 'is the badge or cognisance of Christ, and the very character of a Christian ... He is no Christian man therefore, he is scarce a man, that hath no compassion of other mens miseries ... It argueth a want of love to Christ, when men have no commiseration of the members of Christ, being in want or misery, in distresse, danger or extremitie.'[12] But what was a sign of faith might also be good business, as Perkins, in a characteristically blunt paraphrase of St Luke, reminded his readers: alms-giving is 'the best kinde of thrift or husbandry' because it is a kind of pious usury, 'lending ... to the Lord, who in his good time will return the gift with increase'.[13] Charity, moreover, is clearly recognized as an indispensable adjunct of the social order: extremes of wealth and poverty are created by God specifically in order to provide an occasion for expressions of charitable mercy;[14] and true charity must never be confused with that levelling impulse which seeks to remove social divisions and disturb the proper ordering of the members of Christ's mystical body;[15] rather the exercise of charity acts, by alleviating the wretchedness of the poor, as a necessary plaster to social discontents.

There is of course a good scriptural basis for such a broad social reading of charity: St Paul, in that same passage of 1 Corinthians from which Massinger's Luke draws his mock text, sees patience, humility and self-restraint as aspects of true charity: 'Charity suffereth long, and is kind; charity envieth not; charity vaunteth not itself, is not puffed up. Doth not behave itself unseemly'; and in Colossians he presents charity as a social bond whose effectiveness depends on each person's recognition of his allotted place in the social order:

put on charity, which is the bond of perfectness ... Wives, submit yourselves unto your own husbands ... Children, obey your parents ... Servants, obey in all things your masters according to the flesh ... knowing that of the Lord ye shall receive the reward of the inheritance ... Masters, give unto your servants that which is just and equal. (Colossians 3.14–24; 4.1)

An important part of St Paul's idea of charity is the belief, widely argued in the seventeenth century, that this virtue involves not merely certain positive obligations towards the needy, but also significant restraints on the activities of the affluent – on the sharpness of their business practice, the extravagance of their lifestyle, and the reach of their social ambition. Thus Thomas Adams's tract, *The White Devil* (1613), inveighs against the pretence that alms-giving can atone for commercial overreaching:

It is not seasonable, nor reasonable charitie, to undoe whole townes by your usuries, enclosings, oppressions, impropriations; and for a kind of expiation, to give three or foure the yeerely pension of twentie markes: an almeshouse is not so big as a village.[16]

Equally reprehensible is that 'monstrous pride' which turns the charitable duty of 'hospitality into a dumbe shew' of conspicuous consumption, so that 'that which fed the belly of hunger, now feedes the eie of lust'; 'where lies the wealth of England?' asks Adams, 'in three places, on citizens tables, in usurers coffers, and upon courtiers backes.'[17] Charles Richardson's *Sermon Against Oppression* links hunger for status with prodigal expenditure as another expression of that covetousness which robs the poor to feed the rich:

men having gotten a deale of wealth together, give many hundreth pounds, to buy one degree of honour after another, to make themselves great in the world, & I know not how many thousand poundes, to advance their daughters in marriage, to make them ladies or great personages.[18]

This was a mode of amibition which Massinger had attacked in his first comedy, *A New Way to Pay Old Debts*, where the titanic greed of Sir Giles Overreach is equally manifested in the extravagant style of his housekeeping –

> To grow rich, and then purchase, is too common:
> But this Sir *Giles* feedes high, keepes many seruants,
> ...
> Rich in his habit; vast in his expences. (II.ii.109–10, 112)[19]

– and in his consuming social drive to have his daughter, at whatever cost, made 'right honourable'. Sir Giles is a City parvenu, a usurer villain who has married into the gentry and turned his eyes on landed wealth; but *A New Way* is not strictly a City play. Its country setting is of a piece with its commitment to the aristocratic values of the patron to whom Massinger offered it; accordingly its ideas of charity do not go beyond the old-fashioned conception of noble 'housekeeping' in which the dramatist found the idealized model of a benevolent patriarchal society. *The City Madam*, though it often remembers the earlier play, takes a new direction.[20]

As the sardonic oxymoron of his title suggests,[21] Massinger's London is a society, like his Nottinghamshire, engaged in a furious competition for wealth and status. The model for this society is once again that 'little commonwealth', the family — here converted to a 'house of pride' (II.ii.187). Sir John Frugal's patriarchy has been turned upside down by the ambitious revolt of those 'wise virago's' his wife and daughters (II.ii.166). The dramatized prologue, framed by the commentary of the prentices Tradewell and Goldwire, introduces us to a family whose natural 'shape and proportion' (I.i.20) is already distorted by an ambition which 'Swells my young Mistresses, and their madam mother,/With hopes above their birth, and scale' (lines 16–17). Not content with reducing her prodigal brother-in-law, Luke, to a condition of humiliating slavery (lines 36–48), in which the slightest murmur is construed as 'rebellious' (line 103), Lady Frugal extends her attack on the masculine hierarchy by challenging her own husband's sovereignty. Her consciousness of the implications of this challenge is registered in her openly political language; the making up of marriages, she claims, belongs to the realm of female prerogative:

> And I by speciall priviledge may challenge
> A casting voice ...
> In these affairs I govern.
>
> ...
>
> You may consult of somthing else, this Province
> Is wholly mine.   (II.ii.15–17, 19–20)

Sir John, like some reluctant constitutional monarch, still claims 'the power to do' (line 23) while effectively abandoning it to his wife; and the full extent of the female insurrection is exposed in the marriage treaty which the Frugal women seek to impose on the suitors, Plenty and Sir Maurice Lacie, in a brutal anticipation of the Restoration 'proviso scene'.[22] Encouraged by Stargaze's prophecy of 'rule, preheminence, and absolute sovearigity in women' (lines 84–5), Anne and Mary insist on 'articles' and 'conditions' of the most draconian character, 'obedient Husband[s]' and 'the Countries Soveraignty' (lines 127, 179). Nothing short of complete surrender will serve.

Since Massinger conceives of social hierarchies in terms of a seamless web of duty and obedience, it is entirely fitting that this domestic revolt should be linked with even more extravagant social ambitions. Like Sir Giles Overreach, Lady Frugal is a rebel commander who imagines victory in terms of usurpation rather than revolutionary overthrow; accordingly her ambition turns her City household into 'a little Court, in bravery' (I.i.24) – not merely in 'Variety of fashions' and other forms of conspicuous consumption, but in its ridiculous obsession with the 'addition[s]' of court life, titles, marks of distinction, and nicely graded honorifics (lines 9–11). She has taught her daughters to dream of becoming 'Countesses' (I.i.18); they long for 'Princely Husbands' (III.ii.197) and dismiss Lord Lacie with the contemptuous observation that he is 'but a Lord' – their thoughts 'soar higher' (III.ii.188–9); her very waiting woman nourishes fantasies of precedence which recall Overreach's schemes for humiliating the 'true gentry':[23]

> I hope to see
> A Country Knights son and heir walk bare before you
> When you are a Countess, as you may be one
> When my Master dies, or leavs trading; and I continuing
> Your principal woman, take the upper-hand
> Of a Squire's wife, though a Justice.   (I.i.72–7)

When Sir John's bogus will announces his 'Jubile of joy', Luke continues to cocker up their vanity by promising that they will triumphally revive 'the pomp ... Of the Roman matrons, who kept captive Queens/To be their handmaids' (III.ii.161–3); he answers Lord Lacie's strictures on the 'decorum' by which 'the Court [should be]/Distinguished from the City' (lines 152–3), with a vision of a sumptuous masquing world in which Lady Frugal will appear 'Like *Juno* in full majesty, and my Neeces/Like *Iris*, *Hebe*, or what deities else/Old Poets fancie' (lines 164–6). And even after Luke has scourged their vanity through his wryly chosen role of 'new satirist' in Act IV, Scene iv, Lady Frugal's pride is still sufficiently fantastic to be briefly seduced by his preposterous offer to make them all 'Queens in another climate' (V.i.99); indeed she is deterred only by the revelation that their proposed 'seat of majesty' is to be none other than the dreaded Virginia – a place they wisely reckon fit only for the transportation of 'Strumpets and Bauds' (lines 104, 108).

Actually the intended punishment is by no means arbitrary: in the abortive proviso scene the infuriated Sir Maurice sneeringly suggested that the most fitting husband for their minxships would be 'The general pimp to a Brothel' (II.ii.194); and Massinger means to suggest that their determination to trade their portions and persons for status is no better than a kind of whoredom. It is Dingem, pimp-general to Shavem, who cynically reminds Young Goldwire that in 'marriage, and the other thing too,/The commoditie is the same' (III.i.80–1); and Shavem's term-driving relationship with her clients merely repeats in a lower key the Frugal girls' relationship with their suitors. The hectors, Ramble and Scuffle, come swaggering and roaring to her door in III.i, as Plenty and young Lacie brawled before Frugal's in I.ii; with the assistance of the disguised Goldwire and Dingem, they are humbled and forced to kneel to 'Mistris *Shavem*' and 'Mistris *Secret*' for mercy, as the suitors were meant to prostrate themselves before 'Mistris *Anne* and *Mary*'. Shavem, that 'brave virago' (line 67), relishes her conquest with all the tyrannical extravagance of a Lady Frugal: 'I am their soveraign, and they my vassalls,/For homage kiss my Shoo-sole rogues, and vanish' (lines 65–6). Not surprisingly Shavem's imagination plays on her own dreams of conspicuous consumption – coaches, muskmelons, asparagus, mutton and wine (lines 12–22); and though she hyperbolically affects to prefer prentices to 'Lords ... Commanders,/And country heirs' (lines 86–8), she too is susceptible to the seductions of status and display:

> [*Young Goldwire.*] Thou shalt have thy proper and bald-headed Coach-man;
> Thy Tailor, and Embroiderer shall kneel
> To thee their Idoll. Cheap-side and the Exchange
> Shall court thy custome, and thou shalt forget
> There ever was a St Martins. Thy procurer
> Shall be sheath'd in Velvet, and a reverend Vail
> Passe her for a grave Matron.   (IV.ii.23–9)

The moral of all this seems clear enough: the successive peripeties of Acts IV and V reduce first Shavem's gang and then the Frugal battalion to 'penitent tears' and pleas for mercy; each gets, in Luke's phrase, 'what is fitting' (IV.ii.72); those who offer rebellion against the patriarchal hierarchy, or seek to rise above their ordained place in society are compelled to recognize the iron necessities of decorum:

[*Sir John.*]   Make you good
             Your promis'd reformation, and instruct
             Our City dames, whom wealth makes proud, to move
             In their own spheres, and willingly to confesse
             In their habits, manners, and their highest port,
             A distance 'twixt the City, and the Court.   (v.iii.150–5)

Frugal's conclusion, echoing as it does Lord Lacie's reflection on that fit decorum which divides court from City, seems to fix Massinger's social vision decisively enough – it is simply an urban version of the triumphantly restored patriarchy of *A New Way to Pay Old Debts.*

In fact, however, as befits the dramatist's departure from the country with its fiction of unchanging hierarchies, to the conspicuously mobile world of City commerce, the social ideology of *The City Madam* is a good deal more flexible than this comfortable restoration would imply.[24] A clue to the degree of adjustment involved is given by the clash between Plenty and Sir Maurice Lacie in Act I, Scene ii: it is an image of the conflict between old landed wealth and new money enacted in a whole series of plays from *Arden of Faversham* to *A New Way* itself; Plenty indeed might be a scion of that dynasty which the upwardly mobile Tapwell hoped to found in Massinger's earlier comedy.[25] Lacie taunts Plenty with his humble origins:

             thy great grandfather was a Butcher,
      And his son a Grasier, thy sire Constable
      Of the hundred, and thou the first of your dunghill,
      Created gentleman.   (I.ii.67–70)

In the eyes of Lacie and his page, Plenty's transformation into 'a gallant of the last edition' (line 3), his rich display and pretension to the genteel code of honour, learned 'At the Academie of valour,/Newly erected for the institution/Of elder Brothers' (lines 22–4), mark him as a type of upstart vanity and ambition. Yet Plenty emerges from their flyting with more dignity than his aristocratic antagonist: there is an impressive restraint about his pride in fulfilling the offices of 'a plain Gentleman' (line 49), and in his commitment to an ideal of generous housekeeping which avoids both courtly extravagance and City ostentation (lines 38–60). Where Tapwell was scorned and humiliated for his designs, Plenty, his *arriviste* successor, is endorsed to the point of earning the friendship of young Lacie as well as the respect of

Frugal. Lady Frugal's own upward progress, as her brother-in-law outlines it, is granted a similar acceptance, so long as it remains within the bounds of decorum:

> Your father was
> An honest Country farmer. Good-man Humble,
> By his neighbours ne're call'd master. Did your pride
> Descend from him? but let that passe: your fortune,
> Or rather your husbands industry, advanc'd you
> To the rank of a Merchants wife. He made a Knight,
> And your sweet mistris-ship Ladyfi'd, you wore
> Sattin on solemn days, a chain of gold.
> . . .
>
> thus far
> You were priviledg'd, and no man envi'd it;
> It being for the Cities honour, that
> There should be a distinction between
> The Wife of a Patritian, and Plebean.   (IV.iv.67–74, 77–81)

The decorum insisted on, clearly, is one determined not by inherited rank, but simply by the contingencies of acquired status – it depends, that is to say, solely on the individual's immediate relationship to the social order. In this new scheme the orders of society are imagined as having an immutable and almost abstract existence, quite independent of the arbitrary placing of individuals within them. Lady Frugal's privilege is entirely contingent on her husband's rise, but his trappings of rank in turn are seen as proper not so much to his personal industry as to the dignity of the 'Patritian' order within the City hierarchy. Status, like wealth, then, can be conceived as something lent rather than given, an object of stewardship, another counter in the elaborate system of debt and obligation which makes up the bonds of society. Thus Lord Lacie rebukes Lady Frugal's 'pride ... and stubborn disobedience' as another form of debt-reneging – 'wilfully forgetting that your all/Was *borrowed* from him' (III.ii.60–1, 64–5; my italics).

In such a scheme, downward mobility, though it may invite pity and charity, must be as acceptable as upward. The entire plot of *A New Way* is devoted to rescuing the prodigal Welborne from his fallen condition – the individual's loss of status, however much he may have brought it on himself, is felt to undermine the time-hallowed social order quite as dangerously as the rise of his unscrupulous opponents. No such automatic rescue is extended

to the debtors of *The City Madam*, whether they are collapsed
gentlemen like the prodigal Hoyst, marginal men like the pauper
Penurie, or broken merchants like Fortune, whose career so precisely mirrors Frugal's own:

> You were the glorious Trader,
> Embrac'd all bargains; the main venturer
> In every Ship that launch'd forth; kept your wife
> As a Ladie, she had her Coach, her choice
> Of Summer-houses, built with other mens moneys
> Took up at Interest, the certain road
> To Ludgate in a Citizen. (I.iii.22–8)

The view of society implied is barely distinguishable from that
implied by Timothy Tapwell's register in chalk – 'What I *was* Sir,
it skills not,/What you *are* is apparent' (*A New Way*, I.i.29–30,
my italics); Luke Frugal himself is partly sincere when he speaks
to his tyrannic mistress of 'Forgetting what I *was*, but with all
duty/Remembring what I *am*' (I.i.124–5, my italics), as his later
soliloquy reveals:

> 'tis but justice,
> That I should live the families drudge, design'd
> To all the sordid offices their pride
> Imposes on me
> . . .
> 'tis not fit
> I should look upward, much lesse hope for mercy.
> (III.ii.4–7, 16–17)

In his world a man is only what enterprise and Fortune make him.
   Given such a view of society, it is not surprising that social
identity in *The City Madam* should be understood not in terms of
preordained 'place', but rather as a matter of arbitrarily assumed
roles. Metamorphosis, consequently, becomes one of Massinger's ruling motifs: it is initiated by that first extraordinary
tableau of the Frugal ladies, their extravagant attire transforming them, as the choric prentices point out, from their proper
selves:

> [*Goldwire.*]   Look these
> Like a Citizens wife and daughters?
> *Tradewell.*   In their habits
> They appear other things; but what are the motives
> Of this strange preparation? (I.i.49–52)

The true answer to Tradewell's question is really indicated by the narcissistic self-absorption of their *'several postures, with looking-glasses at their girdles'* (I.i.48 SD) — a self-absorption marvellously exaggerated in Lady Frugal's primping before the mirror of Milliscent's flattery which preposterously re-creates her as 'a Virgin of fifteen' (line 83). What Luke will later call their 'monstrous Metamorphosis' (IV.iv.92) is paralleled in Plenty, who, in the sceptical eyes of the page, is similarly 'transform'd [to] a gallant of the last edition' (I.ii.2–3). At the other extreme is Luke, the erstwhile 'companion/For the Nobility', new clothed in the humble garments of service, whom only the courtesy of Lord Lacie now grants even the bare title of gentility:

> Your hand Master *Luke*, the world's much chang'd with you
> Within these few months; then you were the gallant.   (I.ii.111–12)

Luke himself — it is one reason for his successful imposition on the world — has a sharp ear for those niceties of address which mark the gradations of status — 'your honor' for Lord Lacie, 'Noble' for Sir Maurice, 'Worshipfull Master' for Plenty, 'Master' for Hoyst (I.ii.110, 78–9, 108). But for him they are signs merely of the deference owed to the 'prerogatives' of money — 'Since all the titles, honours, long descents/Borrow their gloss from wealth' (III.ii.157–8); and his meticulousness in the matter only gives decorous expression to that peculiar 'ravishing lechery' with which he excites the prentices in Act II, Scene i — his desire for

> The reverence, respect, the crouches, cringes,
> The musical chime of Gold in your cram'd pockets,
> Commands from the attendants, and poor Porters.   (II.i.83–5)

Money for this revolutionary is at once the leveller of all social pretensions —

> My Lord no sooner shal rise out of his chair,
> The gameing Lord I mean, but you may boldly
> By the priviledge of a gamester fill his room,
> For in play you are all fellows.   (II.i.93–6)

— and the only passport to status and power, the quasi-magical agent of a perfect metamorphosis: 'Have mony and good cloaths, /And you may passe invisible' (II.i.100–1). A man's only proper claim to the 'gallant tincture/Of gentry', he argues, with a passion born of utter conviction, is the ungoverned instinct of acquisition, to 'take boldly,/And no way be discover'd' (lines 51–2, 55–6). Luke's precepts about clothes and status receive comic confirmation in Young Goldwire's theatrical 'device' in Act III, Scene i, when he appears in the role of a Justice of the Peace with Dingem and the Musicians as Constable and Watch;[26] but his philosophy receives its fullest illustration through the disguise-plot contrived by Lord Lacie and Sir John. Hardly is Luke presented as his brother's heir than Dingem and Gettall come to announce, as though in fulfilment of his advice to the prentices, the deferential tributes of the gallant world to this City Croesus:

> The news hath reach'd
> The ordinaries, and all the gamsters are
> Ambitious to shake the golden golls
> Of worshipfull Master *Luke*. (IV.i.20–3)

So complete is his metamorphosis that Luke can soliloquize about what seems, even to himself, an 'entrance to/My alter'd nature' (IV.ii.117–18). The 'wondrous brave ... habit [which speaks him] a Merchant royall' (V.ii.16–17) emblematically takes the place of 'the shape/I wore of goodnesse' (V.iii.25–6); and his transformation is matched by that of the Frugal women who, finding themselves in an upside-down world where 'The Scenes chang'd,/And he that was your slave, by fate appointed/Your governour' (III.ii.92–4), are subject to a second, equally emblematic metamorphosis, through the penitential 'coarse habit' which prefigures their ultimate penitence. 'What witch hath transform'd you?' asks the astonished Milliscent, confronted by this travesty of the 'glorious shape' promised by Luke; 'The world' as the grimly satisfied steward, Holdfast, observes '[is] well alter'd' (IV.iv.23, 21).

But the metamorphoses are not yet complete: in the last act all are restored to their proper shapes, and the vehicle of their restoration is one of the most elaborate transformation scenes outside Shakespeare's late romances. What's involved, as at the end of *The Winter's Tale* or *The Tempest*, is a kind of magic – not one effected by supernatural powers, but one which expresses the mysterious influence of human love. It begins with the Masque of Orpheus, in which a group of dancers mime the story of Orpheus' passage through the underworld; the point of the fable is to illustrate the transforming power of harmony (that characteristic expression of the principle of love) to 'Alter in fiends their nature' (v.iii.45). The incredulity with which Luke responds to this sublime fiction ('in my self I find / What I have once decreed, shall know no change' lines 46–7), is immediately illustrated in the 'magic' tableau of 'spirits' called up by Sir John in his guise of Indian shaman:

Sad musick. Enter GOLDWIRE *and* Tradewell, *as from prison*; FORTUNE, HOYST, PENURIE *following after them*; SHAVEM *in a blew gown*; SECRET, DINGEM, OLD TRADEWELL, *and* OLD GOLDWIRE *with* Serjeants *as arrested. They all kneel to* LUKE *heaving up their hands for mercy.* (v.iii.59 SD)

The effect of this conjuring is to produce a kind of moral metamorphosis – though it is of the opposite kind to that demonstrated in the Orpheus mime:

> This move me to compassion? or raise
> One sign of seeming pity in my face?
> You are deceiv'd: it rather renders me
> More flinty, and obdurate. A South wind
> Shall sooner soften marble. (v.iii.60–4)

It is as though he were turned to stone, as hard, cold and inflexible as a marble statue: the image recalls Lord Lacie's description of the Frugal women in III.ii 'charm'd' by Luke's promises of future greatness – 'Are we all turn'd statues?' (III.ii.178) – and the strange postures in which they were frozen by vanity in I.i. By contrast, the scene's final transformation will show the supposed statues of Plenty and Sir Maurice, 'magically' brought to life as though in response to the love and penitent prostration of Lady Frugal and her daughters. Luke is made to point the moral with didactic insistence:

> *Sir John.*   Does not this move you?
> *Luke.*   Yes as they do the statues, and her sorrow
>   My absent brother. If by your magick art
>   You can give life to these, or bring him hither
>   To witnesse her repentance, I may have
>   Perchance some feeling of it. (v.iii.97–102)

The absent are made present, the lifeless brought to life by love; by repentance, as in *The Tempest*,[27] time past can after all (as Lady Frugal so desperately wishes) be recalled.

Compared with its Shakespearian models, this scene has, it

must be conceded, something schematic about it: it is conspicuously without the numinous suggestion surrounding the restoration of Hermione, or even the tableau of restored children with
which Prospero concludes *The Tempest*. The effect may even be
close to burlesque; but that is not entirely inappropriate, since in
the end this last transformation is merely part of the elaborate
hocus-pocus of 'wonders' (III.iii.120) associated with the
'Indians', and another comic sign of the blinkered vision produced by greed and ambition. Its 'magic' extends no further than
the simple didactic metaphors of Sir John's enacted parable. But
the device seems right, partly because so much of the play's action
has been built upon metaphors of false magic, devil-worship and
idolatry. Closely connected with these is an important vein of
religious parody – and here the point of reference is Jonsonian
rather than Shakespearian.[28]

The life of luxury evoked by Luke in his catechizing of the
prentices is 'inchanting' (II.i.108); the 'charm' of his seductive
promises to the Frugal ladies is presented as a kind of base
Hermetic conjuring:

> only hold me
> Your vigilant *Hermes* with aeriall wings,
> My caducevs my strong zeal to serve you,
> Press'd to fetch in all rarities may delight you,
> And I am made immortall.   (III.ii.168–72)

The real source of immortality, in Luke's fevered imagination, is
of course that 'great Elixar', gold – or rather not so much gold, as
the power it confers, symbolized by the key to Sir John's treasure,
to which he addresses the great mock encomium of the ensuing
scene:

> Thou dumb magician that without a charm
> Did'st make my entrance easie, to possesse
> What wise men wish, and toyl for. *Hermes* Moly;
> *Sybilla's* golden bough; the great Elixar,
> Imagin'd onely by the Alchymist
> Compar'd with thee are shadows, thou the substance
> And guardian of felicity.
>
>   . . .
>
> I am sublim'd! grosse earth
> Supports me not. I walk on ayr!   (III.iii.9–15, 43–4)

Paralleling his 'magic' are the equally gold-centred 'sorceries' of
the prostitute Shavem (IV.ii.20) who offers '*Medæas* Drugs,

Restoratives' to the withered youth of Luke (IV.i.51), and the similarly fraudulent practices of that bombastic 'Oracle' (II.ii.70), Stargaze, who has his own '*Hermes* Moly' in

> the Aphorismes of the old Chaldeans; *Zoroastes* the first and greatest Magi-
> cian, *Mercurius Trismegistus*, the later *Ptolomy*, and the everlasting Prog-
> nosticator, old *Erra Pater*.   (II.ii.87–90)

Fittingly enough, it is as the hierophant of diabolic arcana that Sir John, in his Indian guise, presents himself to Luke:

> The Divel. Why start you at his name? if you
> Desire to wallow in wealth and worldly honors,
> You must make haste to be familiar with him.
> This Divel, whose Priest I am, and by him made
> A deep Magician (for I can do wonders)
> Appear'd to me in *Virginia*.   (v.i.26–31)

This Virginian devil, who seemingly has a taste for puns as well as human sacrifice, demands the blood of 'Christian Virgins' in exchange for pelf.

Extravagant and melodramatic as this idolatry may seem, it does no more than give a horridly literal cast to the proceedings by which Massinger's City world is governed. Young Goldwire, for instance, envisages Shavem's stipendiaries 'kneel[ing]/To thee their Idoll' (IV.ii.24–5); just as Luke recalls the grovelling of beggars before the wealth of the Frugal women as a species of 'idolatrie':

> And going
> To Church not for devotion, but to shew
> Your pomp, you were tickl'd when the beggars cry'd
> Heaven save your honour.   (IV.iv.115–18)

In this context the successive tableaux of kneeling with their desperate appeals for mercy take on a tricky ambiguity: looked at from one point of view they are emblematic illustrations of the harshness of the rich and of the need for charity; viewed in a slightly different way they become enactments of the idolatry of wealth, the deification of status and money power – like the ludicrous kneeling of the Frugal women to 'give thanks' for the prophecies of Stargaze (II.ii.68).[29] Certainly when Sir John Frugal dismisses Penury as an 'Infidel .../In not providing better' for his wife and family (I.iii.19–20), though he is consciously invoking a text from St Paul ('if any provide not for his own, and specially for those of his own house, he hath denied the faith, and is worse than an infidel', 1 Timothy 5.8), we may suspect that it is mainly Penury's neglect of the pieties of commerce that damns him in the merchant's eyes. Massinger's London, in fact, is repeatedly shown as an idolatrous society, whose *mores* are not fundamentally different from those of flesh-trading 'pagans' such as Shavem and Secret;[30] its true mirror is the 'Virginia' conjured up by Sir John Frugal and his fellow 'Indians' – Virginia, the destination of 'Strumpets and Bauds,/For the abomination of their life,/Spew'd out of their own Country' (v.i.108–10), where City madams will purportedly be 'ador'd .../As goddesses' (v.i.117–18); Virginia, whose supposed emissaries, though they at first seem 'Infidells' to their unwilling benefactor (III.iii.78), prove to be the priests of 'sacred principles' (line 126) which are those of London itself – a city where indeed 'All deities serve *Plutus*', the god of riches (line 108).

Act III, Scene iii, where Luke first encounters the Indians, is a conversion scene; and conversion, in Massinger's metaphoric structure, is the last form of metamorphosis, the ultimate magical transformation. Each act of the comedy, in fact, has its conversion scene, beginning with Luke's preaching the virtues of charity and compassion to his brother in a sermon whose eloquence, according to Lord Lacie, 'Our divines' cannot match (I.iii.96): 'it will damn him,' remarks the expectant Hoyst, 'If he be not converted' (lines 80–1). Sir John's ensuing change of heart towards his creditors is capped by his conversion from what Lacie types as his 'Atheist' behaviour towards Luke (line 126). This scene is juxtaposed with Luke's counter-sermon to the prentices, Tradewell and Goldwire, in II.i, persuading them of the pleasures of peculation and prodigality, which ends with the rapt Tradewell's declaration – neatly linking the religious and profane senses of conversion –

> I am converted.
> A Barbican Broker will furnish me with out side,
> And then a crash at the Ordinarie. (II.i.131–3)

The 'Religious, good, and honest' Luke (I.iii.152), as befits his pious front, is named for one of the Evangelists, the reputed author of that saga of conversion, the Acts of the Apostles; but his appearance with the great key to Frugal's treasury at the beginning of Act III, Scene iii, more immediately recalls the iconography of another apostle, St Peter, who bears the key to the Heavenly Jerusalem; for Luke, the key grants access to a material paradise, a 'sacred room' (line 19), a place of 'perpetuall day', (line 24) 'Heavens abstract, or Epitome' (line 31).[31] The 'Indians' appear almost as though magically summoned by his act of idolatrous worship. They have been sent, Luke is to believe, as a charitable testimony by his brother – himself now converted to a life of monastic devotion. Luke is to be responsible 'For their conversion' (III.iii.98), but fears that language may be an obstacle to this holy purpose. Lacie, however, is able to reassure him, with a heavy *double entendre*, 'They have liv'd long/In the English Colonie, and speak our language/As their own Dialect' (lines 99–101). There follows a neat illustration of their linguistic competence: Lacie departs urging Luke to 'Continue ... a pious/And honest man' (lines 102–4), a description which he offers to translate into the 'heathen language' of his own City *mores*: 'That is, interpreted,/A slave and beggar' (lines 104–5); it is a dialect which the 'Indians', hitherto confined to fustian gobbledygook, instantly understand:

> *Sir John.*   You conceive it right,
> There being no religion, nor virtue
> But in abundance, and no vice but want.
>
> (III.iii.105–7)

The 'worldly wisdom' announced by this 'Oracle' (line 108), in his parodic inversion of Luke's earlier sermonizing on charity, is identifiably of the same order as that offered by the play's other 'Oracle', Stargaze (II.ii.70). It is of course richly ironic that 'Indians' should be made the spokesmen for the play's frankest statement of corrupted commercial values, since the one characteristic of Indian peoples, however allegedly brutish, barbarous or savagely idolatrous, on which nearly all commentators agreed, was their indifference to wealth and ignorance of the value of gold.[32] The 'dialect' of Massinger's Indians is merely the dumb language of gold rendered articulate, the true language of the City:

> Temples rais'd to our selvs in the increase
> Of wealth, and reputation, speak a wise man;
>   . . .
> All knowledge else is folly.   (III.iii.109–10, 114)

They profess Luke's own faith with a directness that turns his world upside down, persuading him that 'You are learn'd Europians, and wee worse/Then ignorant Americans' (lines 127–8). The pretended missionary is himself converted – and the agent of his conversion is that same 'Angels' language' which 'ravish'd' Lady Frugal in Stargaze's prophecies (II.ii.63), and which Gettall will hear jingling in Luke's promise of reward ('There spake an Angel', IV.i.44):

> Be confident your better Angel is
> Enter'd your house. (III.iii.115–16)

Sir Maurice's assurance points directly at the play's favourite pun, and creates Luke's conversion as a kind of blasphemous Pentecost, marking his possession by the unholy spirit of gold and its 'tongues of angels'.

Luke's public conversion to the diabolical service of Plutus is a metamorphosis which reveals his true nature – not least to the once credulous Lord Lacie whom Luke's 'cunning shape' made think 'This divell a Saint' (V.ii.3, 5). But ironically it also makes him the agent of the genuine conversion of the Frugal ladies. Though Luke's inquisition in IV.iv is carried out for the pure pleasure of revenge, his posture of satyr-'Satyrist', scourging 'a generall vice' (IV.iv.61–2), brings the City madams to a repentant acknowledgement of their faults of pride and disobedience (lines 149–54) – a penitence which prepares the way for the final conversion of the 'Indians' to their former Christian selves in Act V, Scene iii. In his chastisement of the women, then, Luke is made to fulfil the calling of his Evangelist namesake, becoming, in Lady Frugal's words, 'A rough physician' to their moral sickness; with his harsh purgatives he takes the place of the false 'parcel Physician', Stargaze, whose flattering prescriptions taught his mistress to diet upon pride (II.ii.33–4); and the unintended success of his devilish ministrations gives a kind of ironic confirmation to the opinion of the suitors that 'what's bred in the bone/Admits no hope of cure ... Though Saints, and Angels/Were their Physitians' (II.iii.36–8): where even saints might fail, the pretended saint, with his demonic angel's tongue, paradoxically triumphs.

The effect of his triumph is to restore the Frugal household and its dependants to a state of charity, from whose orphic harmony

Luke's 'sounding brass' alone is excluded. But more than a restoration this is a conversion, for the idea of charity with which the play began has, by its end, been significantly transformed. The virtue trumpeted by Lady Frugal in the opening scene is above all a mode of power, a purchase on gratitude and servility:

> Dar'st thou in a look
> Repine, or grumble? Thou unthankful wretch,
> Did our charitie redeem thee out of prison,
> Thy Patrimonie spent, ragged and lowsie,
> When the Sheriffs basket, and his broken meat
> Were your Festivall exceedings, and is this
> So soon forgotten? (I.i.110–16)

Lord Lacie, indeed, contrasts Luke's enforced slavery with what he sees as the true 'charity to your debtors' exercised by Sir John Frugal under Luke's persuasions (I.iii.123). This scene, the first of the play's tableaux of charity, appears to establish a firm contrast between the City *mores* of the elder brother ('He is a Citizen,/ And would increase his heap, and will not lose/What the Law gives him', I.ii.140–2), and the Christian idealism of the younger. Massinger is trading here not only on the conventionally sympathetic role of the younger brother, but also on expectations set up by his own earlier comedy. For the two Frugals seem initially to occupy the parts of Overreach and his kinsman Welborne. Sir John shares with Sir Giles an appetite for country manors (I.i.6), and a seemingly merciless attitude towards debt slavery:

> I have heard
> In the acquisition of his wealth, he weighs not
> Whose ruines he builds upon. (I.ii.137–9)

> I know no obligation lies upon me
> With my honey to feed Drones. (I.iii.12–13)

His commercial code merely translates into a loftier language the 'Ka me, ka thee' ethics of young Goldwire (II.i.127). Luke, on the other hand, seems to be the champion of a social vision which stresses the bonds of human community over the bondage of debt — bonds honoured in the traditional generosities of patriarchal housekeeping:

> Not as a brother, Sir, but with such dutie
> As I should use unto my Father, since
> Your charitie is my parent, give me leave
> To speak my thoughts.
> ...

> You have many equals; Such a mans possessions
> Extend as far as yours, a second hath
> His bags as full; a third in credit flies
> As high in the popular voice: but the distinction
> And noble difference by which you are
> Divided from 'em, is that you are styl'd
> Gentle in your abundance, good in plentie,
> And that you feel compassion in your bowels
> Of others miseries (I have found it, Sir,
> Heaven keep me thankful for't) while they are curs'd
> As rigid and inexorable/   (1.iii.41–4, 52–62)

While the idea of true status (gentility) as being determined by the fulfilment of social obligation is one which the play will confirm, a closer inspection of Luke's charitable doctrine reveals that it too is compromised by the perception of good works as an agent of power. To spare his debtors, he argues, will do Sir John himself 'a benefit'

> By making these your beads-men. When they eat,
> Their thanks next heaven, will be paid to your mercy.
> When your Ships are at Sea, their prayers will swell
> The Sails with prosperous winds, and guard'em from
> Tempests, and pirates: keep your ware-houses
> From fire, or quench'em with their tears
>   . . .
> Write you a good man in the peoples hearts,
> Follow you every-where.   (1.iii.101–6, 107–8)

Charity here becomes at once a kind of thrift or prudence and another mode of ambitious self-advertisement, distinguished from conspicuous consumption only by the accident of its effect. To be a charitable beadsman, as the 'Beadsman-brother' (III.ii.1), Luke, best knows, is merely to wear an enforced livery. In this sense his first response to his inheritance in Act III is not necessarily to be seen as an entire hypocrisy: in his vision of debtors become devoted beadsmen, Luke is savouring the first delights of power:[33]

> And now me thinks I see
> Before my face the Jubile of joy,
> When it is assur'd, my brother lives in me,
> His debtors in full cups crown'd to my health,
> With Pæans to my praise will celebrate.
> For they well know 'tis far from me to take
> The forfeiture of a Bond.   (III.ii.130–6)

And it is precisely to this corrupted ideal of alms-giving that the trio of debtors appeal in their flattering prophecies of Luke's exalted future as a Lord Mayor, outdoing Gresham in munificence: 'Hospitals,/And a third Burse erected by his Honour ... We his poor Beads-men feasting/Our neighbours on his bounty' (IV.i.72–3, 77–8). At least part of his objection to Sir John's scheme for conversion of the Indians must be that it is presented as 'testimony' of his brother's 'religious charitie' rather than his own. All that the 'Indians' do is to instruct Luke in the logic of his self-absorption: the charitable dispensation of wealth may be an exhibition of power, but money is the thing itself: 'All humane happinesse consists in store' (IV.ii.133). In so far as he continues to speak the language of charity ('What's mine is theirs', IV.i.38), it is only for the pleasure of luring his victims into a confidence which renders them even more pathetically vulnerable to his power: to the prentices and their suburban hangers-on he seems to show himself 'a second *Anthony*' in 'magnificent bounties' (IV.ii.40–1) the more to enjoy their despair when he throws them into Bridewell; to the debtors he offers 'charity' and 'patience' purely to enhance the pleasure of consigning them to his old debt-hole, the Counter, where the only benefactions will be the Sheriff's basket 'And a Coal-sack for a winding-sheet' (IV.iii.60); and having reduced the Frugal women to his own condition at the beginning of the play, dressing them in coarse cloth and forcing them to 'serve one another' (IV.iv.136), he crowns his masterpiece of ironic revenge by offering them up to sacrifice in a deal which the 'Indians' present as a black parody of charitable alms-giving:

> *Lacie.* Know you no *distressed Widow*, or *poor Maids*,
>   Whose want of dower, though well born, makes 'em weary
>   Of their own Country?   (V.i.47–9, my italics)

If Lady Frugal and her daughters are forced to take Luke's old place, he himself begins to talk the language of Sir John: where the elder brother dismissed the debtors as 'Drones' undeserving of his 'honey', the younger expels Milliscent and Stargaze as 'useless drones' (IV.iv.138); where Sir John feared that his mercy to the debtors would be laughed at as a 'foolish pity/Which mony men hate deadly' (I.iii.115–16), Luke rejects the appeals of Old Goldwire and Old Tradewell with the reflection:

> Should I part
> With what the law gives me, I should suffer mainly
> In my reputation. For it would convince me
> Of indiscretion.
> . . .
> They cannot look for't, and preserve in me
> A thriving Citizens credit.   (v.ii.38–41, 43–4)

'Conscience' and 'wealth,' he declares, as though passing his own comment on the play's ruling parable, 'are not always neighbours' (lines 37–8). The City world of which Luke has come to be the spokesman is in fact a world without neighbourhood where 'hospitality' to poor neighbours is 'a virtue/Grown obsolete, and uselesse' (v.i.144–5); a world of appetitive individuals, each of whom 'lives wisely to himself' (v.iii.13), bound to those around him only by the links of commercial obligation and legal contract:

> If there be law in London your fathers Bonds
> Shall answer for what you are out.   (IV.ii.90–1)

> Your bonds lie
> For your sons truth, and they shall answer all.
> . . .
> I have your Bonds, look too't.
>   (v.ii.44–5, 51)

Even Luke's old patron, Lord Lacie, finds the very estate from which his title comes a forfeit to remorseless law. The peak of Luke's ecstasy in the counting-house scene was his discovery of 'A mannor bound fast in a skin of parchment,/The wax continuing hard, the acres melting' (III.iii.36–7), and now the bond proves to be Lacie's:

> And it please your good Lordship. You are a noble man
> Pray you pay in my moneys.
> . . .
> Look you to your Bonds.   (v.ii.67–8, 78)

The tone is distinctly Shylockian; but the bitter humour is infused with Massinger's characteristic sensitivity to the accents of caste hatred; the heavy stress on 'good' suggests an equivoque which sarcastically undercuts the carefully chosen honorific offered by one for whom nobles (gold coins) are the only proper tokens of nobility.

    The banquet with which Luke ends his reign is constructed as a pageant of anti-charity. Traditionally the banquet is a symbolic celebration of human community, an exhibition of that hospitality by which the wealthy acknowledge their stewardship of wealth and their charitable duty towards all their neighbours. Luke's, by contrast, is only for himself:

> I will sit
> Alone, and surfet in my store, while others
> With envy pine at it. My Genius pamper'd
> With the thought of what I am, and what they suffer
> I have mark'd out to miserie. (v.i.145–9)

As he sits at his feast he reflects mockingly on his beadsman-brother's charity:

> Let my brother number
> His beads devoutly, and believe his alms
> To beggars, his compassion to his debters,
> Will wing his better part, disrob'd of flesh,
> To sore above the firmament. (v.iii.26–30)

He revels, Overreach-like, in the benefits of his own uncharitable rigour:

> And so I surfet here in all abundance;
> Though stil'd a cormorant, a cut-throat, Jew,
> And prosecuted with the fatal curses
> Of widdows, undone Orphans, and what else. (v.iii.31–4)

The tableau of pleading beggars conjured up by the Indian magus to challenge his compassionate instincts merely gratifies Luke's triumphant self-esteem:

> This move me to compassion? or raise
> One sign of seeming pity in my face?
> . . .
> 'Tis my glory
> That they are wretched, and by me made so,
> It sets my happinesse off. I could not triumph
> If these were not my captives. (v.iii.60–1, 67–70)

It is Luke's most magniloquent speech, the moment at which he most closely approaches the grandiose villainy of Sir Giles; but it is his most ridiculous moment too. The 'magic' banquet and the pantomimes of 'spirits' which accompany it, are reaches of Sir John's supposed Indian 'art' which parodically recall the 'wonders' of Prospero's brave new world; just as the animated statues of Plenty and Young Lacie imitate the mysteriously en-livened image of Hermione in Leontes' Sicily. But the magic here

Charity and the Social Order in *The City Madam*

is of a kind which would deceive only those blinded by the self-absorption of pride and greed. The hard-headed commercial realism which animated Luke from the moment of his conversion proves to be as fertile a source of fantastic self-delusion as the ladies' preposterous vanity; the gulling hypocrite, the great disguiser, is gulled by the most transparent disguise of all – gulled, indeed, to the point where he is made to be his own judge and pass his own irrevocable sentence ('may I ne're find pity' v.iii.58). To be denied pity is to be denied compassion, fellow-feeling, to be cast out, in effect, from the charitable community of humankind: behind the tableau of beggars at the feast lies the last of Massinger's controlling parables, Dives and Lazarus:

There was a certain rich man, which was clothed in purple and fine linen, and fared sumptuously every day: And there was a certain beggar named Lazarus, which was laid at his gate, full of sores, And desiring to be fed with the crumbs which fell from the rich man's table. (Luke 16.19–21)

And over the figure of the departing Luke (as over the demented Sir Giles), hangs the shadow of the damned and outcast Dives cut off by a great gulf of despair, even from the proffered mercy of those he has wronged: 'I care not where I go, what's done, with words/Cannot be undone (v.iii.146–7).

NOTES

1 iv.iii.46–7; all citations from *The City Madam* are based on *The Plays and Poems of Philip Massinger*, ed. Philip Edwards and Colin Gibson (5 vols., Oxford, Clarendon Press, 1976), vol. 4.

2 1 Corinthians 13.1; biblical citations (except where otherwise indicated) are based on the King James version. It is worth noting, in view of its preoccupation with charity, that *The City Madam* was first licensed on 25 May 1632, and may therefore have been intended for performance in the week of 11 June, the feast of St Barnabas. St Barnabas, who in Acts 4.36–7, sells his property in order to distribute the proceeds amongst the poor, has a particular connection with charity; the Gospel for the day is John 15.12 ('This is my commandment, That ye love one another'). Performance on St Barnabas's Day would give a special intensity to Frugal's final proclamation of mercy: 'This day is sacred to it' (v.iii.126). The feast was omitted from the 1552 Calendar, but the service was retained, and in 1636 Bishop Wren issued an order that 'ministers forget not to read the collects, epistles, and gospels appointed for ... St Barnaby's Day' – see J. H. Blunt, *The Annotated Book of Common Prayer* (London, Oxford and Cambridge, 1876).

MICHAEL NEILL

3   Cf. Mary's sneer at those who think 'the happinesse of mans life consists/In a mighty shoulder of mutton' (I.i.153–4).

4   Psalm 58.4; cited from the Prayer Book version.

5   In the light of the play's satiric denigration of inspiration in favour of charity, it may be worth noting that St Paul's encomium on charity seems to exalt it above the pentecostal gifts: 'Though I speak with the tongues of men and of angels ... And though I have *the gift of* prophecy, and understand all mysteries, and all knowledge; and though I have all faith ... and have not charity, I am nothing' (1 Corinthians 13.1–2).

6   Cf. my article, 'Massinger's Patriarchy: The Social Vision of *A New Way to Pay Old Debts*', *Renaissance Drama*, n.s. 10 (1979), 185–213.

7   Cf. also I.iii.118; II.ii.68 SD; III.ii.94; IV.iii.3; and perhaps IV.ii.103; IV.iv.140–1.

8   W. K. Jordan, *Philanthropy in England, 1480–1660: A Study of the Changing Pattern of English Social Aspiration* (London, Allen and Unwin, 1959), p.146; for a detailed discussion of the process by which charity became progressively institutionalized see Gareth Jones, *History of the Law of Charity* (Cambridge, Cambridge University Press, 1969), chapters 1–5.

9   Jordan, pp.77ff.

10 Jordan, pp.18–19, 152ff.

11 Anonymous, *Three sermons or homelies to moove compassion towards the poore* (1596); Henry Smith, *Sermons* (1599), quoted in Jordan, pp.168–9.

12 Thomas Gataker, *A sparke toward the kindling of sorrow for Sion* (1621), quoted in Jordan, p.186.

13 William Perkins, *Works* (1605) quoted in Jordan, p.152; cf. also the sermon by William Whately, *Sinne no more* (1628), quoted p.184: 'Bountifull and mercifull actions are the best bargaines, and the best purchases.'

14 See Whately, in Jordan, p.184: 'let your abundance supply their wants, whom God therefore hath called to want, that he might give you occasion of declaring the abundance of your charitie'; cf. also Edward Dering's argument that 'men ... are made rich for no other reason than they may give to the poor' (p.153).

15 See for instance Jordan's account of Thomas Lever's teaching (pp.163–4).

16 Quoted in Jordan, p.192.

17 *Ibid*, p.193.

18 Quoted in Jordan, p.192.

19 Citations from *A New Way to Pay Old Debts* are based on Edwards and Gibson, vol. 2.

20 For a reading which emphasizes the new City alignment of Massinger's later comedy, see Martin Butler, 'Massinger's *The City Madam* and the Caroline Audience', *Renaissance Drama*, n.s. 13 (1982), 157–87.

21 Cf. Luke's 'Madam-punck' (II.i.102), and Hippolita's contemptuous

phrase in Ford's *'Tis Pity She's a Whore*, 'your goodly Madam Merchant' (II.ii.49) – quoted from Derek Roper's Revels edition (London, Methuen, 1975). 'Madam' had the double sense of 'a lady of rank' and 'affected fine lady' (*OED*, sb.3a,c); Massinger plays with both meanings.

22 Butler, 'Massinger's *The City Madam*', p.166, points out that the provisos take the appropriately City form of a mock indenture.

23 *A New Way*, II.i.78–89; cf. also Anne's ambition to have 'Some decay'd Ladie for my Parasite,/To flatter me, and rail at other Madams' (*City Madam*, II.ii.123–4).

24 Cf. A. G. Gross, 'Social Change and Philip Massinger', *Studies in English Literature* 7 (1967), 329–42; Gross declares 'I think it is possible to advance, *though it is not possible adequately to support*, an hypothesis that in the decade that passed between writing these two plays Massinger's social views matured decidedly' (p.341, fn.; italics added); I would take issue with his qualification.

25 Cf. Tapwell's boast to Welborne:

> poore *Tim Tapwell* with a little stocke,
> Some forty pounds or so, bought a small cottage,
> Humbled my selfe to marriage with my *Froth* here;
> Gaue entertainment ... [to whores, and canters,
> Clubbers by night].
>   ...
>   The poore Income
> I glean'd from them, hath made mee in my parish,
> Thought worthy to bee *Scauinger*, and in time
> May rise to be *Ouerseer* of the poore;
> Which if I doe, on your petition *Welborne*,
> I may allow you thirteene pence a quarter,
> And you shall thanke my worship.
>   (*A New Way*, I.i.59–63, 65–71)

26 The parallel entry of 'Sheriff, Marshall, *and Officers*' to Goldwire, Tradewell and their accomplices at IV.ii.72 only reinforces this point.

27 See my discussion of *The Tempest* in 'Remembrance and Revenge: *Hamlet, Macbeth*, and *The Tempest*', in Ian Donaldson (ed.), *Jonson and Shakespeare* (London and Canberra, Macmillan/Humanities Research Centre, 1983), pp.35–56. Butler, 'Massinger's *The City Madam*', p.185, speaks of the conclusion of the play as 'an epiphany' fulfilling 'a sacramental pattern'.

28 Despite Massinger's long apprenticeship with Fletcher, Jonson was his principal mentor in comedy; it is interesting to note that (as Anne Barton argues in *Ben Jonson, Dramatist* (Cambridge, Cambridge University Press, 1984), pp.259, 279–81)) the master was engaged in his own reassessment and reworking of Shakespeare's romances at about the same time.

29 See above, n.7.

30 See Goldwire's use of the term, II.i.110.

31 Since Luke vainly imagines it a key to heaven, it may be worth

recalling, as a source of additional irony, the key to the bottomless pit given to the fifth angel in Revelation 9.1.

32   On this point see Gary B. Nash, 'The Image of the Indian in the Southern Colonial Mind' in Edward Dudley and Maxmilian E. Novak (eds.), *The Wild Man Within* (Pittsburgh, University of Pittsburgh Press, 1972), pp.55–86; Benjamin Keen, 'The Vision of America in the Writings of Urbain Chauveton'; Haydn White, 'The Noble Savage Theme as Fetish'; and Arthur J. Slavin, 'The American Principle from More to Locke'; all in Fredi Chapelli, *et al.* (eds.), *First Images of America: The Impact Of the New World on the Old*, 2 vols. (Berkeley, Los Angeles and London, University of California Press, 1976), vol. 1, pp.107–20, 121–35, 139–64; and A. L. Rowse, *The Elizabethans and America* (London, Macmillan, 1959), pp.27, 199–200. Naturally the Indians' supposedly communalist societies and their alleged indifference to pelf were most emphasized by primitivists like Montaigne ('Of the Cannibals') who wished to present them as possessing the felicities of the Golden Age, denied to Europeans by the doubtful gift of civilization. But even those with a clearer commercial vision, like the Virginia Council, rejoiced in the innocence of a people from whom the English 'doe buy ... the pearles of the earth, and sell to them the pearles of heaven' (Nash, p.57); more hostile later commentators tended to denigrate their material carelessness as 'improvidence'; but even Captain John Smith, who found them 'Generally covetous of Copper, Beads, and such like trash' did not credit them with any proper sense of value (*Works*, ed. Edward Arber (Birmingham, English Scholar's Library, 1884), p.361): Smith's observations echo the astonishment of John de Verrazano (1524) who found that the Florida Indians esteemed copper above gold which, because of its indifferent colour, 'is counted the basest' (see Richard Hakluyt, *The Principal Navigations Voyages Traffiques and Discoveries of the English Nation*, 12 vols. (Glasgow, MacLehose, 1903–5), vol. 8, (1904), p.433. The popular image of the Indian attitude to wealth in Massinger's day is probably still best represented by the feckless negligence of Othello's 'base Indian' throwing away a pearl 'richer than all his tribe'. Butler, 'Massinger's *The City Madam*', pp.177–85, emphasizes the Indian's reputation for Devil-worship and argues that this makes them 'a visual sign' of Luke's damnability – but the Devil they adore speaks good English.

33   For charity as a way of ensuring posthumous fame, see Jordan, pp.143–239, 215–28.

The Distinctive Voice of Massinger

ANNE BARTON

(Reprinted from *The Times Literary Supplement*, 20 May 1977, pp. 623–4.)

PHILIP MASSINGER died in 1640, fifteen years after his friend and collaborator John Fletcher. According to Aston Cokayne, who celebrated the curiosity in a poem, Massinger was buried in Fletcher's grave at St Saviour's, Southwark. This interment proved oddly symbolic. At least thirteen plays in which Massinger was a secret but important sharer were to be printed in the Beaumont and Fletcher Folio of 1647, without acknowledgement of his authorship. Moreover, as Fletcher's reputation gradually declined from its seventeenth-century height, it took Massinger's with it. Except for *A New Way to Pay Old Debts* and *The City Madam*, comedies which stand apart from the rest of the canon, Massinger's very considerable body of dramatic work has all too readily been dismissed in the twentieth century as that of a ponderous and untalented imitator: a man who exploited Fletcher's dubious, tragicomic mode without being able to extract from it even those limited and suspect theatrical virtues of which 'decadence' was capable in the hands of its chief creator.

T. S. Eliot, in 1920, at least liberated Massinger from Fletcher, but only in order to establish him as the villain of the seventeenth-century dissociation of sensibility – an artist hurrying us, fatally, down the primrose path to Milton. According to Eliot, Massinger's 'personality hardly exists'. 'Massinger's tragedy may be summarized for the unprepared reader as being very dreary', while 'what distinguishes Massinger from Marlowe and Jonson is in the main an inferiority'. Eliot's verdict, even more severe than that of Leslie Stephen in the 1870s is generalized and highly questionable, but it effectively annihilated Massinger for two generations of readers. Twenty years later, the anonymous

ANNE BARTON

author of *The Times Literary Supplement* article which marked
the third centenary of Massinger's death, could think of nothing
to say about his subject except that no one any longer read him,
not even in the universities, but that his plots were surprisingly
expert and he might have been a success in Hollywood. The only
recent critical book devoted to Massinger (T. A. Dunn, 1957) not
only accepts Eliot's point of view, but contrives to apologize for
concerning itself with Massinger at all, except as a somehow
representative figure.

According to the calculations of Philip Edwards and Colin
Gibson, Massinger was associated with the writing of no fewer
than fifty-five plays, of which thirty-three survive. Fifteen were
all his own work, and he published ten of them, in quarto editions, in his lifetime. There are indications that, towards the end
of his life, he contemplated a modest, personal collection of his
work – at least, he had eight of the quarto plays bound together
in a single volume, perhaps for presentation to a patron – but he
seems never to have aspired to the dignity of Folio publication.
Even in his own time, Massinger does not appear to have been a
very popular dramatist. In his fine essay, 'Massinger the Censor'
(1962), Philip Edwards points to the defensiveness of the
commendatory verses attached to *The Renegado* and *The
Emperor of the East*, and to the dramatist's own, somewhat
embarrassing humility in the Prologue to *The Guardian*. Even
sadder, perhaps, are the lines which Thomas Jay addressed to 'his
worthy friend Mr. Philip Massinger, upon his Tragaecomaedie
stiled, the Picture':

> you can endure
> To heere their praise, whose worth long since was knowne
> And justly to, prefer'd before your owne.
> I know you would take it for an injury,
> (And 'tis a well becomming modesty)
> To be paraleld with *Beaumont*, or to heare
> Your name by some to partiall friend writ neere
> Unequal'd *Jonson*; being men whose fire
> At distance, and with reuerance you admire.
> Do so and you shall find your gaine will bee
> Much more by yeelding them prioritie
> Than with a certainety of losse to hould
> A foolish competition.

No doubt true, at least with respect to Jonson, but it is none the less hard to believe that Massinger did not wince as he obediently prefixed this poetic offering to the quarto of that good and thoughtful play, *The Picture*. Commendatory verses in the early seventeenth century are usually made of more enthusiastic stuff.

Not until 1759 did anyone think it worthwhile to bring out a collected edition of Massinger's unaided plays. In 1805, Coxeter's edition was superseded by Gifford's and for a time, Massinger's reputation seemed to be in the ascendant. The Romantics, without being uncritical, none the less took him seriously. Coleridge, whose high opinion of Massinger's verse is especially interesting ('the nearest approach to the language of real life at all compatible with a fixed metre'), returned to the subject on a number of occasions. In the theatre, Sir Giles Overreach was one of Kean's greatest parts and, during one performance, reduced Byron to nervous hysterics.

Then, a critical reaction set in, followed by that theatrical and academic neglect of Massinger's work which has persisted, on the whole, up to the present. During the first half of the twentieth century, while Jonson, Marlowe, Webster, Dekker, Fletcher, Peele, Lyly, Shirley and other dramatists were all reaping the benefits of modern editorial attention, Massinger continued to face his dwindling public in Gifford's early nineteenth-century text, or in selected editions deriving from it. The new Clarendon Press *Massinger* has been sorely needed for a long time.

Now that it is at last complete, it is a pleasure to report that the edition prepared by Professor Edwards and Professor Gibson is a model of what such things should be: a splendid, scholarly achievement that is intelligent, thorough and humane. It does Massinger himself a great service, and it is also of incalculable value to students of Jacobean and Caroline drama generally. The editors have built upon (and generously acknowledged) the unpublished Oxford doctoral dissertation (1931) and other papers of the late A. K. McIlwraith, to whom the task of editing Massinger was originally assigned. In their treatment of the text and its apparatus, they have followed the principles and practices of Fredson Bowers, as established in his edition of the dramatic works of Dekker. Their edition as a whole, however, is in the great Oxford tradition of the Herford and Simpson *Ben Jonson*, a tradition which it honourably extends.

The editors offer an excellent general introduction concerned with Massinger's life and theatrical career, and with some of the fluctuations of his literary reputation. Each play is prefaced by a full account of its sources, date, stage history and text. There are a number of significant new discoveries recorded here. The final volume contains not only a glossary and a list of Massinger's spellings but a detailed, extremely well judged, and *indexed* commentary. Readers will find the latter provocative as well as informative. Although it may initially seem startling, ultimately it is very reassuring to find one's attention being directed (in the commentary to *The Fatal Dowry*) to a *News of the World* headline of 1971. Massinger's tragic tangles are not so artificial after all. They still occur. And the editor, in noting the parallel, demonstrates that he has been living with his author as a whole, and not merely as a textual problem.

Although Professor Edwards has, elsewhere, published two important interpretative essays, no attempt has been made by the editors to provide formal, critical introductions to the fifteen unaided plays and the two collaborations (*The Fatal Dowry* and *A Very Woman*) which they include. They content themselves with the establishment and elucidation of Massinger's text, and with the provision of the factual material needed for an intelligent approach to the plays. The edition seems certain, however, to spark off a much-needed critical re-evaluation of Massinger's work as a whole. It provides an incentive to read through his dramatic work in chronological order – including the sixteen plays written in collaboration with Fletcher and others, which lie outside the scope of this collection – and to discover in the process that Massinger does indeed possess a striking and well-defined artistic personality but that his work is far more interesting and complex than has generally been supposed.

Cyrus Hoy's linguistic tests have convincingly separated Massinger's hand from Fletcher's in many of the collaborative plays. Even without reference to Hoy's criteria, however, it is usually possible to sense when one is listening to Massinger's voice. Sometimes, as in *The Little French Lawyer*, his attitude towards the plot and characters is so much at odds with that of his collaborator as to create a self-contradictory play. Despite a later, overall revision by Massinger, it remains obvious that the two dramatists were constitutionally incapable of treating Champernel, 'a veteran naval warrior', in compatible ways. This disagreement matters. For Fletcher, Champernel is nothing more than a rich old man whose marriage to a young woman means that he has to endure the scoffs and pranks of the gallant who has courted her unsuccessfully. In its last acts, the play bounds along merrily to a conclusion in which the gallant, Dinant, after some earlier attempts on the wife's chastity have failed, triumphantly outwits the newly married pair. Loftily, he spares her honour, but humiliates her and puts her firmly in her place.

This is an archetypal comedy plot, deprecating December/May marriages and involving the victory of the young man over the *senex*. It becomes disturbing only because Massinger, who wrote all of Act I, could not help introducing Champernel as a tragic figure. The scene in which the old sea-dog, returning from his wedding, is coarsely baited in the street by Dinant and a friend does not make amusing reading. Champernel, shamed before the bride he loves and respects, is utterly powerless to retaliate because he has lost a leg and had one arm disabled in a sea-fight. The young men finally reduce him to tears of impotent rage which have more to do with the frustration of Lear, trying to retain his manhood when confronting Goneril and Regan, than with the emotions of a comic *senex*. The episode generates interest in Champernel, and makes Dinant positively repulsive, in ways that can neither be forgotten nor accommodated within the preordained course of the comedy. It is a little as though Meredith's *The Amazing Marriage* had run full tilt against the attitudes of Wycherley's *The Country Wife*.

Act I of *The Little French Lawyer* is quintessential Massinger. It makes one wonder how often Fletcher, who seems to have preferred to relinquish the prickly business of beginnings to his collaborator, actually rejoiced over the opening scenes he was given. Massinger's characteristic – although by no means uncritical – affection for soldiers is plainly in evidence here, and so is his interest in the emotionally unendurable situation. Champernel's helplessness, the mounting sense of claustrophobia as he is obliged to stand and take an excruciatingly painful verbal assault which he can neither arrest nor counter, and from which he cannot run away, is echoed everywhere in Massinger's work: in the magnificent but appalling last scene of *Believe As You List*, in the trapped anguish of Domitian in *The Roman Actor* and Sforza in *The Duke of Milan* when they are taunted by the woman they love and hate, in Overreach at the end of *A New Way to Pay Old Debts*, or in Malefort of *The Unnatural Combat* when he is confronted (after her rape by his 'friend') with the dying wreck of the daughter he himself has incestuously desired. Equally characteristic is the protracted debate on revenge and the justification of private affairs of honour with which *The Little French Lawyer* commences. None of these things, as it happens, really interested Fletcher and, despite a few rather inhibited gestures by Massinger in later scenes, they are issues left puzzlingly undeveloped in the remainder of the play. One sees why collaborations such as *The Custom of the Country*, in which Fletcher and Massinger worked for the most part on separate aspects of a multiple plot, are on the whole more satisfactory.

Although Massinger's dependence upon surprise seems to have been as great as Fletcher's, it was significantly different in purpose and effect. Massinger is far less concerned with fifth-act discoveries of identity than he is with the concealment of motivation or true character. In play after play, the theatre audience is made to flounder and misunderstand its way through a subtle and intelligent plot which often seems to be invested with the kind of complexity and ambiguity which other dramatists bestowed upon their verse. We are not much more privileged than the characters themselves. Massinger may even construct traps out of our theatrical preconditioning, as he does with Bellisant's confident assertion of her invulnerability and self-control in *The Parliament of Love*. One anticipates that she will meet the fate of Shakespeare's Angelo, Middleton's Duchess in *More Dissemblers Besides Women*, or Chapman's Eudora in *The Widow's Tears*, because in comedy this kind of pride almost always foreruns a devastating assault by the life force. Instead, Bellisant effortlessly proves as good as her word.

In general, when Massinger withholds a character's real name or motive, he does so for reasons that would have been less congenial to Fletcher than to the author of *The Faerie Queene*. In Book I, Spenser hurls both the reader and Red-Crosse into an encounter with a nameless giant: a 'monstrous masse of earthly slyme'. Only after we have been made to experience, and have tried to assess, Orgoglio's nature in action is the name which defines him finally released. The technique, one to which Spenser frequently resorts, is part of the way his poem educates its readers in the complexities and difficulties of moral judgement. Massinger shares much of Spenser's seriousness, his view of life as a constant test of the self, involving a series of problematic discriminations and an unflagging alertness. Like Spenser, he is a moralist who refuses either to simplify existence or to offer his public – as the authors of morality drama did – an omniscience possible in fiction but not in life. Characters such as Luke Frugal in *The City Madam*, Francisco in *The Duke of Milan*, Montreville in *The Unnatural Combat*, or Marullo in *The Bondman* all convict us, as well as their associates in the play, of lack of vigilance and perception, when they come to show their true faces.

Massinger's insistence upon the need to evaluate and plumb human actions, together with his sense of the difficulty of arriving at just judgement, or even of a comprehension of all the facts, has a profound effect upon his drama. Structurally, it impels him in play after play towards formal trial scenes and debates. Verbally, it produces innumerable comparisons between life and the theatre; images of the world as a stage which stand out not only because of their frequency, but for their alien quality in dialogue which otherwise seems singularly lifelike and non-metaphoric. It is as though Massinger were determined to stress the correspondence between the spectators and characters, warning us that in a world where everyone, at least in some degree, is putting on a public performance, it is wise not to trust in appearances, but to try to understand. *The Roman Actor* is indeed a brilliant tragedy (RSC and National Theatre, please note) but perhaps it pleased Massinger as much as it did – 'the most perfit birth of my Minerua' – because it is the play in which the related ideas of life as arraignment and as theatre are most elaborately and perfectly conjoined.

Coleridge described Massinger as 'a Democrat', and liked to see him as an early Whig incongruously associated with Fletcher, the Tory ultra-Royalist. Since S. R. Gardiner devoted his attention, over a hundred years ago, to Massinger's politics, a good deal of notice has been taken of him as a critic of kings. It seems certain that Massinger did aim a few covert shafts at Charles I, and at royal policies of which he disapproved. 'Democrat', however, is obviously a misnomer. Ben Jonson might (in *The New Inn*) permit a chambermaid to marry a lord: Marullo in *The*

Bondman turns out, like Spenser's Pastourella or his Salvage Man, to be of gentle birth. There is something inveterately patrician about Massinger, a bias which emerges not only in the social conservatism of his two city comedies, but in his essentially aristrocratic ideal of rationalism and self-control. Yet his ingrained obsession with liberty – in particular, the freedom of the mind – greatly complicates this attitude.

Timoleon, to a large extent Massinger's spokesman in *The Bondman*, proclaims all men who 'would usurp on others liberties,/Rebels to nature, to whose bounteous blessings/All men lay clayme as true legitimate sonnes'. Slavery can be justified only as society's way of punishing confirmed vice. *The Bondman* itself is scarcely a Marxist manifesto. The leader of the slaves' revolt is a disguised gentleman manipulating the lower classes for his own, essentially non-political, ends. He does not even respect his followers, and with reason. Massinger insists that the slaves themselves are corrupt and greedy – just the sort of people who, according to Timoleon's definition, *ought* to be made to serve the virtuous because such service is a proper penance for being so awful. (The possibility that what one is may be a depressing consequence of one's social condition was something that Massinger, along with virtually every other dramatist in the period except Shakespeare, was not prepared to entertain.) The Syracusan aristocracy, on the other hand, is not virtuous either.

To a large extent it deserves what it gets when the social order suddenly turns upside down. Marullo drives this point home in his impassioned explanation to the aristocrats of how 'your tyranny/Drew us from our obedience'. The whole speech pleads for a return to an older way of life, one in which Massinger himself obviously believed. It presents a nostalgic view of the good society, based upon a number of idealized Penshursts dotted over a landscape. In such great houses, Marullo claims, 'Lords were styl'd fathers of Families,/And not imperious Masters'. They used even their domestic animals kindly, but they regarded their human servants as 'almost equall with their Sonnes'.

The lady Cleora is the best of the aristocrats in *The Bondman*. She is honourable and, by comparison with such harpies as Olimpia and Corisca, considerate of her maidservant. She begins the play, none the less, by arrogantly confusing men with beasts in just the way that Marullo and Timoleon deplore. What she describes as the 'meaner qualitie' are apparently fit only to contend

> Who can indure most labour; plough the earth,
> And think they are rewarded, when their sweat
> Brings home a fruitfull Haruest to their Lords;
> Let them proue good Artificers, and serue you
> For use and ornament, but not presume
> To touch at what is Noble.

Exactly this kind of haughtiness leads her, when her lover Leosthenes reads her a condescending lecture on chastity before he swans off to the wars, not only to resent his mistrust – which she is entirely right to do – but to bind herself by an absurd vow not to speak and to blindfold her eyes until his return. What she anticipates as 'the glorious splendor of my sufferings' is calculated to exalt her and humiliate Leosthenes, 'the people ioyning with you in the wonder'. Events, however, take a different course. Again, Massinger is cautious. Cleora does not believe that Marullo, with whom she falls in love, is really a slave. Her father, brother and lover, on the other hand, do. Cleora has a bad time of it before she can be allowed to exchange the tiresome Leosthenes for a man with whom it may be possible for her to be happy.

The Bondman's conjunction of the issue of political freedom with that of freedom within a love relationship is typical of Massinger. In both *The Maid of Honour* and *The Bashful Lover*, a woman roundly informs a reigning prince that her mind and affections are out of his province, and inviolably her own. Cleora is only one of a number of women in the plays who are tormented by the jealousy and possessiveness of a lover or husband determined to deprive them of their independence of being.

Sforza, in *The Duke of Milan*, would prefer the wife on whom he dotes to be dead rather than to survive him. Mathias, in *The Picture*, employs sorcery in order to spy on Sophia, who has given him not the slightest cause for suspicion, during his absence. Theodosius, in *The Emperor of the East*, moves from an extreme of uxoriousness to one of hate simply because his empress gives away a handsome apple he sent her, without consulting him first. All of these men sin against Massinger's ideal of marriage as a frank and reciprocal relationship based on mutual respect and trust. Their great love, looked at rightly, is only a form of self-worship.

Although no one would ascribe a Shakespearian depth of characterization to Massinger, his men and women are none the less living and real. Significantly, he seems to have preferred as central characters people past their first youth. Many are already married, almost all have a personal past, often secret, which is of consequence to the action. Massinger's insistence that man should be guided by reason, not by his passions, a dictum hammered home in play after play, is orthodox enough. He never loses sight, however, of the fact that what is set down so in Heaven tends to be excruciatingly difficult to achieve on earth. It is not just that legal, political and social institutions inhibit man's freedom in ways that are bad as often as good, or that self-control is a difficult and demanding ideal.

The mind forges fetters for itself. A character like Sforza is sane, balanced, magnanimous and courageous on every subject but one: his wife. This self-imposed bondage makes him a prisoner of the irrational. Camiola, at the end of *The Maid of Honour*, after having done the right thing for the wrong reason when she paid Bertoldo's ransom, compounds her mistake when she abandons the world for the religious life, in order to 'deserve mens prayse, and wonder too'. Overreach, as Hazlitt recognized, cannot disentangle his contempt for the landed aristocracy from his adulation, and the result is ruin. Even the noble Charalois, whose self-restraint seems as impressive as his filial piety in the early scenes of *The Fatal Dowry*, and far superior to the blustering of his well-meaning friend Romont, loses his way in the pursuit of Honour. When he forces Rochfort, the just judge, to condemn his own daughter to summary execution for adultery, arguing that 'A Iudge should feele no passions', he forgets that he himself was saved from perpetual imprisonment in Act I precisely because Rochfort did feel, and act upon, emotions which had nothing to do with the strict course of law. The whole play is a subtle examination of the vexed relation between personal and institutionalized justice.

I do not think that one can read through the seventeen plays collected in the Clarendon Press edition without being impressed both by the force and singleness of this artistic personality, and by the range and variety of Massinger's output. Between such cheerful romps as *The Great Duke of Florence* or *The Renegado* (Massinger's *Entführung aus dem Serail*), and the sombre splendours of *Believe As You List* and *The Roman Actor*, the distance is, in one sense, very great. Yet the same sensibility – thoughtful and essentially grave, concerned to probe and analyse, both passionate and restrained – is reflected in all of them, even as it is in the very different city comedies. There is a sense in which *The Roman Actor* is more pessimistic about the power of art to correct and inform its audience than any other play written between 1580 and 1642. Yet there was something in Massinger which refused to abandon the effort, while insisting that the game should not be played with marked cards. This is why he places his audience, too, at risk.

Coleridge's praise of Massinger's dramatic verse, excessive though it may seem, is fundamentally accurate. Massinger never once needs to use prose, not even for low or comic scenes, because his flexible and beautifully cadenced verse is accommodated to the requirements of the most ordinary conversation as perfectly as it is to impassioned speech. Magnificent lines such as Ford bestows upon his characters in their extremity – 'So falls the standard/Of my prerogative in being a creature' – are not to be found in Massinger. On the other hand, he could give his audience the moving and truthful simplicity of Marcelia's speech at the end of *The Duke of Milan*: 'Oh, I haue fool'd my selfe/Into my graue', or the poignant words of the former king Antiochus, now a galleyslave, as he calmly proves an identity that is no longer of any use to him by revealing to old friends the secret of a ring that once was his:

> *Antiochus.*   I will
> make a discoverie of a secret in it
> of wch you yet are ignorant. pray you trust it
> for kinge Antiochus sake into my handes
> I thancke your readines. nay drie your eies,
> you hinder els the facultie of seeinge
> the cunninge of the lapidarie. I can
> pull out the stone, & vnder it you shall finde
> my name, and cipher I then vsde ingraven.
> *Cornelia.* 'tis most apparent. though I loose my life for't
> theis knees shall pay their dutye.
> *Antiochus.*   by noe meanes.
> for your owne sake bee still incredulous
> since your faith cannot saue mee.

For all its deceptive simplicity, this is dramatic verse of a very high order. It is theatrical in the best sense, the bones and sinews of stage action. Its qualities can be fully understood only if you speak it aloud. It is not easy to write. Nor is it, for all Eliot's complaints about the essential frigidity of Massinger's technical skills, emotionally impoverished. Coleridge announced boldly, during a crisis in the writing of English verse tragedy, that aspiring poets would do better to model themselves on Massinger than on Shakespeare. One poet may have tried. When Shelley fails to convince, in *The Cenci*, it is usually because he is remembering Shakespeare. His most effective lines, however, seem to spring from an entirely beneficial admiration of Massinger, as when Beatrice and her mother, in prison, bind up each other's hair before going to execution: 'How often/Have we done this for one another;/Now we shall not do it any more.'

It is curious, in a way, that Eliot should have attacked and condescended to Massinger in the way he did. After all, the poetic style of this supposedly 'dissociated' sensibility does not sound like that of people 'speaking verse'. At the same time, it contrives for much of the time to suggest what Eliot asked from verse drama: 'a deeper reality than that of the plane of most of our conscious living'. It seems, in many respects, to be the equivalent of that poetic medium for which Eliot himself was searching in the plays written after *Murder in the Cathedral*, a medium which he signally failed to find. If it does nothing else, the Clarendon edition should demonstrate the impossibility of putting Massinger (in Eliot's words) 'finally and irrefutably into a place'.

Index

Index

Blackfriars Theatre, 11, 13, 117
Boccaccio: ultimate source for *The
Maid of Honour*, 98–9; *De
Casibus*, 122, 127
Boccalini, Traiano: *The New-Found
Politicke*, 140–2 (nn. 5, 6, 12)
Bolton, Edmund: *Nero Caesar, or
Monarchy Depraved*, 144
Bouwerie Lane Theatre: performance
of *The Roman Actor*, 10
Bowers, Fredson: edition of Dekker,
223; on *The Fatal Dowry*, 126
Bradshaw, John: defence of
Parliament's actions at trial of
Charles I, 167
Brathwaite, Richard: *Mercurius
Britannicus*, pamphlet play, 165
Browning, Elizabeth Barrett: *The
Book of the Poets*, on Massinger's
style, 26
Brutus, Marcus Junius, 166
Buckingham, George Villiers, first
Duke of, 143–4, 148
Byron, George Gordon, 6th baron:
reaction to Kean as Sir Giles, 223

Caesar, Julius, 145, 166
Caligula, 139, 167
Calvinism, 195
Cambridge, University of, 143
Campbell, Thomas: Massinger's
dramatic eloquence, 26;
mentioned, 10
Carew, Thomas: *Coelum
Britannicum*, 152, 154; figure in a
literary quarrel, 12–13
Catholicism, 164, 195
Chaloner, Thomas, 166
Chapman, George: share in *Rollo,
Duke of Normandy*, 66;
mentioned, 125
Bussy D'Ambois, 119; and *The
Maid of Honour*, 107
*The Conspiracy and Tragedy of
Charles, Duke of Byron*, 119
The Tragedy of Chabot, 119
The Widow's Tears: compared with
The Parliament of Love, 226
Charles I, 118, 132, 143–67, *passim*
Claudius, 139
Cockpit (or Phoenix): Massinger's
plays for, 2, 12, 117
Cokayne, Sir Aston: indignation at

unacknowledgement of
Massinger, 2, 51; prefatory poem
to *The Emperor of the East*, 15;
mentioned, 221
Coleridge, Samuel: opinion of
Massinger, 4, 10, 28, 223, 227,
231–2
Colman, George, 10
Cotton, Sir Robert, 144
Courthope, W. J.: on Massinger's
style, 26
Coxeter, Thomas: edition of
Massinger, 223
Cromwell, Oliver, 158
Curio, Gaius Scribonius, 166

Daborne, Robert: 'tripartite' letter
with Massinger and Field, 51
Davenant, Sir William, 12
de casibus tragedy: pattern of in *The
Roman Actor*, 120
Dekker, Thomas: share in *The Virgin
Martyr*, 51, 120; mentioned, 223
Dio Cassius: *Roman History*, source
for *The Roman Actor*, 125
Domitian, 139, 167
Dorislaus, Isaac, 143
Dunn, T. A.: on Massinger's style, 9,
27; book on Massinger, 222
Dyce, Rev. Alexander: attribution of
The Prophetess to Fletcher, 90

Edwards, Philip: on Massinger's art,
97–8; on *The Maid of Honour*,
113; reading of *Believe As You
List*, 132, 134; compares *Perkin
Warbeck* and *Believe As You List*,
133–4; on Massinger's
defensiveness and humility, 222
Eichmann, (Karl) Adolf, 128
Eliot, Sir John: denounces
Buckingham as England's
Sejanus, 143; mentioned, 144,
166
Eliot, T. S.: opinion of Massinger, 4,
15, 221; on Massinger's style, 9;
condemnation of Massinger, 171;
praise for *The Fatal Dowry*, 15,
for *The Unnatural Combat*, 16;
Murder in the Cathedral, 232;
compared with Massinger, 232;
mentioned, 10
Elizabeth I, 132

234

Index

Elizabethan Poor Law, 195
Elton, Oliver, 10
Enright, D. J.: on *A New Way*, 181
Essex, Robert Devereux, 2nd Earl of,
143

Farnham, Willard, 122
Felton, John, 144–5
Field, Nathan: 'tripartite' letter with
Massinger and Daborne, 51
share in: *The Fatal Dowry*, 51; *The
Queen of Corinth*, 66
Filmer, Sir Robert: *Patriarcha*, 166
Flamininus, Titus, 118
Fleay, F. G., 118
Fletcher, John: as Massinger's
collaborator, 48–9, 51–80, 221;
compared with Massinger, 26,
175, 188; influence on Massinger,
114; death of, 71, 88, 117;
definition of tragicomedy, 112;
mentioned, 84, 223, 227
share in: *Beggars' Bush*, 73–4; *The
Custom of the Country*, 60–5;
The Double Marriage, 65–6; *The
Elder Brother*, 67–8; *The Fair
Maid of the Inn*, 71; *The False
One*, 67–8; *The Little French
Lawyer*, 55–60; *The Prophetess*,
88–97, passim; *The Queen of
Corinth*, 66; *Rollo, Duke of
Normandy*, 71–3; *The Spanish
Curate*, 53–5; and *Thierry and
Theodoret*, 74–7.
A Wife for a Month: compared with
Thierry and Theodoret, 76
Ford, John: possible contributor to
The Fair Maid of the Inn, 66;
prefatory poem to *The Great
Duke of Florence*, 15; compared
with Massinger, 231; mentioned,
12, 125
Forman, Simon, 11
Fothergill, Robert, on *A New Way*,
171
Frederick V, Elector Palatine, 132
Frewen, Thomas: extracts from *The
Bondman*, 12

Galba, 139
Gardiner, S. R.: on Massinger's
politics, 227
Gataker, Thomas, 218, n. 12

Gibson, Colin: projected survey of
Massinger criticism, 5; on sources
of *The Roman Actor*, 122, 124
Gifford, William: edition of
Massinger, 10, 223
Gill, Roma: influence of Machiavelli
in *Believe As You List*, 130, 133
Glasgow Citizens Theatre:
performance of *The Roman
Actor*, 117
Globe Theatre, 117
Gosse, Edmund: opinion of
Massinger, 9, 26, 28
Gosson, Stephen: fear of violent effects
of playing, 159
Gough, Thomas: Massinger as *poeta
elegantissima*, 14
Greg, W. W., 118

Hallam, Henry: praise of Massinger,
4, 10
Hannibal, 118
Harbage, Alfred, 118
Hardy, Thomas: *Tess of the
D'Urbervilles*, compared with
Believe As You List, 120
Harvey, Robert: prefatory poem to
The Roman Actor, 14, 121–2
Hayward, Sir John: *Life of Henry IV*,
143
Hegel, G. W. F., 130
Hemminge, William: *Elegy on
Randolph's Finger*, 13
Henrietta Maria, 152
Henry, Prince of Wales, son of James I,
150
Henslowe, Philip: 'tripartite' letter
from Massinger, Field, and
Daborne, 51
Herbert, Sir Henry: lost Massinger
plays, 2; licensing of *Believe As
You List*, 117–18, 127, 133;
refusal to license *The King and the
Subject*, 118; mentioned, 84
Herbert's Office Book: no entry for
The Maid of Honour, 84
Herford, C. H. and Percy and Evelyn
Simpson: Jonson edition as model
for Clarendon Massinger, 223
Hobbes, Thomas: *Behemoth*, on
overeducated gentry as a cause of
the Civil War, 167: *Leviathan*,
170, n. 50

235

Index

Hogan, A. P.: on Paris's ambition in *The Roman Actor*, 122

Horace, 123

How, William: excerpted material from *The Great Duke of Florence* and *The Maid of Honour*, 12

Hoy, Cyrus: on Massinger's share in the Beaumont and Fletcher canon, 1–3, 224; on rhetorical formulae in Massinger, 174

Hyde, Edward, 145

Independents, 167

James, I, 143, 147, 166, 190

James, Richard: librarian to Sir Robert Cotton, 144–5

Jay, Thomas:
prefatory poems to: *A New Way*, 14; *The Picture*, 3, 222; *The Roman Actor*, 14, 121

Jonson, Ben: compared with Massinger, 3–4, 188, 221; influence on Massinger, 84–8, 112, 114; on influence of Tacitus, 140; member of Arundel's circle, 145; rogues in plays of, 185; share in *Rollo, Duke of Normandy*, 66; mentioned, 12, 222–3

The Alchemist: echoed in *The Maid of Honour*, 87; compared with *The Maid of Honour*, 112, with *A New Way*, 181

Catiline, 139

Epicoene: possible influence on *The Maid of Honour*, 87

Epigrams, 140

The New Inn, 227

Sejanus: opening possibly echoed in *The Maid of Honour*, 86; source for *The Roman Actor*, 119; influence of Lucan in, 146; compared with *The Roman Actor*, 157

Volpone: compared with *A New Way*, 189

Jordan, W. K.: on seventeenth-century philanthropy, 195

Juvenal: *Saturae* and *The Roman Actor*, 122, 124

Kean, Edmund: as Sir Giles Overreach, 4, 223; desire to produce *The*

Unnatural Combat, 16

Keats, John, 10

King's Men: Massinger's association with, 2, 85, 117

Knights, L. C., 10, 85

Lamb, Charles: excerpts from Massinger in *Specimens of the English Dramatic Poets*, 4

Leggatt, Alexander: on *A New Way*, 171

Lepidus, 141

Lipsius, Justus: editor of Tacitus, 142

Livy, 139

Long Parliament, 166

Lucan: *Pharsalia*, 145; mentioned, 144, 146, 167

Lydgate, John: *The Falls of Princes*, 127

Lyly, John, 223

Machiavelli, Niccolò: *The Prince* and *Believe As You List*, 130–1; mentioned, 142, 150

Malone Society, 132

Marie di Medici, 166

Marlowe, Christopher: *Tamburlaine*, 185, 190; compared with Massinger, 221; mentioned, 12, 29, 223

Marston, John: *The Dutch Courtesan*, compared with *The Little French Lawyer*, 56

Marten, Henry, 166

masque: in the Caroline period, 152

MASSINGER, PHILIP: as collaborator, 1–3, 51–80, 221; Clarendon edition of, 2–4, 221–32, *passim*; dramatic style of, 9–37, 77–80; one volume edition, ed. Colin Gibson, 4; tercentenary of his death, 221–2; canon, 2–3, 51–2, 222; revival of his plays in the Restoration, 3; death and burial of, 221

PLAYS OF SOLE AUTHORSHIP:
Alexius the Chaste Gallant (lost), 3

The Bashful Lover, 2–3, 229

Believe As You List: compared with *The Roman Actor*, 118–21, 131, 134; revision of, 132–3; discussed, 126–34; mentioned, 2, 78, 225, 227, 231

236

Index

Index

Index

Monteverdi: *L'Incoronazione di Poppea*, 163
Morality plays, 119, 188
Moseley, Humphrey: collector of Massinger plays, 3
Mozart: *Entführung aus dem Serail*, 231
Mullany, Peter F.: on *The Maid of Honour*, 89
Muret, Marc-Antoine, 141
Murry, John Middleton: *The Problem of Style*, 10

National Theatre, 227
Neill, Michael: on *A New Way*, 171
Nero, 139, 141, 145, 167
Nero, anonymous play of 1624: relation to *The Roman Actor*, 146–8; mentioned, 150, 155, 161–2
News of the World, 224

Oldys, William: excerpts from Massinger in *The British Muse*, 4
Orpheus, 205–6
Otho, 139

Painter, William: *Palace of Pleasure*, source for *The Maid of Honour*, 84–5, 87, 98–9, 110
Peele, George, 223
Pentecost, 211
Perkins, William, 196
Petition of Right, 144
Petrarch: *Secretum*, 122; Petrarchanism, 179
Phelips, Sir Robert, 143
Philip II, King of Spain, 117, 132
Phoenix (or Cockpit): Massinger's plays for, 2; performance of *The Maid of Honour* at, 84
Piso, 145
Plautus, 161
Plutarch, 139
Presbyterians, 167
Protestantism, 164
Puritanism, 159, 196

Queen's Men, 13

Refutation of the Apology for Actors (1614), by 'I.G.', 169, n. 38
Restoration comedy: 'proviso scenes'

in, 198
Reynolds, John, 160–1
Reynolds, John Hamilton: on Massinger's style, 26
Richards, Nathaniel: *Messallina*, discussed, 162–5, mentioned, 139
Richardson, Charles: *Sermon Against Oppression*, 197
Richman, David, 122
Rowley, William: *See* Webster, John; and Middleton, Thomas
Royal Shakespeare Company, 227

St John's College, Oxford, 12
St Luke, 209
St Paul, 193
St Peter, 210
Salgádo, Gámini: on *A New Way*, 173
Salisbury Court Theatre: performance of Richards's *Messallina* at, 164
Savile and Greneway: English translators of Tacitus, 140
Schoenbaum, Samuel, 118
Schopenhauer, Arthur, 134
Scott, Thomas, 160
Sebastian, King of Portugal, 117–21, 126–34, *passim*
Selden, John, 144–5
Seneca: *Thyestes*, 150; mentioned, 107, 142, 144, 146, 163
Seneca the Elder: *controversiae* as source for *The Queen of Corinth*, 68
Shakespeare, William: first Folio, 85; compared with Massinger, 4, 26, 79, 112–13, 188, 230; influence on Massinger, 84–6, 114; mentioned, 13, 19, 104, 139
All's Well That Ends Well: parallel to *The Maid of Honour*, 46–7, 85–7, 109, 113; mentioned, 112
Antony and Cleopatra, 119
As You Like It: parallel to *The Maid of Honour*, 86, 109; compared with *A New Way*, 178
Cymbeline: source of, 87
Hamlet, 69
Henry IV, 126; Part 2: Falstaff's rejection seen in reverse in May's *Julia Agrippina*, 149

239

Index

Index